I0795919

POSTCARD HISTORY SERIES

Lake Geneva

IN VINTAGE POSTCARDS

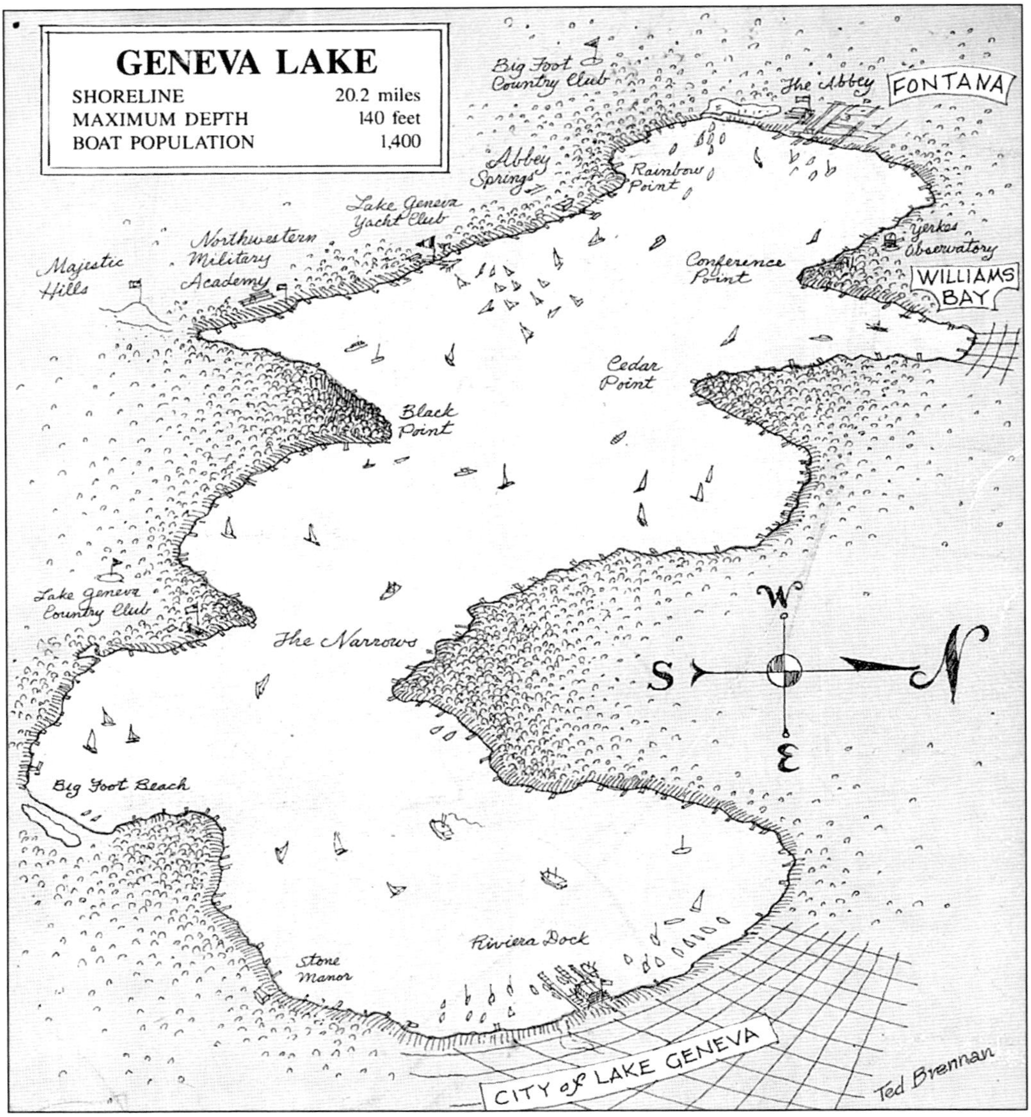

Local artist and sailor Frederick "Ted" S. Brennan created this map of Geneva Lake around 1988. After a full career in the industrial design field, Ted turned to his true love of drawing. His legacy lives on through the many images of boats and Geneva Lake that Ted had completed over several decades. (Courtesy of Maude Brennan.)

POSTCARD HISTORY SERIES

Lake Geneva

IN VINTAGE POSTCARDS

Carolyn Hope Smeltzer and Martha Kiefer Cucco

ARCADIA
PUBLISHING

ISBN 978-0-7385-3398-8

Published by Arcadia Publishing
Charleston, South Carolina

Printed in the United States of America

Library of Congress Catalog Card Number: 2005920683

For all general information contact Arcadia Publishing at:
Telephone 843-853-2070
Fax 843-853-0044
E-mail sales@arcadiapublishing.com
For customer service and orders:
Toll-Free 1-888-313-2665

Visit us on the Internet at www.arcadiapublishing.com

Carolyn wishes to dedicate this book to Bob Kelly, who introduced her to lake living and lake golfing over a decade ago; Kathleen Archibald Simon, who shared Geneva Lake childhood memories and her passion for the lake for over three decades; Joan Meyer, a Chicago friend who follows her to the lake in all seasons; and to her many lake friends, who made Geneva Lake feel like home.

Martha wishes to dedicate this book to her husband Rich, who has shared her dream of living at Geneva Lake, and to her parents and family for all of the wonderful weekend and summer memories of sailing, boating, and friendships throughout the years.

Carolyn and Martha, together, dedicate this book to those who preserved and to those who will continue to preserve the lake's beauty and history so future generations can enjoy the magic, beauty, and relaxation of Geneva Lake.

Contents

ACKNOWLEDGMENTS

The authors would like to thank Bob Kelly for encouraging Carolyn to research Geneva Lake's history and for creating opportunities for her to discover vintage postcard collectors at the lake. In this way, Carolyn met and developed a working friendship with coauthor Martha, who also believed lake history could be learned through postcards.

Many people contributed their time and knowledge to help with historical clarifications and technicalities. Special thanks go to Katie Alder, Doug Bearder, Marianne Bestler, Jim Brown, Emily Cucco, Joan Freytag, Joanne Gabriel, Marlyn Glass, George Hennerley, John Kiefer, Larry Larkin, Terry Leahy, Carol Ann Lothian, Mary Myers, Ted Pankau, Jane Pegel, Samantha Polek, Lucy Sandy, Laura Torhorst, Bob and Mary Winter, and the wonderful librarians at the Lake Geneva, Williams Bay, and Fontana libraries. Also, a very enthusiastic group of postcard collectors generously loaned their treasures to help others see into the past through their photos and cards. A very special thanks to all of you!

Helen Brandt, curator of the Geneva Lake Museum, deserves acknowledgement for graciously editing this book for historical accuracy. At its founding in 1984, the Geneva Lake Museum was located in the 1940 home of Mr. and Mrs. Peter Messe. Today, the museum is located at 255 Mill Street in downtown Lake Geneva. The Geneva Lake Museum and the Lake Geneva Library house original vintage postcards for viewing as well as many other artifacts from the past.

Additional thanks go to John Pearson, Midwest publisher at Arcadia Publishing, who has fond childhood memories of visiting the Geneva Lake home of his grandparents' friends and Elizabeth Beachy, acquisitions editor, for believing that the history of Geneva Lake could be told and visualized through postcards and that *Lake Geneva in Vintage Postcards* would be of interest to lake residents, frequent visitors, and first time discoverers of Lake Geneva.

ABOUT THE AUTHORS

Carolyn Hope Smeltzer is a nurse, a partner at PricewaterhouseCoopers, and a trustee for Advocate Healthcare System, Sisters of Charity of Leavenworth Health System, Illinois Liver Foundation, Loyola University Board of Regents, and Linden House of the Poor Handmaids of Jesus Christ. This is Carolyn's third book. Her first, *Ordinary People, Extraordinary Lives: the Stories of Nurses* (Sigma Theta Tau International, 2003) was coauthored with Frances R. Vlasses and highlights through photography the silent, yet powerful, stories of nurses. Her second book, *Chicago's Nurse Parade* (Arcadia Publishing, 2005), relives Chicago's "largest shortest parade" through images. This Nurse Parade lasted a decade, from1948 to 1958, and was Chicago's "best kept secret" for over half a century.

Carolyn is fortunate to have been able to write stories and contribute to the history of three of her passions: nurses, Chicago, and Lake Geneva. She is equally fortunate to enjoy her robust city life in Chicago, be connected with nurses from around the country, and enjoy friends, swim, and golf in the beauty of her Geneva Lake country home. Her vintage look is riding around Lake Geneva in a convertible, with golf clubs in the passenger seat, listening to Elvis Presley.

Martha Cucco is a real estate broker at Keefe Real Estate, Inc. in Walworth County, Wisconsin. Her interest in local history, combined with her knowledge of the area, helped her contribute to this book. Her hobbies (besides collecting vintage photos and postcards of the Geneva Lake area) include photography, sailboat racing, golfing, singing, and hiking the shore path with her golden retrievers. A volunteer with various local organizations, she is currently active with the Lake Geneva Garden Club and the "Music by the Lake" program at Aurora University. The postcards and images in this book, unless otherwise credited, are from Martha's extensive collection.

INTRODUCTION

Is it Lake Geneva or Geneva Lake? That's a good question, and the answer is that it is definitively . . . both! Historically, the rule of thumb is that the city itself is called Lake Geneva, while the lake is technically called Geneva Lake. The confusion arises when people refer to the water as Lake Geneva. Originally called "Bigfoot Lake" or "Big Foot's Lake" by the Potawatomi Indians, it was written in early history books that this land was surveyed in the early 1800s by John Brink. Struck by the beauty of the area, he was reminded of Seneca Lake, near Geneva, New York. Thinking that it deserved a better name than Big Foot, he entered it in his field notes as Geneva Lake. Researchers, however, have not been able to confirm this through written records, nor is the exact date that Geneva Lake was given its new name apparent.

Geneva Lake, which was formed by a glacier, is unlike any other inland lake. Called Kishwauketoe, it was home to the Oneota Indian tribe as long ago as 1,000 B.C. The lake had no river, railway, or road access. In 1831, the first white man visited the lake while traveling between Fort Dearborn and Fort Winnebago. Throughout the years the lake, surrounded by the towns of Lake Geneva, Fontana, and Williams Bay, became the home of many visitors because of its beauty, wildlife, farm lands, lake fish, and recreation.

Chief Big Foot and his Potawatomi Indian tribe were evicted from the lake in the 1830s and sent to Kansas. Although Chief Big Foot has not inhabited Geneva Lake for over a century, his memory and significance have not been forgotten. Indian gravesites and sacred burial grounds have been preserved and marked. The lake area is home to numerous Chief Big Foot statues and the name Big Foot graces local restaurants and diners, landmarks, parks, golf courses, and beaches.

Lake civilization began in 1836 when Christopher Payne, a Belvedere pioneer, claimed water power and built the first log cabin. Lake Geneva land, surveyed in 1837 with earlier lake ownership confirmed in 1839, was sold for $1.25 per acre. Soon after the land sales were confirmed, sawmills were built, and walnut trees were floated to the mills, cut into lumber, and used to build the town.

By 1840, Lake Geneva had two hotels, two general stores, three churches, and a distillery. Many families rented lakefront land from farmers who placed little value on the land close to shore. Tents, homesteads, and small cottages were set up as the lakefront became a place to raise families in the summer, escape the summer city heat, enjoy friends at the fire pit, and have fun in the lake.

Following the Civil War, the town became a resort for wealthy Chicago families. Mansions were built and railroad transportation began. The Great Chicago Fire of 1871 caused many to move year round to their summer lake home while their Chicago homes were being rebuilt. The construction and maintenance of these mansions, as well as household employment, created more jobs and industry in the town that had already developed a business of shipping tons of lake ice to the Chicago markets. Lake Geneva became known as the "Newport of the West," hosting many visitors from Mary Todd Lincoln and Albert Einstein to Generals Sherman and Sheridan.

Aside from its fascinating history, Geneva Lake displays a rich beauty in all seasons. The beauty of the lake's clear water reflecting the sun or the moon is only enhanced by individuals enjoying lake recreation. In the summer, the lake is alive with all types of boaters, sailors, fisherman, swimmers, and walkers along the shores. Hot air balloons and gliders can be seen in the blue skies over the clear water. Golfers find the hills and terrain challenging; horseback riders enjoy the woods and fields, while farmers find the land rich in value. In the fall, the lake water reflects the leaves' autumnal colors, and the land has the added beauty of bright orange pumpkin patches springing up in the fields as the town hosts Oktoberfest.

After the birds, geese, and ducks migrate from the lake in fall, winter brings new excitement as the sparkling lake freezes and invites ice boaters, fishermen, pilots with air planes on skis, and snowmobiles to enjoy its frozen water and the beauty of snow-covered trees and ground. Shots can be heard as skeet shooters and hunters enjoy their sport. During the winter, the lake is host to ice sculpting, snow shoeing, and skiing.

Spring at the lake represents a new beginning. Buds blossom, flowers are planted, and campers return. Boats and white piers once again appear in the clear sparkling water. In the spring, the lake is alive with everyone preparing for summer recreation and relaxation.

Today, Geneva Lake's Victorian buildings, mansions, cottages, and camps are remembrances of past lake life. Historic classic wooden boats, a steamer, and the old railway markings of train stations are reminders of past lake transportation. More important than these landmarks are the families and campers that have vivid memories of enjoying lake living for generations.

We invite you to appreciate Geneva Lake memories and moments in time, along with the lake's historic beauty in all seasons. Experience lake living by viewing lake mansions, cottages, associations, camps, and towns surrounding the lake. Enjoy lake excitement by seeing images of lake transportation and recreation and appreciate the beauty of Geneva Lake through waterfront scenes. Understand the sentiments that accompany these images by reading the stories that are captured with the postcard visuals in *Lake Geneva in Vintage Postcards*.

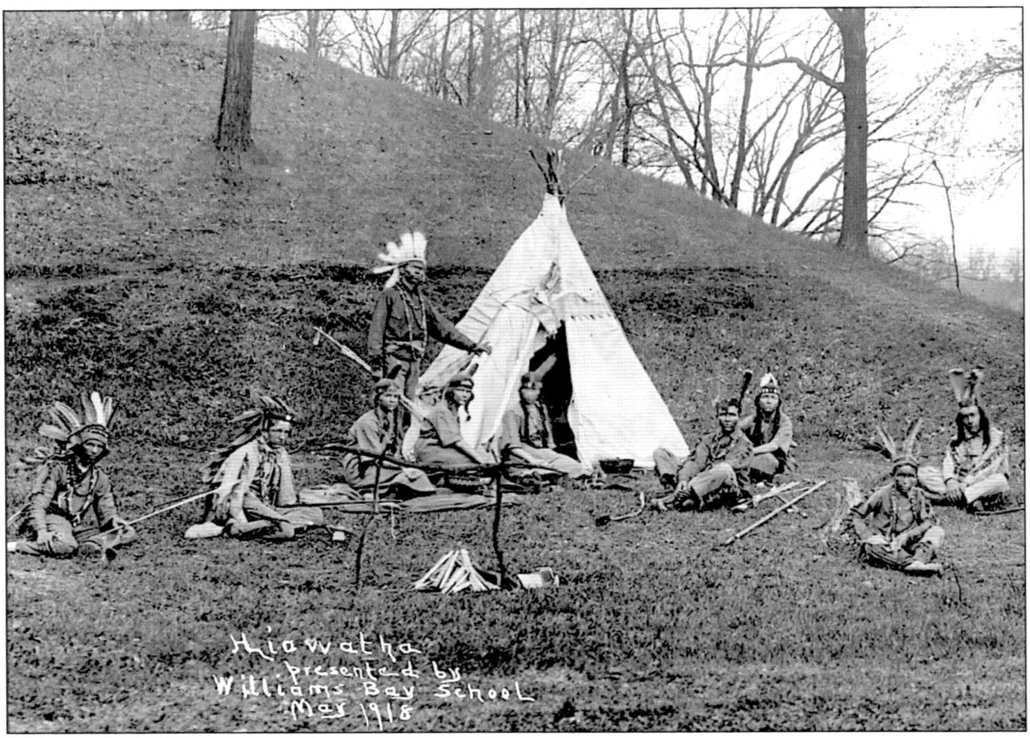

One

THE MAGIC OF LAKE LIVING

Geneva Lake, "Newport of the West" since 1836, has beautiful mansions of yesteryear as well as contemporary homes of today, all dotting its beautiful lake shore. The shore is also lined with cottages, camps, and a unique walking path. The majority of cottages have been grouped into associations or clubs named after the neighborhoods or cities of the families' original dwellings. Today, a number of these homes, mansions, camps, and associations exist, with renovations, just as they did then. Others are newly built homes, sometimes on the footprint of the original cottages or houses. Some of the mansions and associations will be highlighted to illustrate the magic of lake living.

The men who built the original estates around Geneva Lake were the forerunners of Chicago's business and industry from 1870 to 1920. Though some are not as familiar, others are still household names, including Sheldon Sturges, founder of the Northwestern Bank of Chicago; Montgomery Ward Thorne; Philip K. Wrigley; Norman W. Harris of Harris Bank of Chicago; F. L. Maytag of Maytag Washing Machines; John M. Smyth;. P.J. Healy of Lyon & Healy Music Co.; Levi Z. Leiter, cofounder of what later became Marshall Field and Co.; R.T. Crane of Crane Plumbing; Ignatz Schwinn, founder of the bicycle company; Oscar Meyer; John Borden, Arctic explorer and member of the family that owned the dairy products company; Martin Ryerson of Ryerson Lumberyards; and James Hobart Moore, coorganizer of the Rock Island Railroad, the American Can Co., and Nabisco.

Dr. Maxwell, a prominent Chicago surgeon, built a mansion in the City of Lake Geneva in the spring of 1856; he had acquired the land in 1849. The property was named The Oaks in honor of the century-year-old oak trees on his property. The Oaks had tall windows, broad entrances, elaborate ornamental wood moldings, marble fireplaces, and a grand staircase. The mansion gave testimony to Dr. Maxwell's presence as a community leader and "The Father of Lake Geneva." His home welcomed many visitors throughout the years. The Oaks was one of the sites for the courtship between Nancy Davis and Ronald Regan. Today the property is a bed-and-breakfast inn known as The Golden Oaks. The owner combined her own Irish name, Golden, with the mansion's historic name.

Black Point was built in 1888 as Conrad Seipp's family summer home. Mr. Seipp, a brewer from Germany, became very successful in 1871 as his South Side Chicago brewery, unlike many others, did not burn in the Chicago Fire. The home was built by architect Adolph Cudell. Black Point had 20 rooms in all, including 13 bedrooms. The property expanded over 100 acres with a small farm and a thousand feet of wooded lakefront. Although the original land has been subdivided, the mansion is owned by fourth-generation members of the Seipp family. This mansion can be seen from many points on the lake and is listed on the National Register of Historic Places. Many of the furnishings are originals from 1888. Black Point is cited by the Wisconsin Historical Society Magazine as "the best surviving example of the great summer houses in Wisconsin and probably also Illinois."

Stone Manor (officially Younglands) was built in 1899–1901 by Otto Young. Mr. Young made his fortune buying real estate along Chicago's State Street after the Great Chicago fire. This mansion was an 18,000 square-foot magnificent Italianate palace with a 250-foot veranda and an expansive lawn. The mansion had gold-plated fixtures, a ball room, basement bowling alley, and a miniature golf course. Stone Manor, a private home until 1939, has since been a private girl's school, an elegant French restaurant, and is now a multi-unit condominium

House in the Woods, built in 1905–1906, was designed jointly by architect Howard Van Dorn Shaw and artist-muralist Frederick Clay Bartlett. The home was a surprise birthday present for the owner's wife. Ladies Home Journal, June 1909, featured a two-page photo collection of House in the Woods. The mansion has been cited as one of the "Best 12 Country Homes in America."

While the wealthy were building mansions, like Angel's Flight, Alturia, Healy Estate, and Westgate, middle-class families were also creating cottages and associations, making lake living affordable. Cottages sprung up when families from the same "back home communities" started homesteading, tenting, building, and forming lake associations. Many of these cottages did not have bathrooms or running water. The families tapped into the natural spring water or dug wells. Many of the associations had "common out houses" located behind the cottages.

Today many of these associations are still on the lake and are under the same name as in prior years: Belvidere Park, Elgin Club, Harvard Club (1875), Rockford Camp (now known as Dartmouth Woods), Chicago Club (1879), Abbey Springs, Indian Hills, Club Unique, Country Club Estates, Cedar Point Park, Glenwood Springs, Buena Vista Park, and The Gardens. Many of these cottages have been renovated and, for the most part, winterized. These associations gained a reputation as excellent places to raise families in the summer; families made a one-time trip to the lake, staying all summer, while the father commuted to work by rail. Regardless of whether the house is a historic mansion, contemporary home, or cottage, they all represent stories of the magic of lake living.

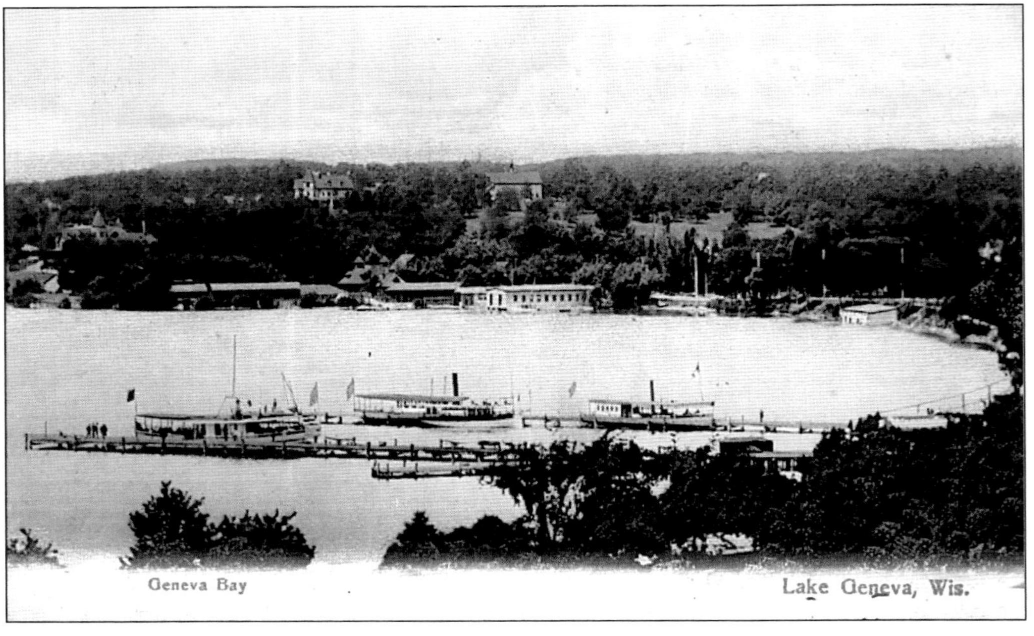

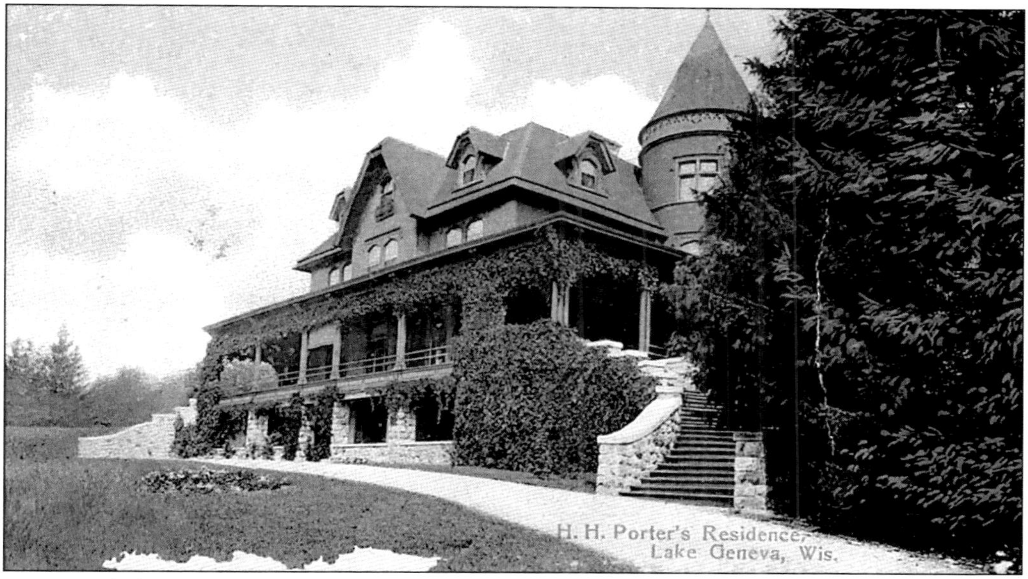

In 1870, Shelton and Frances Sturges built Maple Lawn, the first mansion on Geneva Lake. Their yacht, *Arrow*, was the first private steamboat on the lake. Maple Lawn was purchased in 1890 by Henry H. Porter. Located about a half block west of what is now Library Park, it had a five-story turret. Porter remodeled the square turret to make it round and built the Annex, a large residence. He also bought the land between the estate and Library Park; it eventually became the home of Porter's daughter, Katherine, and her husband, George Isham. The mansion remained in the Porter-Isham heirs' ownership until 1947 when the property was sold and subdivided. The house was razed in 2004.

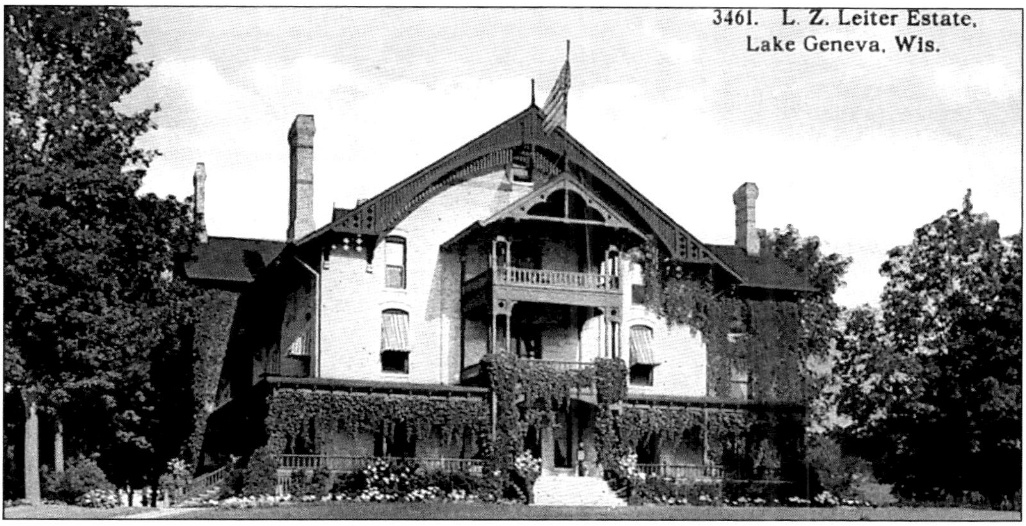

Levi Z. Leiter built his summer home, Linden Lodge, in 1879. Leiter was a partner in the Field, Leiter & Co. stores, which later became Marshall Fields. A large Dutch windmill, six-stories high with forty-foot arms, could be seen from the lake. It was used for pumping water and providing power. The home was demolished in 1939 and the property subdivided into the Lake Geneva Manor Association.

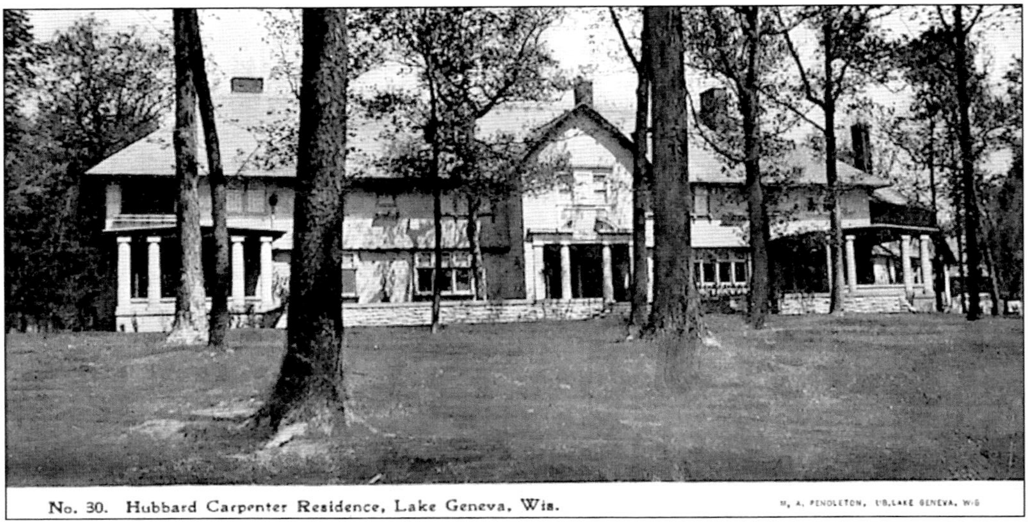

Rehobeth was built in 1906 by the Carpenter family. A unique feature of this home was an open passageway from the back of the house to the front, called a "dog-trot;" one could view the lake right through the house. Hubbard and Rosalie Carpenter used this as their summer home until 1954, when it was sold. It was razed by its new owner, J. Rockefeller Prentice, grandson of J.D. Rockefeller, and became part of the nearby Country House estate. The property remains within the family.

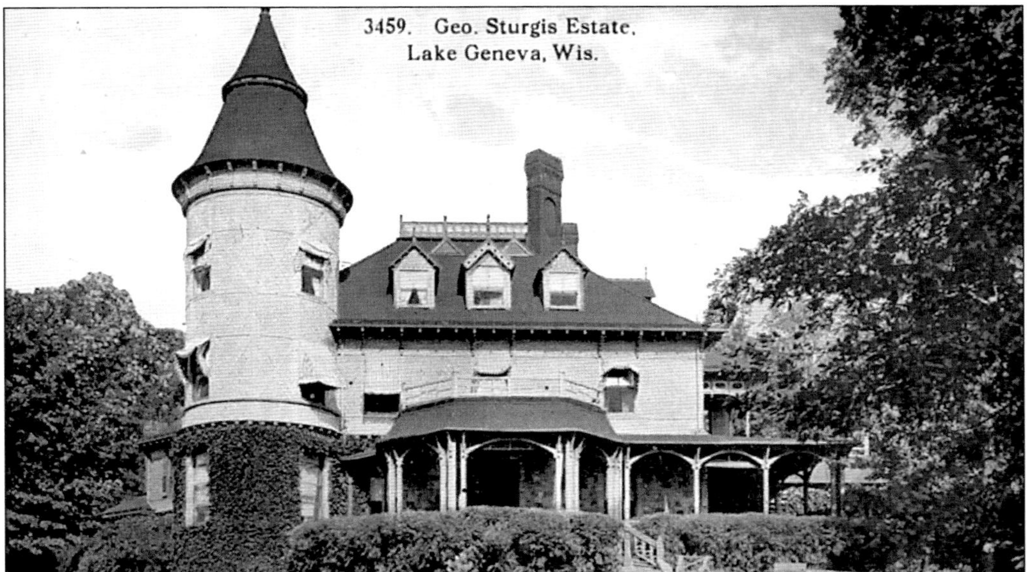

Snug Harbor was built by Mr. and Mrs. George Sturges in 1881 on property which had been part of brother Shelton Sturges' 90-acre holdings. The large three-story rambling Victorian-style home was perfect for their family of eight children. It later became Covenant Harbor Bible Camp, and the main house was used as camp guest facilities. Flames destroyed the mansion in 1957, but the large covered boathouse on the lakefront still remains. (Courtesy of the Joy Peterkin Rasin Collection.)

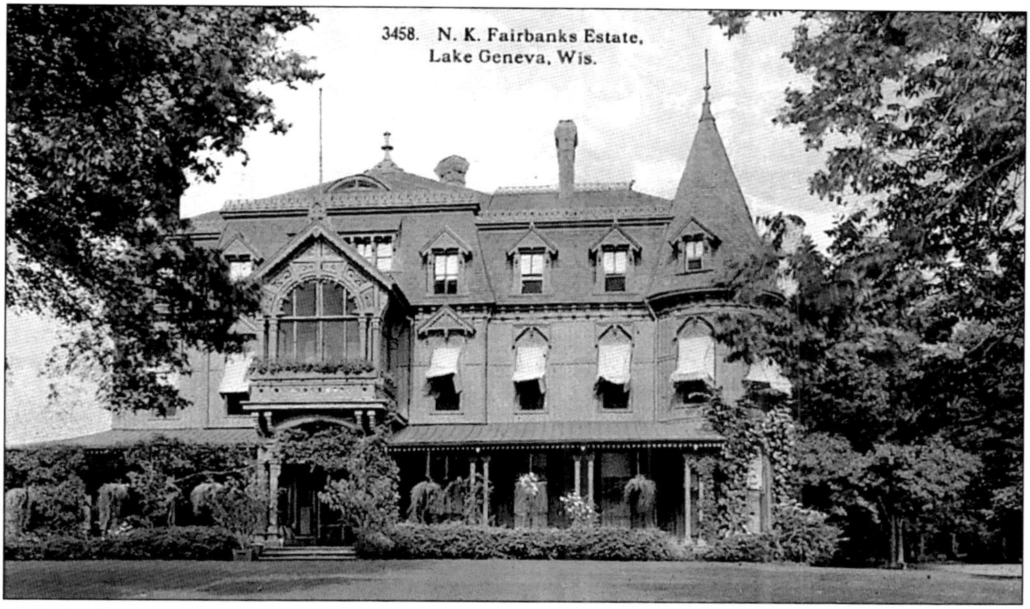

N.K. Fairbanks' summer home, Butternuts, was built in 1874, but consumed by fire in 1875. This 1916 card shows the second home that was constructed with its later addition of a three-story turret. The land was sold and subdivided in 1955, and the home was torn down. Part of the property is now Geneva Bay Estates, while the rest is Forest Rest subdivision.

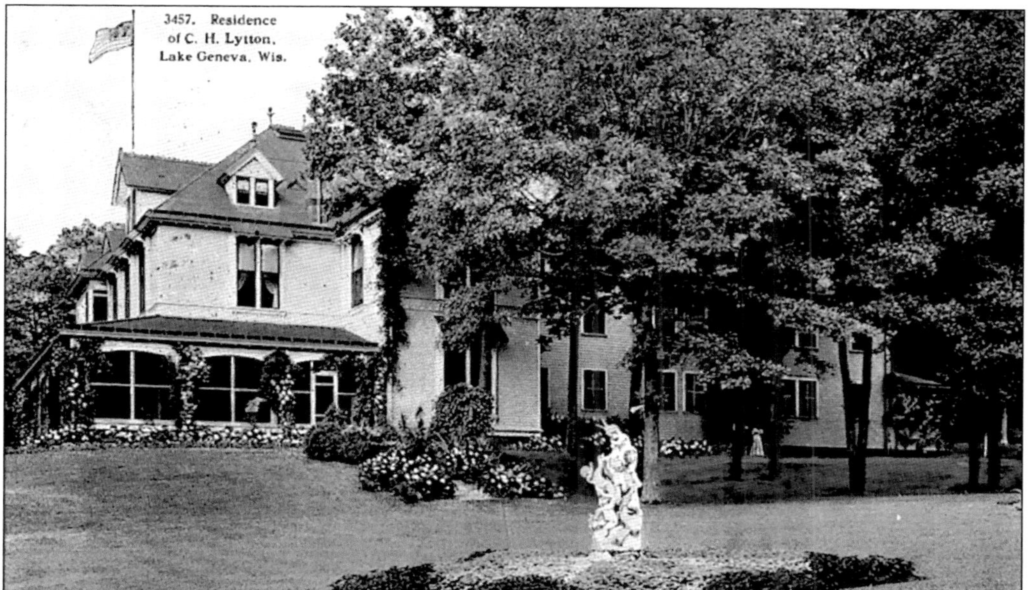

This 1914 postcard shows Roselyn Lodge, built in 1882. Retailer Henry Lytton was the home's second owner at this time. Originally called Gay Lynne, it had several owners after Mr. Lytton, and the name was changed again to Hillcroft. In 1927, Phillip K. Wrigley purchased the property, and his family used it as a summer retreat and later as a guest house. It was sold and a new home built in its place in 1981.

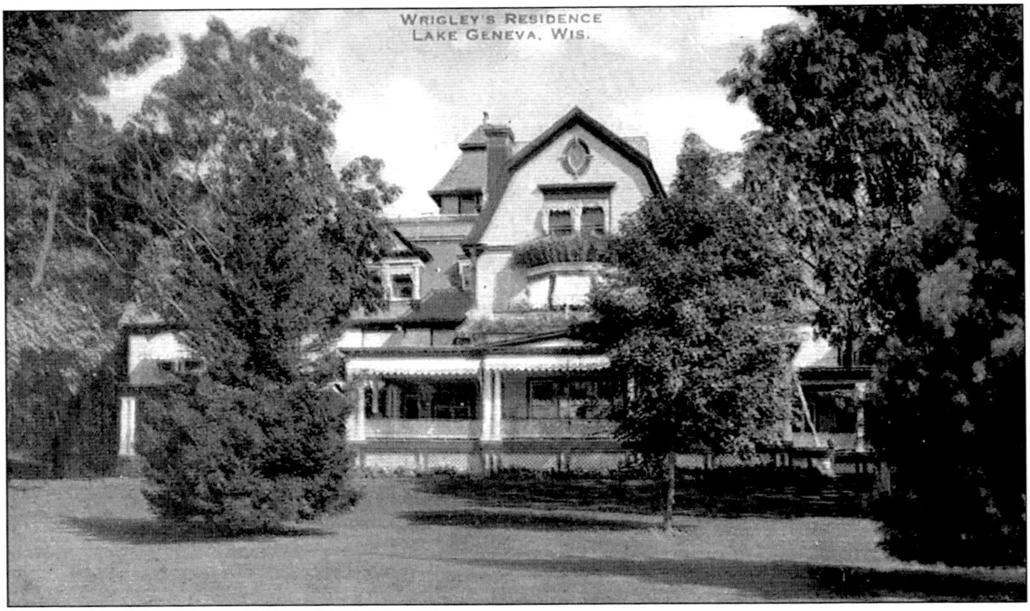

Green Gables was built in 1892 by millionaire C.K.G. Billings. The home was subsequently owned by banker William Mitchell and later the Wrigley family, who in 1955 tore it down and built a new modern brick home of Georgian design in its place. The home has recently undergone a major restoration.

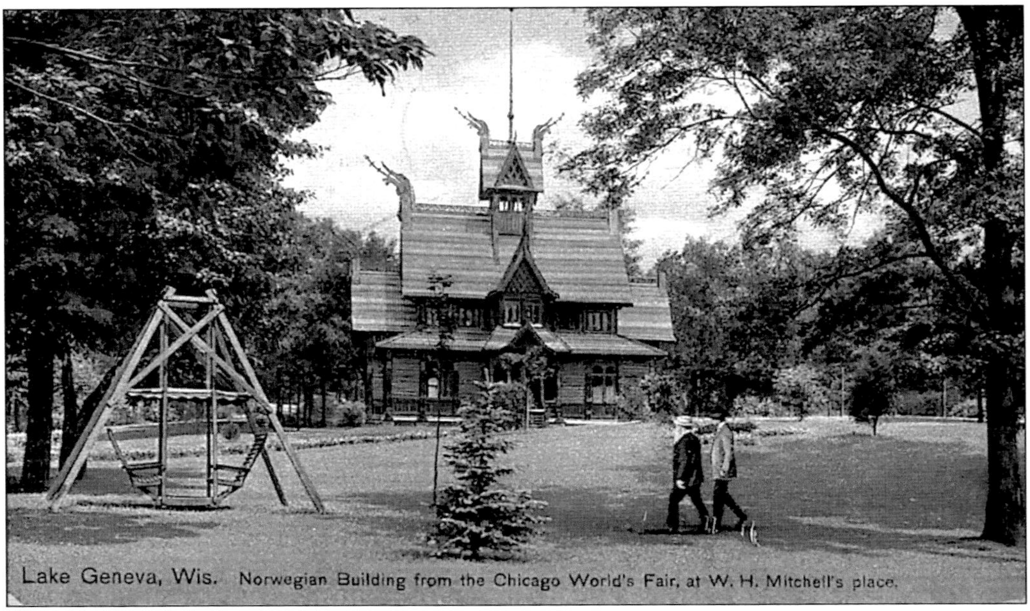

Originally built for the Columbian Exposition of 1893, the Norwegian Building was added to the C.K.G. Billing grounds. Moved to the lakeshore after the exposition ended, it was an authentic replica of a Norse church built entirely of native woods and held together with wooden pegs. It remained a landmark until the 1930s when the building was moved to Little Norway near Mount Horeb, Wisconsin.

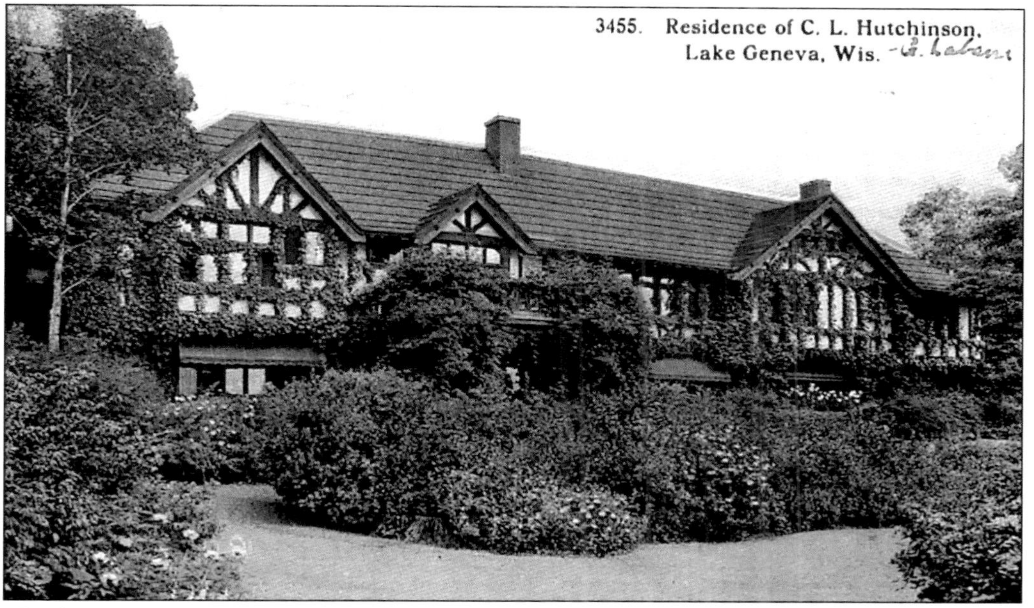

This home on Geneva Lake's north shore no longer looks as it did on this card, postmarked in 1914. Horticultural Hall founder Charles Hutchinson built it in 1902. The estate, which was named Wychwood by Mrs. Hutchinson in reference to the "wych-hazel" that grew in many places on the grounds, was turned into a wildlife sanctuary in 1926. In 1932, the property was given to the University of Chicago as an experimental and research station for students, although it was maintained as a refuge for native plants and birds. Wychwood was sold again to Clarence Mitchell, a banker from Chicago, in 1957. It was remodeled in the 1950s with the upper story removed to "modernize" it into a ranch-style home. Shortly thereafter it was sold to William Wrigley.

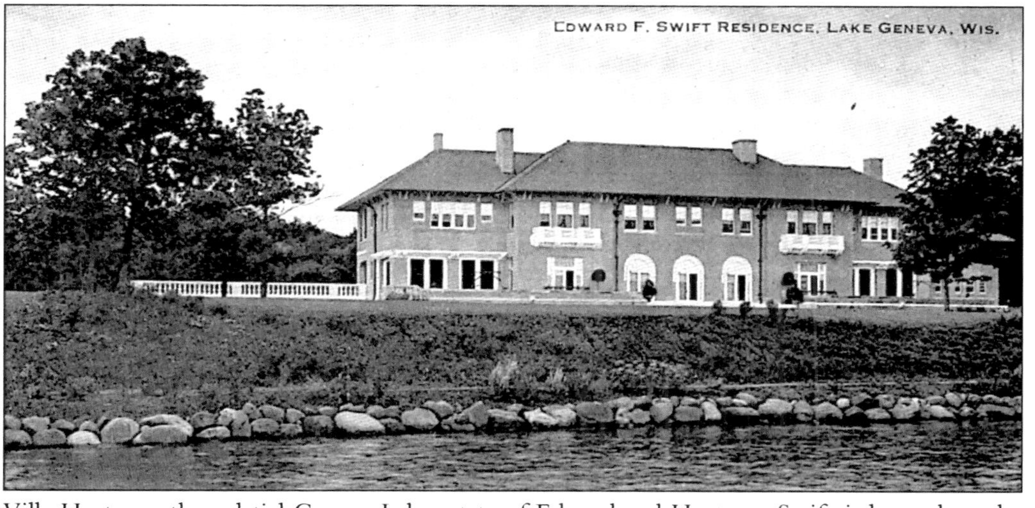

Villa Hortense, the palatial Geneva Lake estate of Edward and Hortense Swift, is located on the east end of the Narrows. Built in 1906, it was owned by the Swifts (of the meat-packing family) until 1922, when it was purchased by Silas Llewellyn. Over the years it has changed hands several times and, known today as Edgewood, is easily recognizable on the North Shore. (Courtesy of the Nancy Geldermann Williams Collection.)

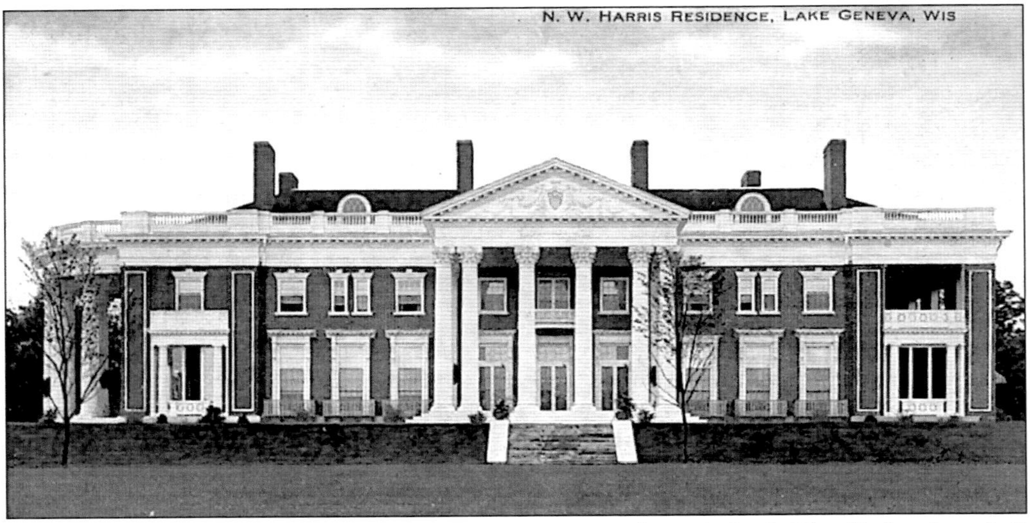

Wadsworth Hall was built in 1905 by Norman W. Harris of Harris Bank. The 50-foot-long hall, built in the classical Greek style, has a 12-foot open stairway leading to a large landing from which stairways rose toward each end of the building. Walden Shaw bought the estate in 1920 and renamed it The Stenning. In the 1930s, it became the estate of Daniel Peterkin and his wife, who was Shaw's daughter. The grounds of the estate were landscaped by the Olmstead brothers, who later designed New York's Central Park.

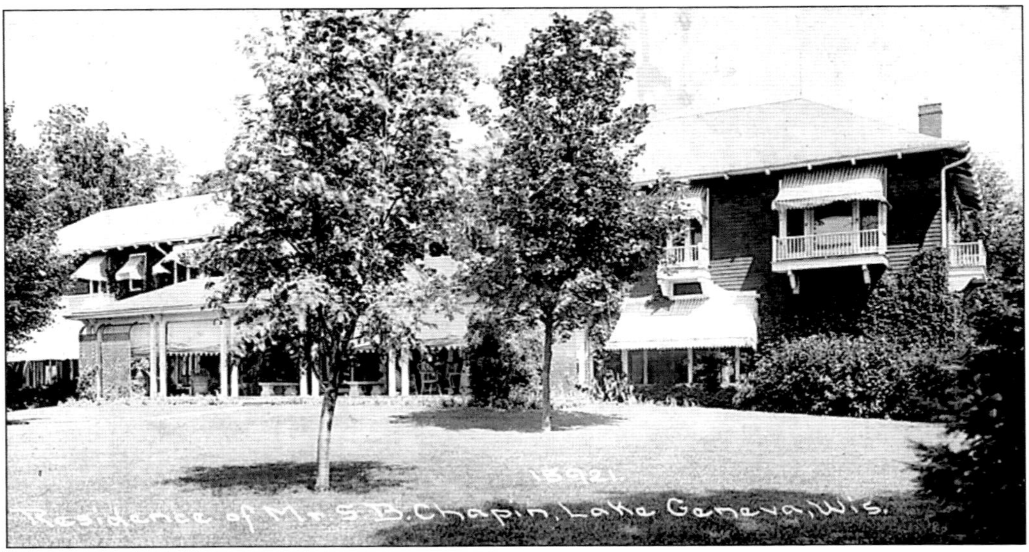

S.B. Chapin built his Flowerside Inn and Farm in 1898. A prominent businessman and community contributor, Mr. Chapin founded Geneva Lake's Water Safety Patrol in 1927; the volunteer service group has prospered and is still going strong. A blend of American- and English-style country homes, one of the most unique features was the built-in pipe organ in the living room. (The organ was recently donated to the Indiana University School of Music for installation in their concert hall.) Originally from Chicago, Chapin and his wife traveled from New York to Geneva Lake every May for 57 years, bringing their children and servants for the summer. (Courtesy of the Joy Peterkin Rasin Collection.)

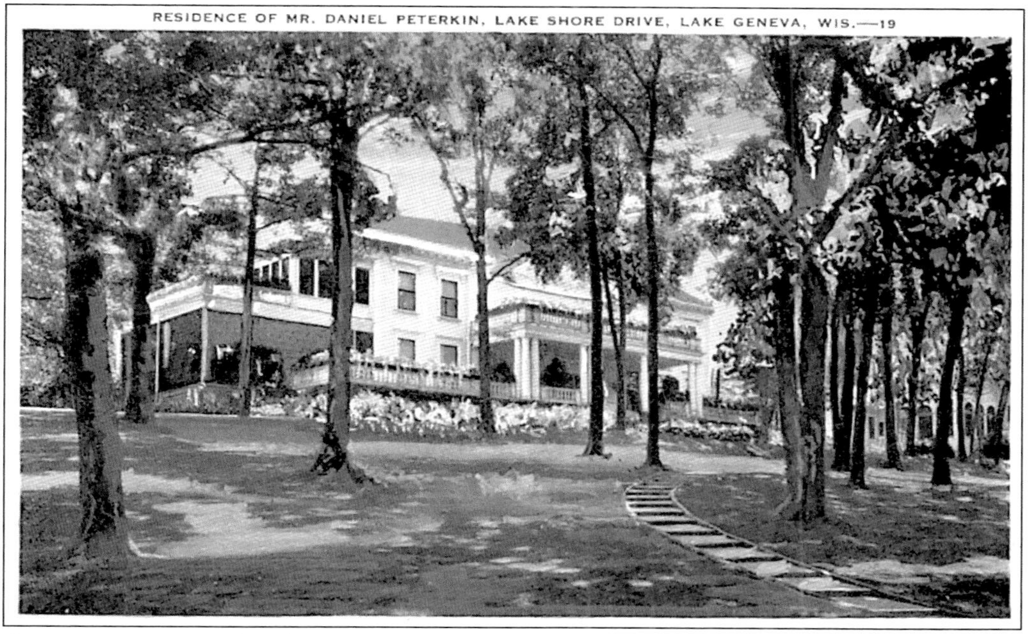

Oak Lodge was purchased by Mr. Daniel Peterkin, president of Morton Salt Company, and his wife from the Barnard family in 1920. So named because of the hundreds of oak trees on the 10.5-acre lakefront property, it was recognized as one of the most beautiful estates on Geneva Lake due to the efforts of the head gardener, Charles Flemming. (Courtesy of the Joy Peterkin Rasin Collection.)

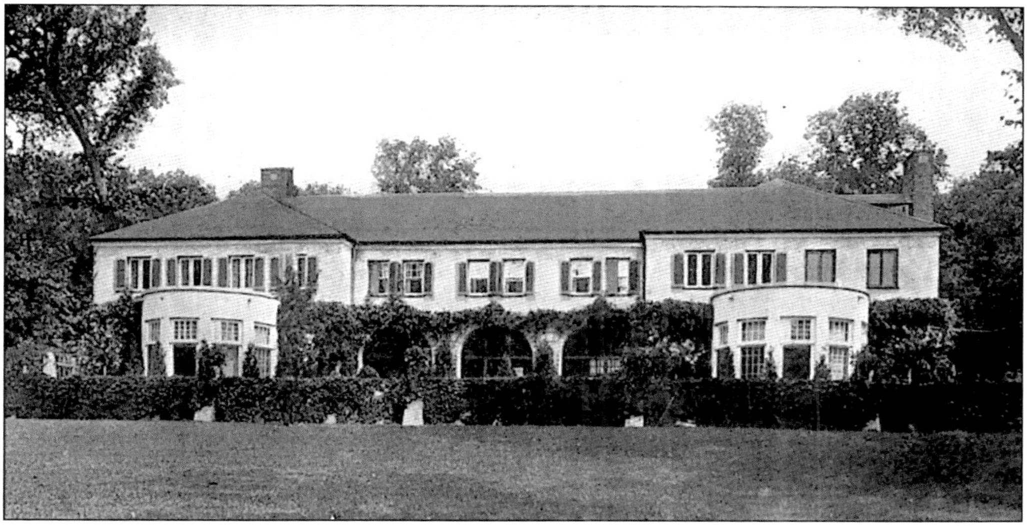

In order to keep the house as a surprise birthday gift for the owner's wife, House in the Woods was built under a circus tent (borrowed from P.T. Barnum's Circus, which wintered in Delavan, Wisconsin) in the winter of 1905. Mr. and Mrs. A.C. Bartlett, the owners and a philanthropic artistic family, donated a large art collection to Chicago's Art Institute, including Surat's painting, La Grande Jatte. Bartlett's son Frederick, a noted artist, created murals on the walls of the unique "u"-shaped mansion's inner court.

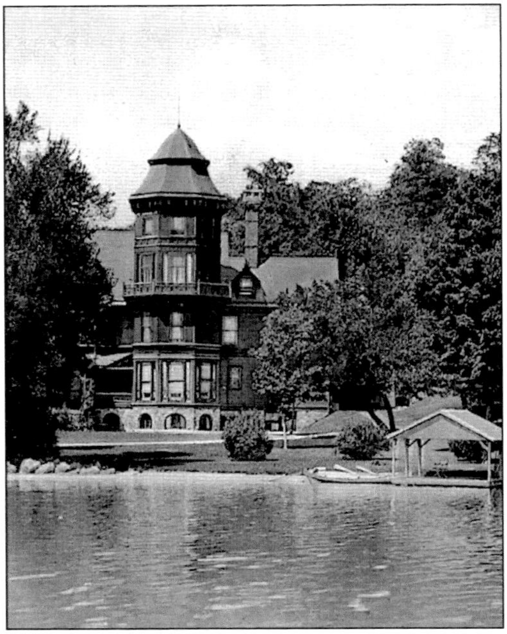

Built in 1884 on the Narrows' north shore and named The Folly, this unusual home had a four-story tower and was built of redwood. Owner Samuel Allerton was in the cattle business, and it was through his efforts that the Union Stockyard was founded. The Folly was torn down in 1925 after Mrs. Allerton's death.

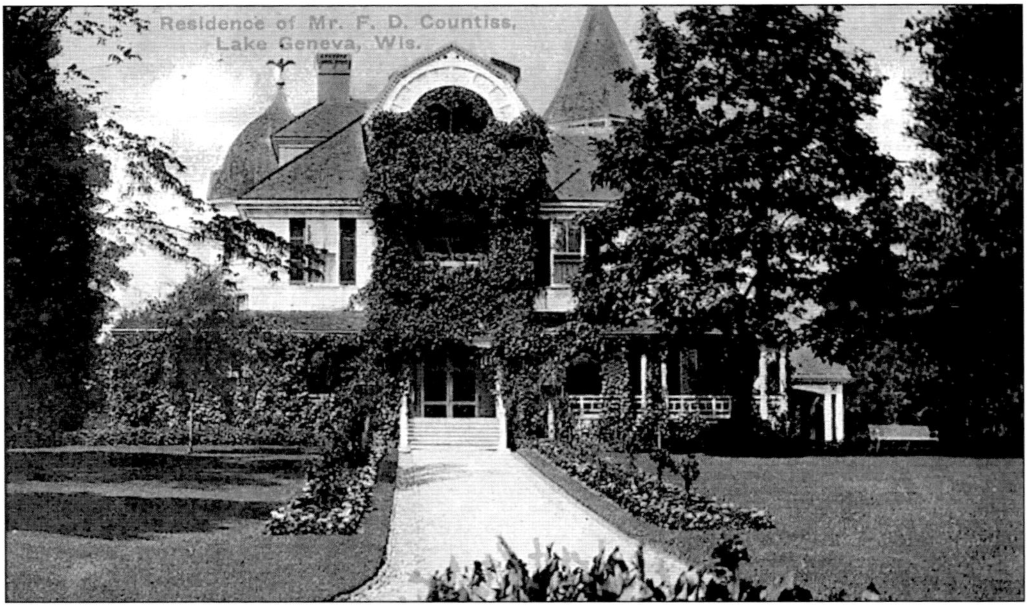

Two Alta Vistas have occupied this site. The first, a wooden structure completed in 1882 and pictured in this 1906 postcard, was built for Orrin Potter, one of the founders of Union Steel. This rambling Victorian structure was engulfed by fire in 1919. Shortly thereafter, it was purchased by William Pelouze, owner of the Pelouze Scale and Balance Company. He collaborated with famous architect Howard Van Dorn Shaw to immediately build a new Alta Vista. In its place arose a palatial Italian-style white-stucco villa with a tile roof. The Pelouze family owned it until 1954, when the surrounding land was subdivided. The main house is still recognizable today.

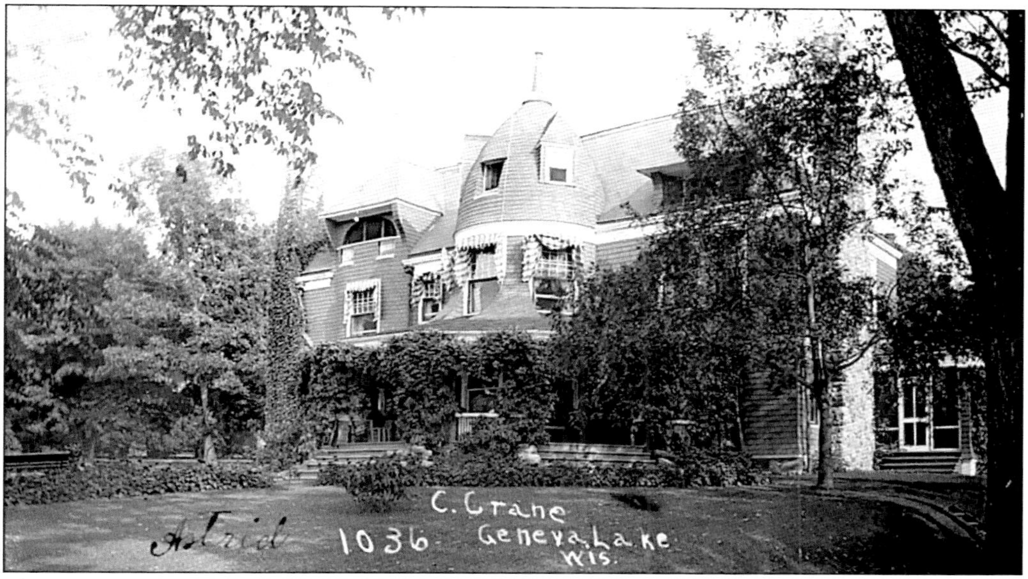

El Nido (The Nest) was built around 1887 for Herbert Crane. It was situated immediately east of the R.T. Crane home known as Jerseyhurst. The Crane estate consisted of four major lakeside residences (only one, Glen Mary, now renamed Windwood, still stands) with many out-buildings on approximately 95 acres, including the area off the lake that is part of the golf community now known as Geneva National. (Courtesy of the John P. Urlakis Collection.)

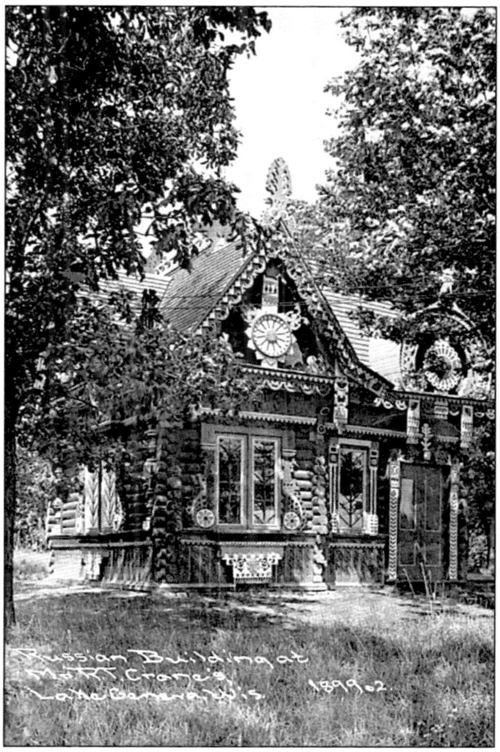

The Russian Building was brought from the St. Louis World's Fair of 1904 by Charles R. Crane. Mr. Crane, having traveled extensively in Russia, had a large collection of Russian artifacts. He greatly admired this replica of a Russian peasant's cottage with its intricate carvings. When Russia withdrew its exhibits from the fair for political reasons, Charles was quick to purchase this structure and move it to the Jerseyhurst grounds, where it was used to host afternoon teas. (Courtesy of the Jerry Glass Collection.)

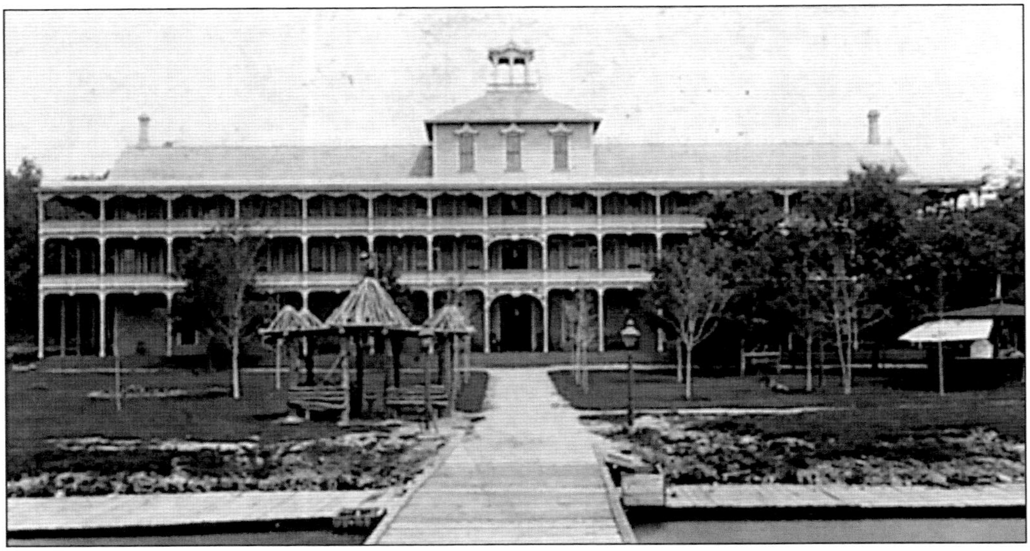

Opened in 1880 as a temperance resort, this four-story hotel was advertised as being the largest in the Midwest. Named the Pishcotaqua Park House Hotel, the Potawatami word for "sparkling waters," it was purchased by John S. Cooke of Chicago in 1890. Following four other failed entrepreneurs, Mr. Cooke put a new slant on the marketing and clientele, and with the trains from Williams Bay bringing Chicagoans to the area, profits started to rise. Unfortunately, a smoldering cigar caught fire and the bowling alley, billiard hall, ice house, barn, and carriage house were all lost. The hotel was remodeled and reopened in 1891 at near capacity, but the success was short-lived as another fire destroyed the entire hotel in December of 1892. John Cooke then switched to gentleman farming, rebuilt the relatively new billiard hall as a residence for his family, and renamed it Ara Glen. The home now graces the shoreline, but most of the property was subdivided. For many years the estate was the site of Camp Augustana. Today most of it is known as Knollwood subdivision, though some belongs to the Ara Glen subdivision, while another part is the Chapel on the Hill Church. (Courtesy of the Brown-Gabriel Collection.)

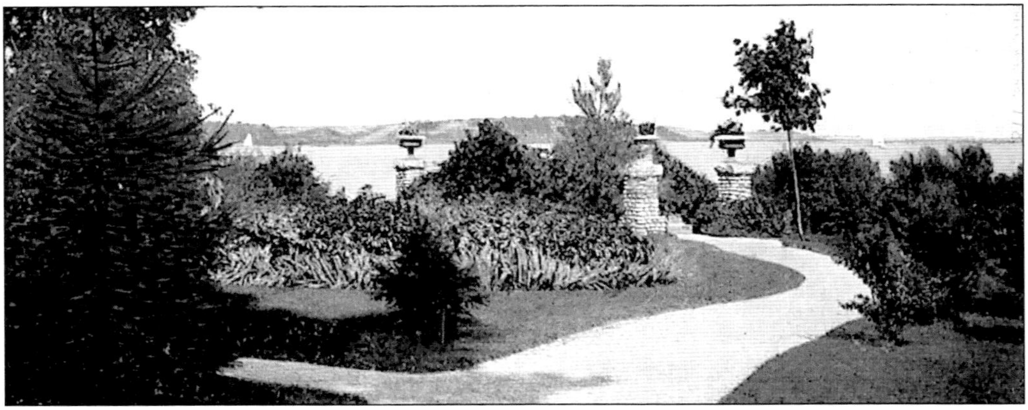

When Edward Uihlein became the owner of Villa Palatina in 1899, he changed the name to Forest Glen. With the help of landscape architect Jens Jensen, he enhanced the fertile land that contained numerous springs by creating extensive gardens with waterfalls and ponds. The mansion had a disastrous fire in 1922, and subsequently the land was sold and subdivided. Part of this estate became the subdivision now known as The Gardens.

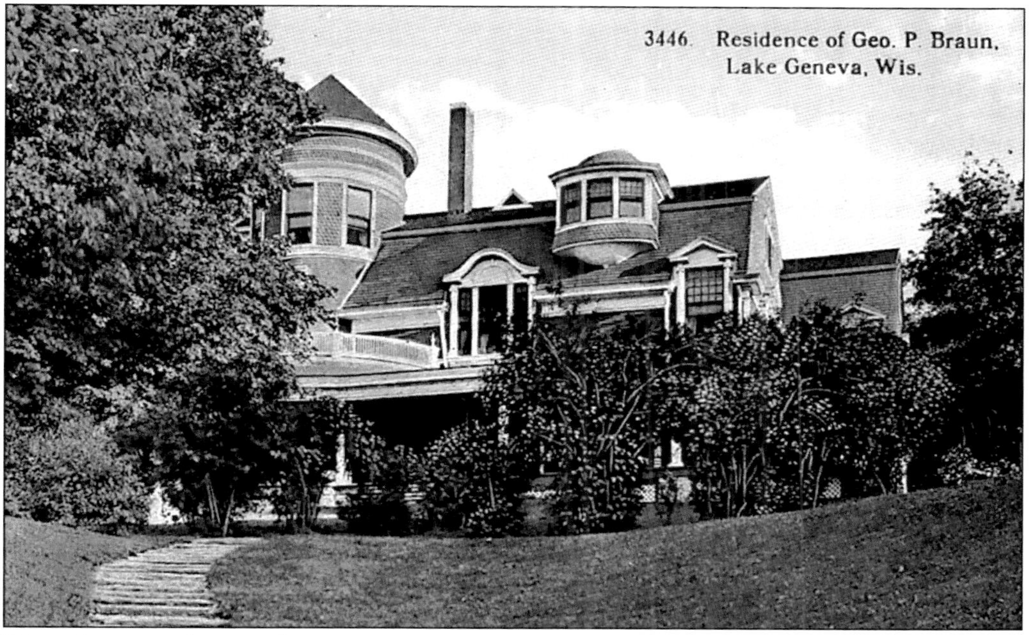

The Echoes was the main house on the 62-acre estate which is now Brookwood Association. This beautifully maintained South Shore showplace was designed by Henry Lord Gay and completed in 1896 at a cost of $18,000. It is a splendid example of the Queen Ann style. The original owner was George P. Braun, who made his fortune producing oleo and margarine in the late 1800s.

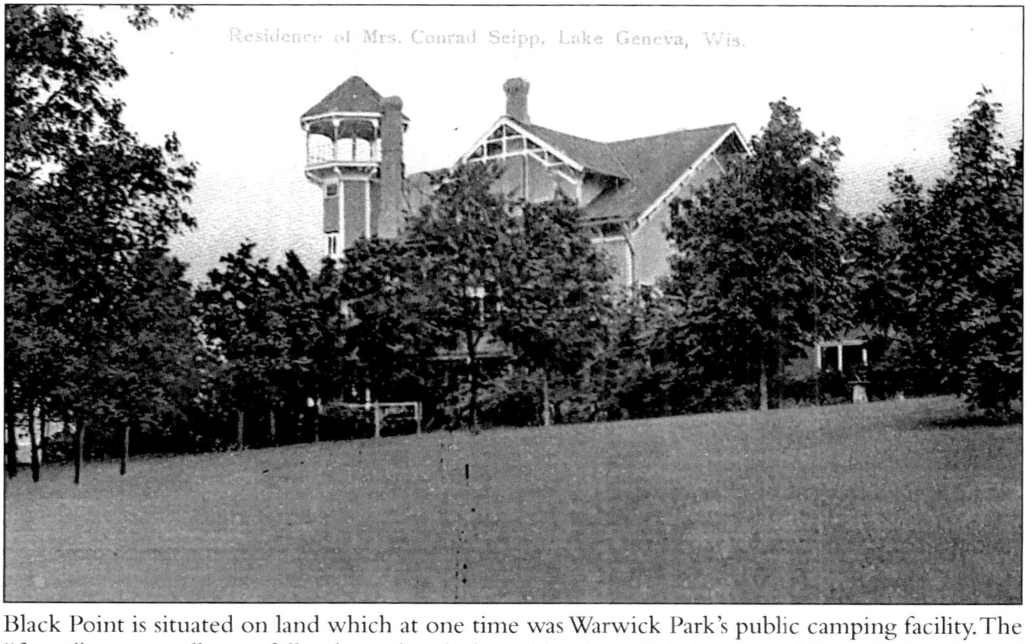

Black Point is situated on land which at one time was Warwick Park's public camping facility. The "forest" was actually carefully planned and planted by the original owners, Mr. and Mrs. Conrad Seipp. Today the house, still owned by the Seipp's descendants, is almost totally obscured by huge firs and pines which cover the point.

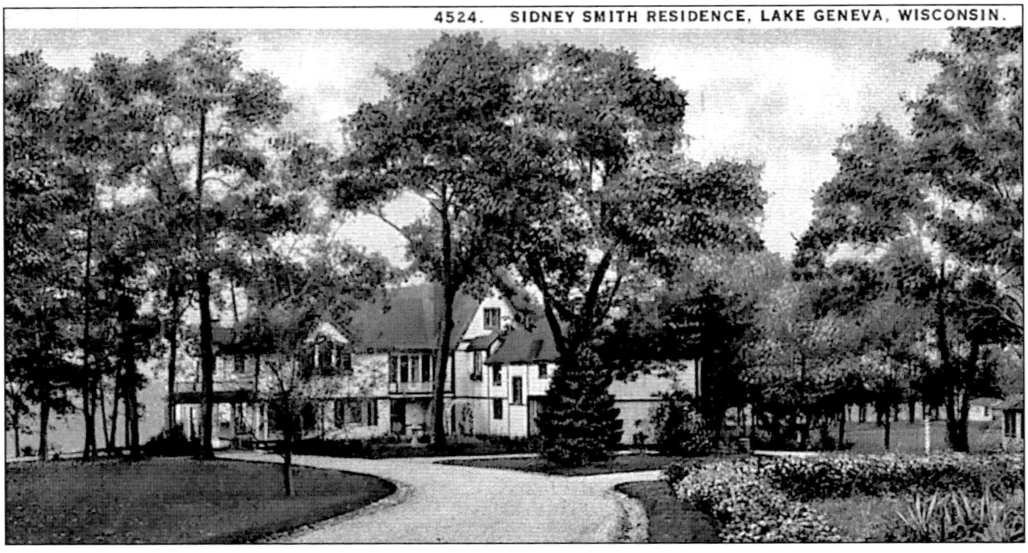

Sidney Smith was the cartoonist who created "Andy Gump," a popular cartoon character. "The Gumps" started running in the Chicago Tribune in 1917, and was the Tribune's first daily cartoon strip. At various times, Sidney Smith owned two homes on Geneva Lake, including Trudehurst (originally called Glen Arden), shown on this 1925 postcard.

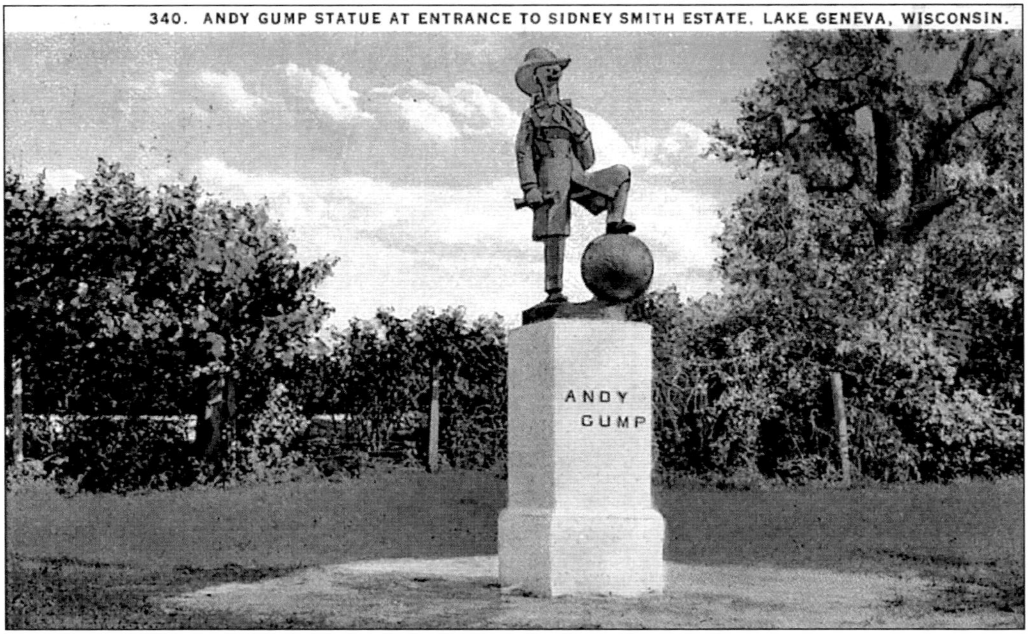

This bronze Andy Gump statue was a gift from the Chicago Tribune to Mr. Smith in 1924, and was displayed on the lawn of his Geneva Lake home. The unveiling of the statue came in conjunction with the announcement of a tongue-in-cheek "Gump for President" campaign. (He lost to Calvin Coolidge.) After Mr. Smith died in a car accident in 1935, the new owner of his estate later donated the statue to the City of Lake Geneva. Flat Iron Park became Gump's new home in the 1940s.

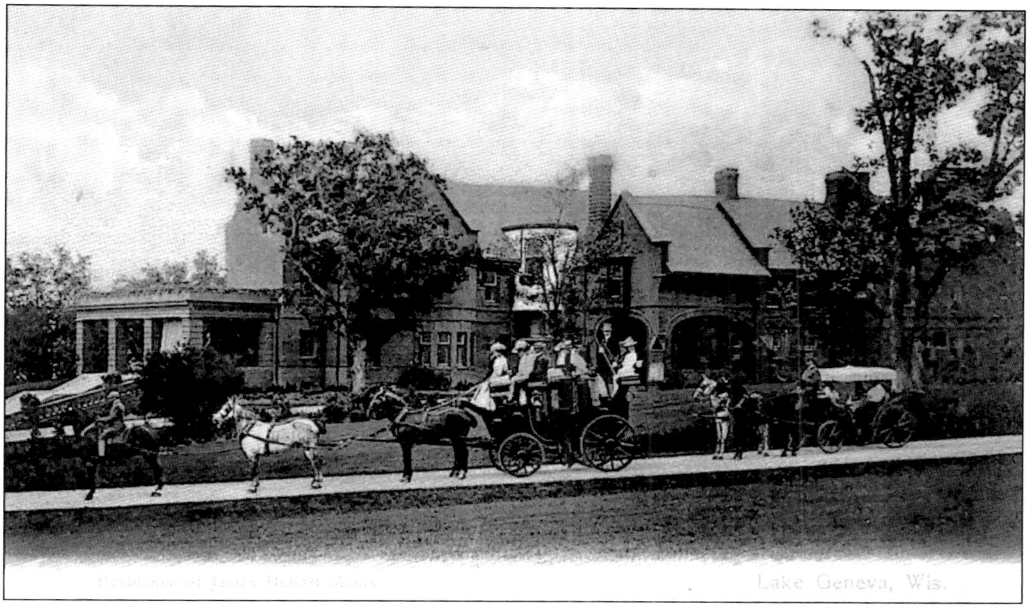

Of the 30 or so buildings that originally made up the Moore estate, Loramoor, only a few remain today; they are presently private homes of the Loramoor Association. Horse lover James H. Moore (1852–1916) owned the Diamond Match Company and the National Biscuit Company.

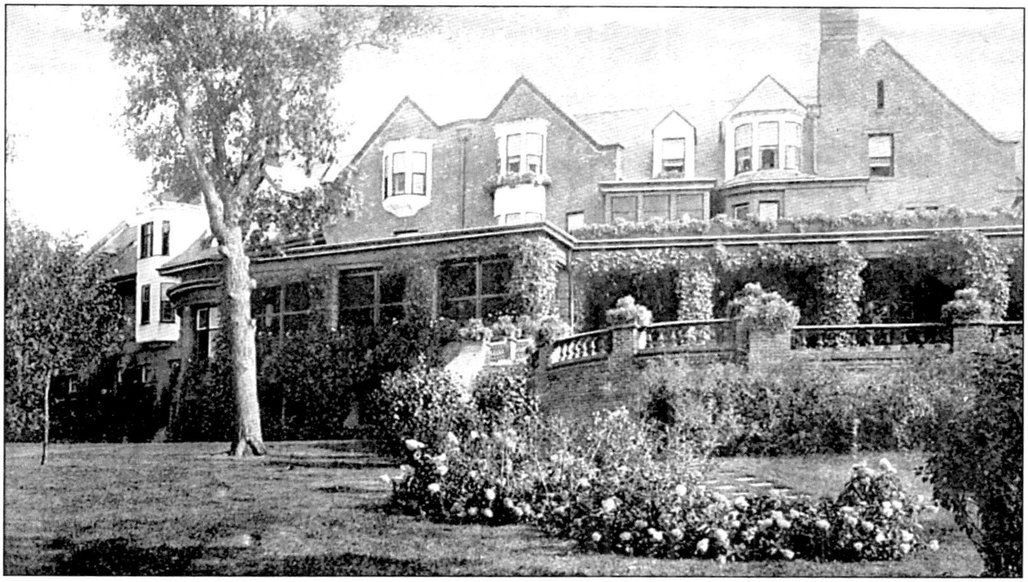

The 27-room main house of the Moore estate was torn down in the late 1970s after being used as a monastery for 30 years by the Franciscan Friars. (Courtesy of the Jerry Glass Collection.)

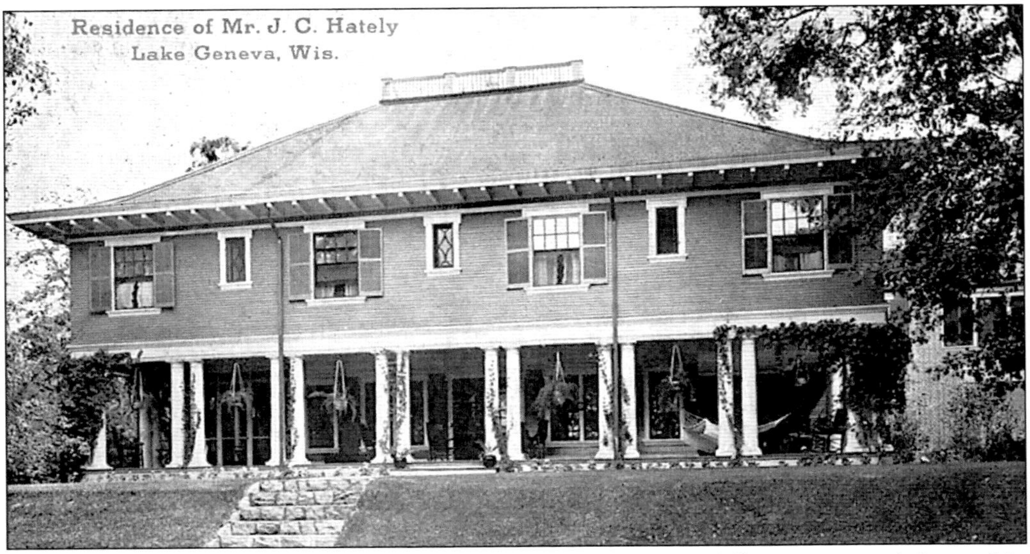

Mr. John Hately built the Galewood Estate in 1893. After many different owners, it burned in 1928. In 1930 the new owner, Mrs. Jessie Bartlett Hooper, built a magnificent Spanish-style villa and named it Casa del Sueno, Spanish for House of Dreams. She sold it to the Starck family, owners of the Starck Piano Company. The Starck family was the first to live in the mansion after construction. For many years, the home was owned by Lee Phillip (Chicago television personality) and William Bell (creator of the daytime soap operas *The Young and the Restless* and *The Bold and the Beautiful*). It has had many renovations, but is still known as Casa del Sueno.

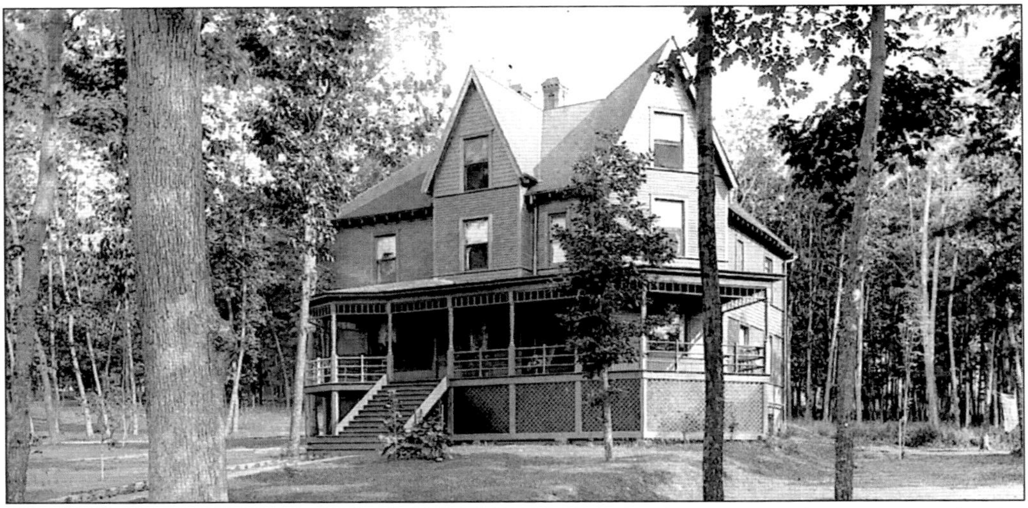

Originally named Six Oaks, this Victorian home was built by Professor David Swing around 1884. As the pastor of the Fourth Presbyterian Church in Chicago, he was best known as "Reverend Swing." Famous for his inspirational sermons, he was sometimes controversial, but well-loved by his congregation. His home, which remains on the lakefront today, features a pulpit area at the top of an immense staircase where he would speak to his followers. Swing's daughter and son-in-law took possession after his death in 1894 and re-named it Swinghurst. They resided there until 1934 when the property was sold and subdivided. (Courtesy of the Geneva Lake Museum.)

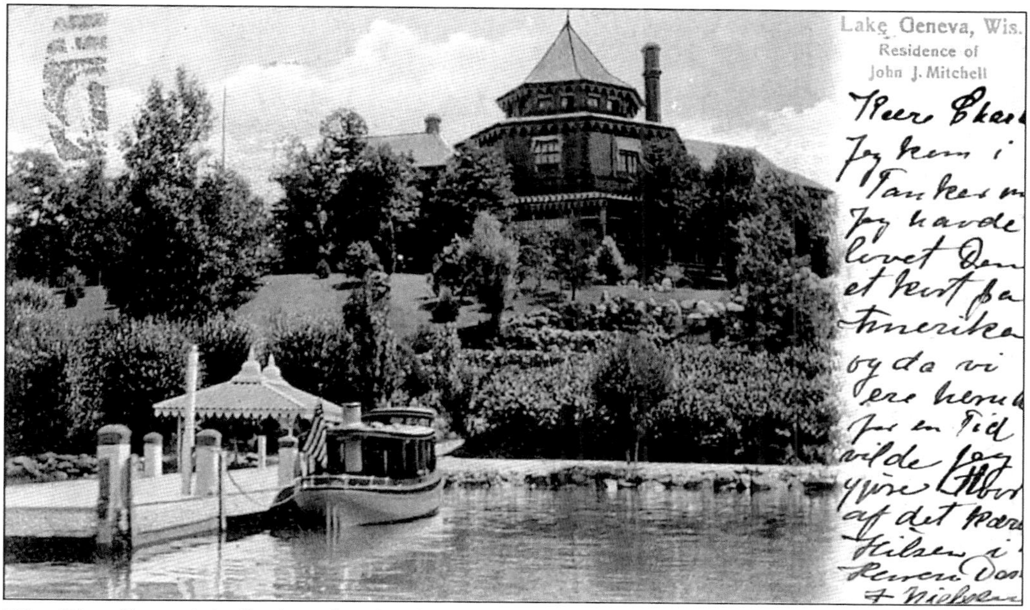

F.R. Chandler originally bought this home, Ceylon Court, from the Ceylon Government at the close of the 1893 Colombian Exposition in Chicago. The exotic hand-carved mansion was dismantled in Chicago and shipped by train in 26 boxcars to the shores of Geneva Lake. Located on the point of land at the north end of Buttons Bay, Ceylon Court was acquired by John J. Mitchell, founder of the Continental Illinois National Bank, in 1901. After the tragic deaths of Mr. and Mrs. Mitchell in an auto accident, F.L. Maytag, the washing machine manufacturer, purchased the estate. In 1958, the furnishings and hand-carved wooden trim of Ceylon Court were auctioned off and the house was razed. The property is now known as Maytag Point.

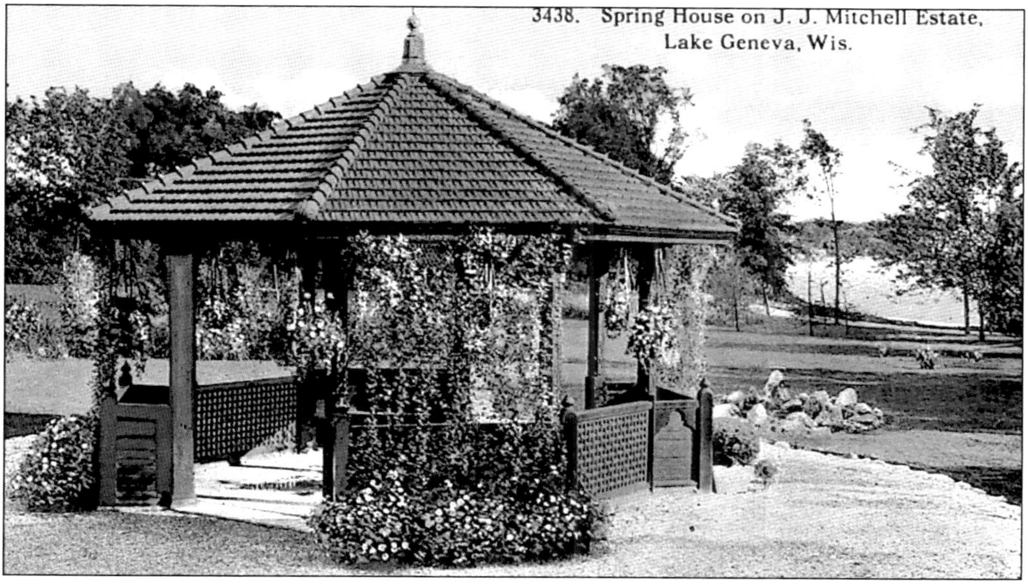

The Spring House on the Ceylon Court Estate was constructed to imitate the main house, which was a replica of a Buddhist Temple and featured 19 different woods native to Ceylon.

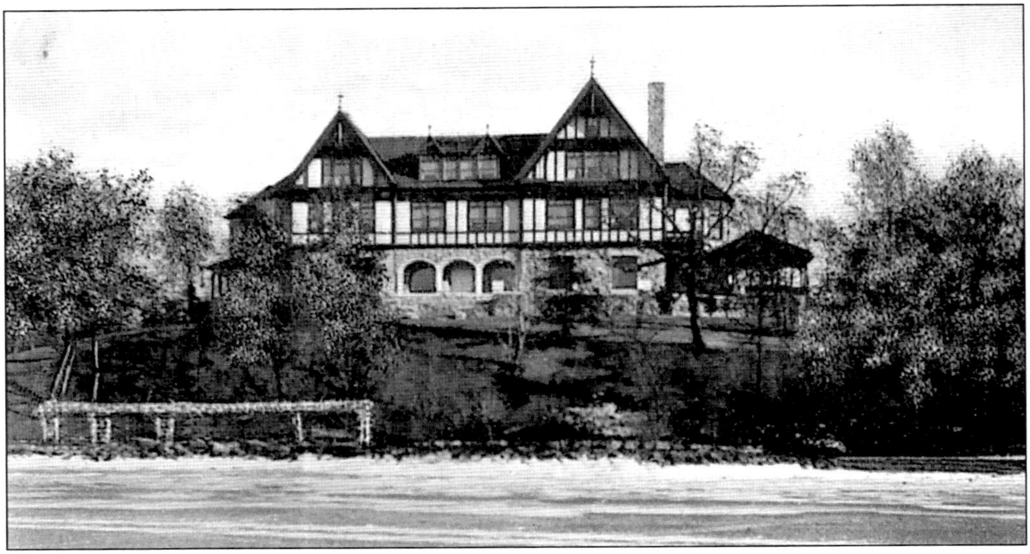

Harrose Hall was built in 1898 by Harry and Rosalie Buckingham Selfridge on the east lake shore next to Ceylon Court. The massive stone and wood mansion was rarely used because the family moved to London, England, where Harry established the famous Selfridges of London department store. The name Harrose (derived from Harry and Rosalie) was changed to Somerset when Lawrence and Eleanor Countiss Whiting purchased the mansion in the late 1920s. Although the land was subdivided, the home remained in the Whiting family until it was torn down in 1975. It is now the site of Somerset Condominiums. (Courtesy of the Joy Peterkin Rasin Collection.)

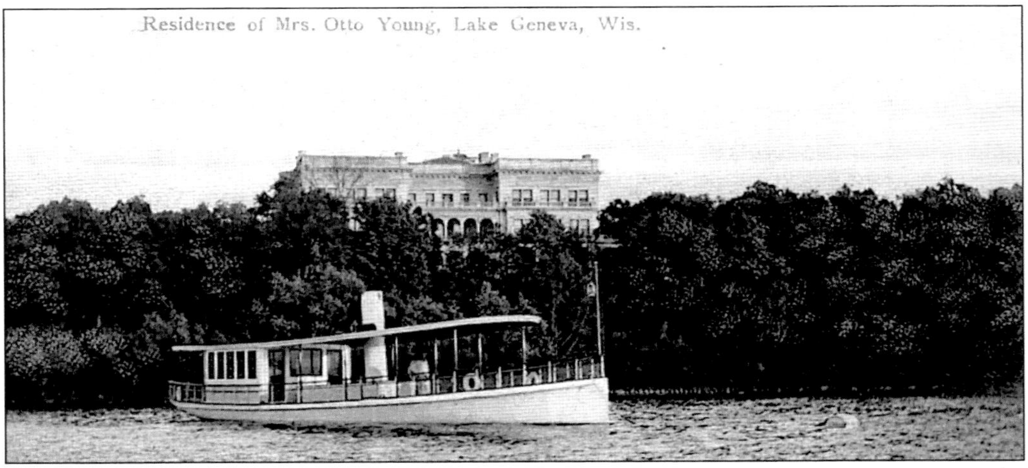

Originally named the Younglands, Stone Manor was built by Otto Young. Construction on the four-story mansion reportedly cost more than one million dollars at the turn of the century. It contained 50 rooms on seven levels and included a dining room that seated 100, a nine-hole miniature golf course, a bowling alley, and a roof garden. In 1898, Mr. Young commissioned the building of a steamboat which he named the *Olivette* in honor of his wife. In 1930, the boat was rechristened the *Polaris*, and it remains the oldest boat in operation on the lake today. Young died in 1906, and his wife in 1916. The property was acquired by one of their four daughters, Cecelia, who deeded it to her daughter Gwendolyn Koch in 1938.

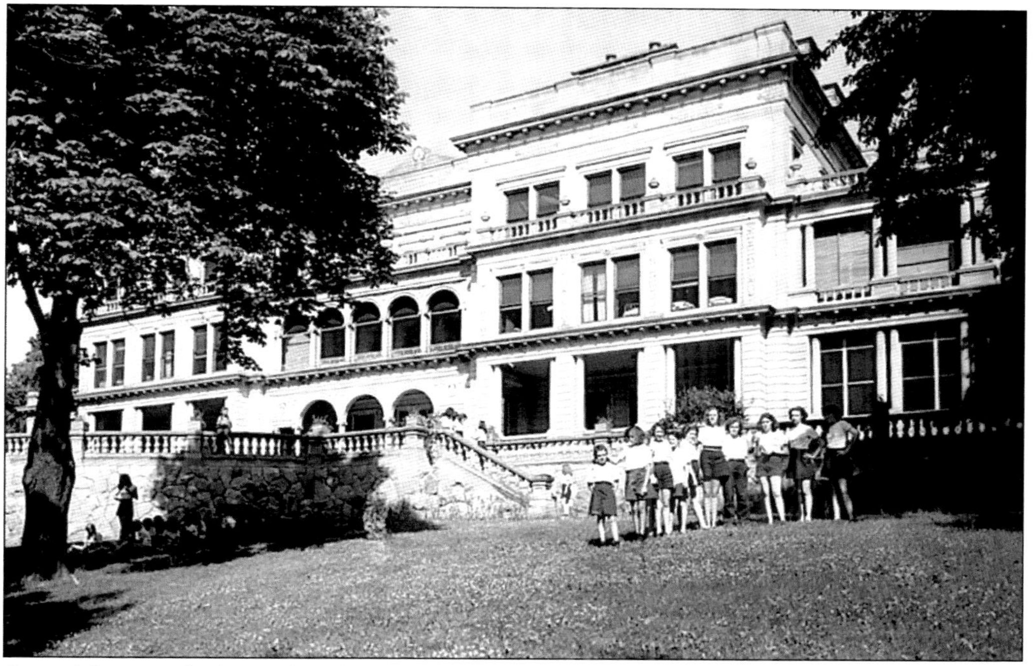

Gwendolyn Koch donated eight acres and the mansion, Younglands (Stone Manor), to the Episcopal Order of St. Anne. They operated a church camp and school for girls there from 1938 through the 1940s. The property was involved in several court actions over ownership from the 1950s to the 1980s.

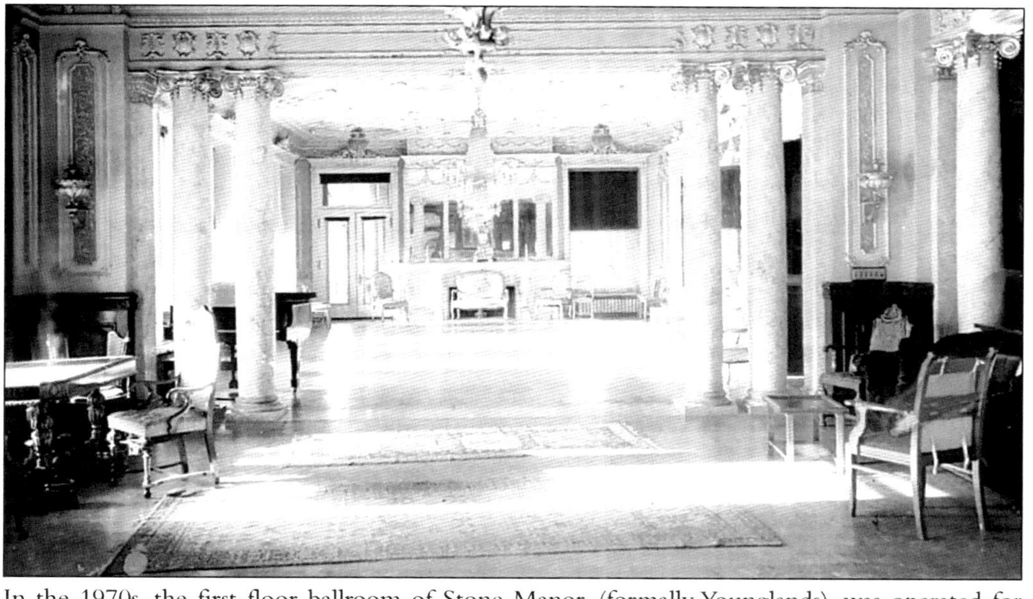

In the 1970s, the first-floor ballroom of Stone Manor, (formally Younglands), was operated for a short time as an elegant French restaurant known as the Stone Manor Inn. The building was refurbished in the 1990s to its original splendor and is now luxury condominiums. (Courtesy of the Jerry Glass Collection.)

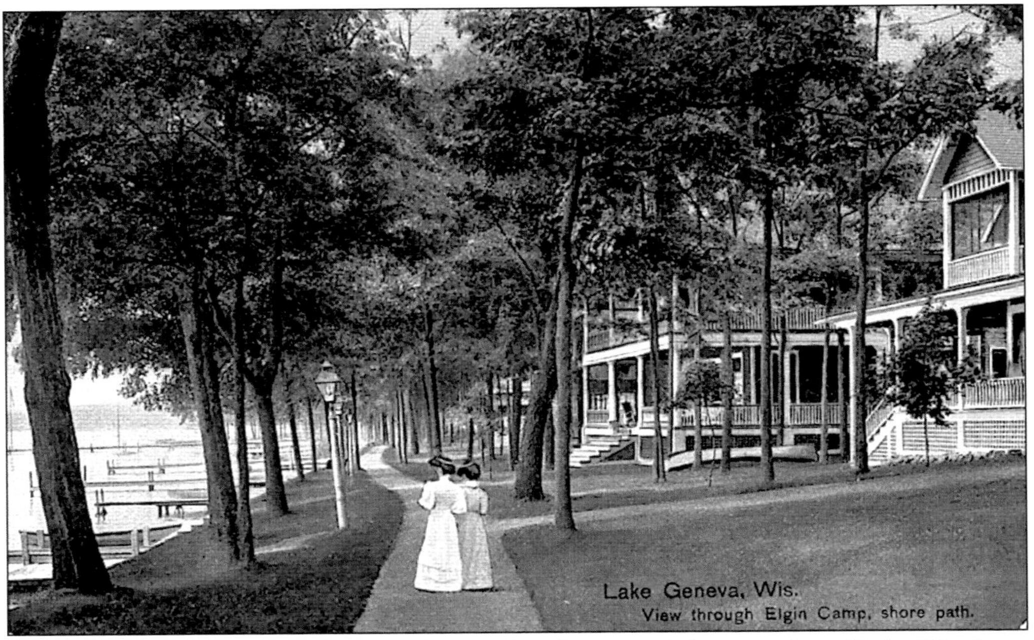

The Elgin Club territory was originally purchased by two fishermen from Elgin, Illinois, to provide shelter during their fishing trips. Since the parcel of land they bought was larger than they needed, they formed a club to share the property. Elgin Club currently consists of 18 homes, some of which are among the oldest on the lake. (Courtesy of the Stephen P. Beers Collection.)

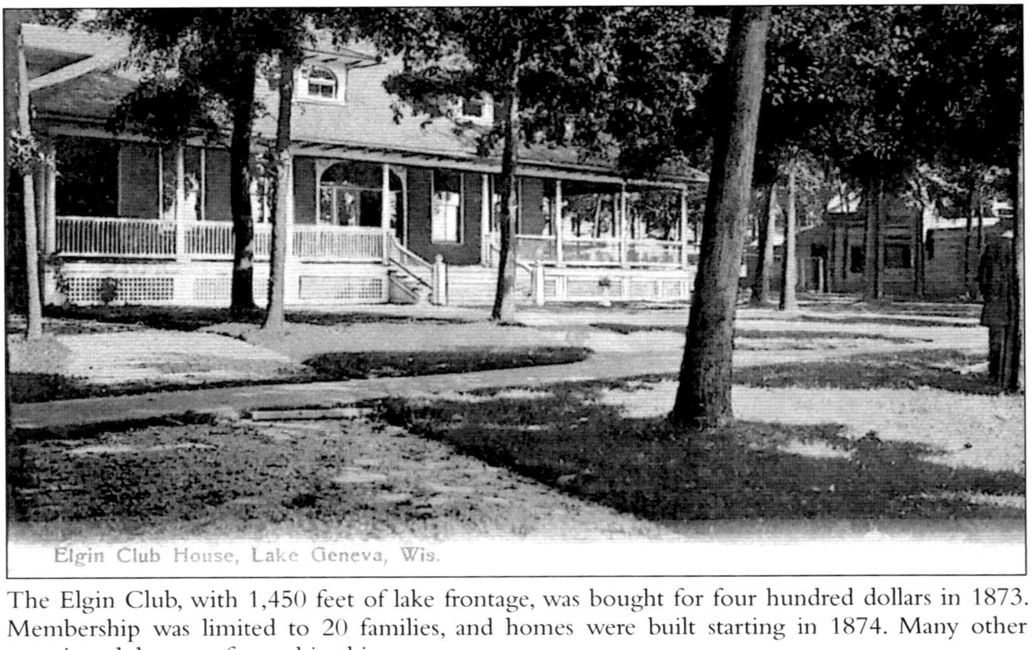

The Elgin Club, with 1,450 feet of lake frontage, was bought for four hundred dollars in 1873. Membership was limited to 20 families, and homes were built starting in 1874. Many other camping clubs were formed in this same manner.

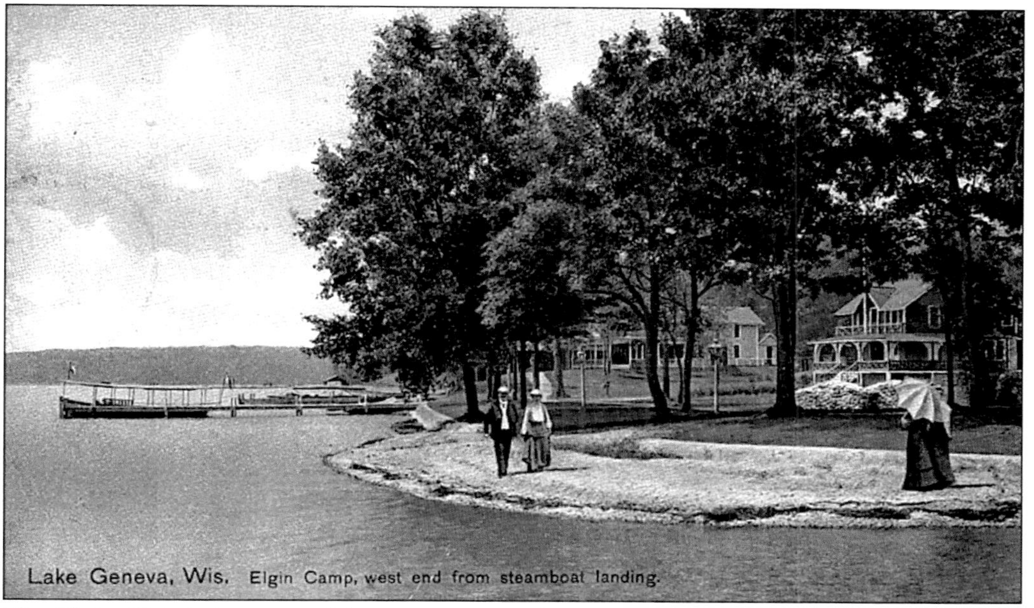

The Elgin Club is just one of the associations still in existence on Geneva Lake. Many of the members are descendents of the original home owners. Clubs such as this one played a major role in the growth and development of the lake.

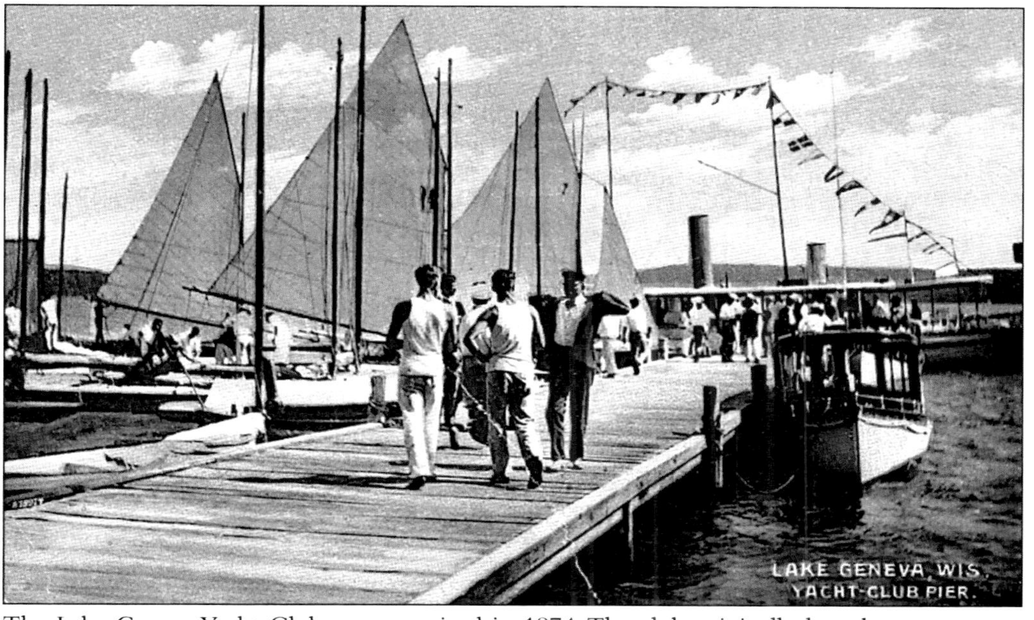

The Lake Geneva Yacht Club was organized in 1874. The club originally leased property near the Elgin Club from 1906 to 1915 when it was formed by a merger of the West End and Geneva Lake clubs. In 1926, the LGYC purchased and remodeled an old residence on the south shore in Fontana, which became its new headquarters. When this lease expired in 1967, Ernst Schmidt, commodore from 1931 to 1935, donated a 112-foot strip of the lakeshore next to his Geneva Lake Boat Company where the present clubhouse was built.

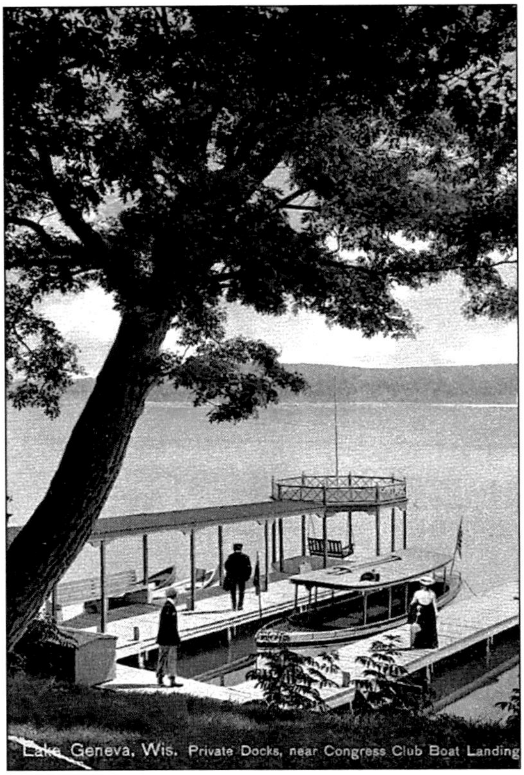

When the Chicago fire spared the area where Ashland, Marshfield, and Paulina Streets met Congress Street, residents of this area got together in 1882 and formed the Congress Club. Shortly thereafter, a semi-circle of beautiful summer homes was created along with a dining hall and clubhouse.

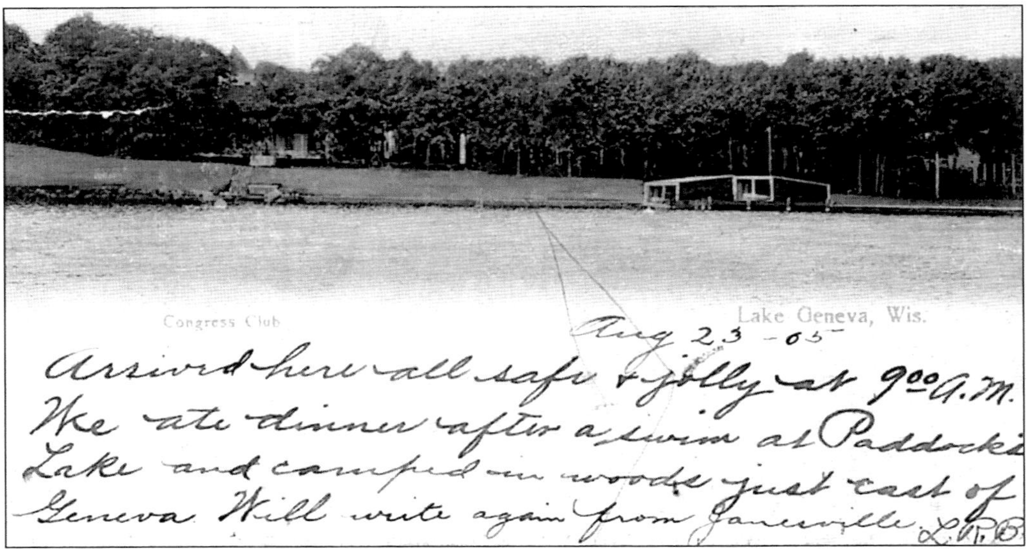

Back then, the majority of cottages were not well insulated and certainly not winterized. Most did not have individual kitchens; instead they had one main dining hall. These homes, many occupied by descendents of the original owners, are still intact today. While greatly updated to modern standards, the charming homes of Congress Club still retain the original color scheme of white with dark green trim.

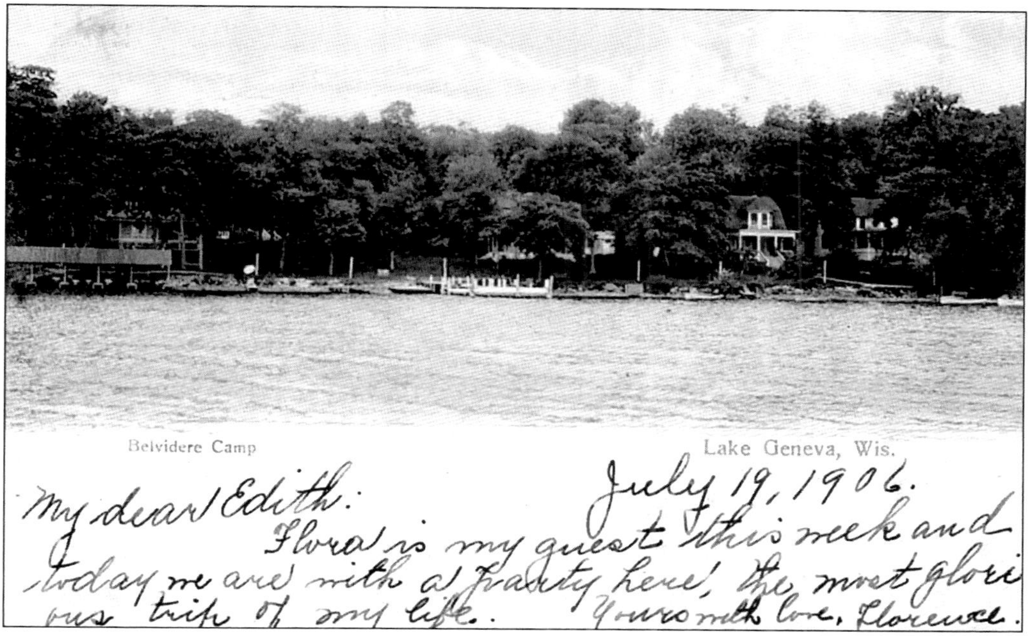

The Belvidere Camp was located on the north edge of Fontana after being founded in 1875 by 27 families from Belvidere, Illinois. Originally a tent campground, the 28 lots were divided among the members by draws. Large horse barns once stood where the parking lot is today; they were built to accommodate the horses, tents, carriages, and buggies used for the two-day trip from Belvidere. Today it is known as Belvidere Park.

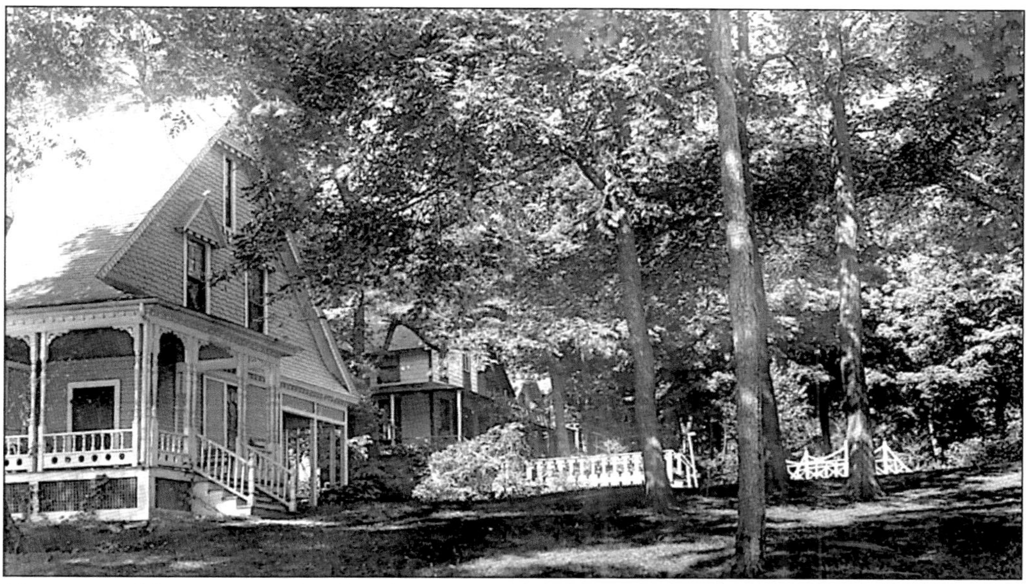

(Courtesy of the Brown-Gabriel Collection.)

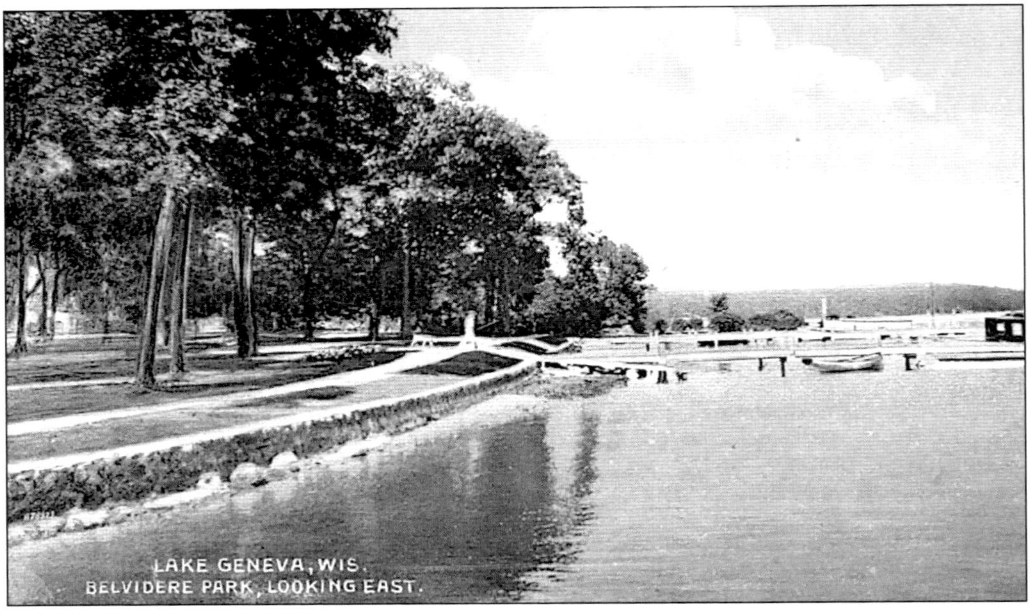

Belvidere Park was the first club on the lake, once a part of Edward Uhlien's estate, Forest Glen. (Courtesy of the Robert Webster Sr. Collection.)

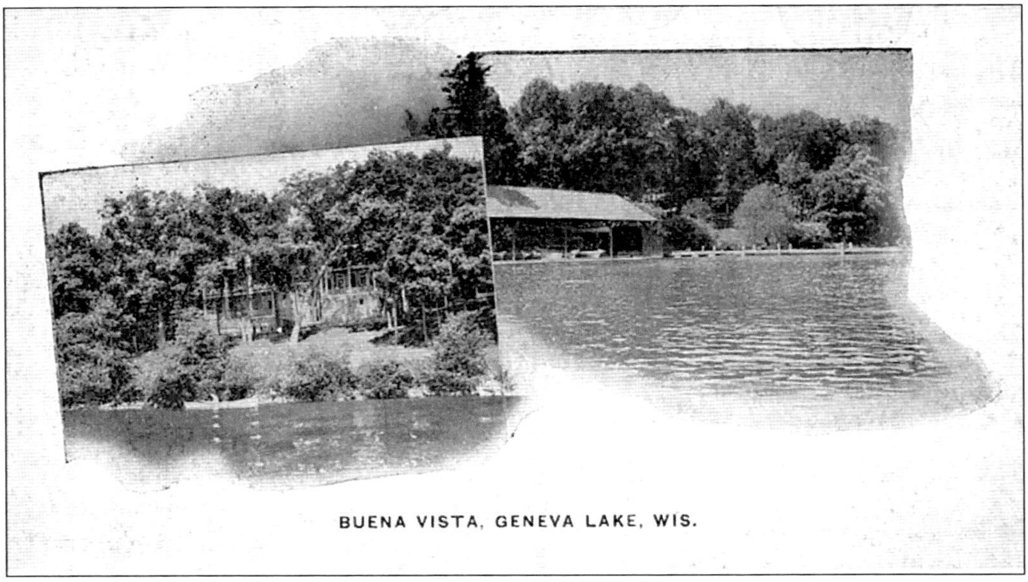

Buena Vista was begun in 1901 by Warren F. Furbeck, who was a private secretary to Charles T. Yerkes, the streetcar magnate. Many of the cottages in Buena Vista were owned by the developer and rented to guests, but in most instances, space was leased to campers who brought their own tents.

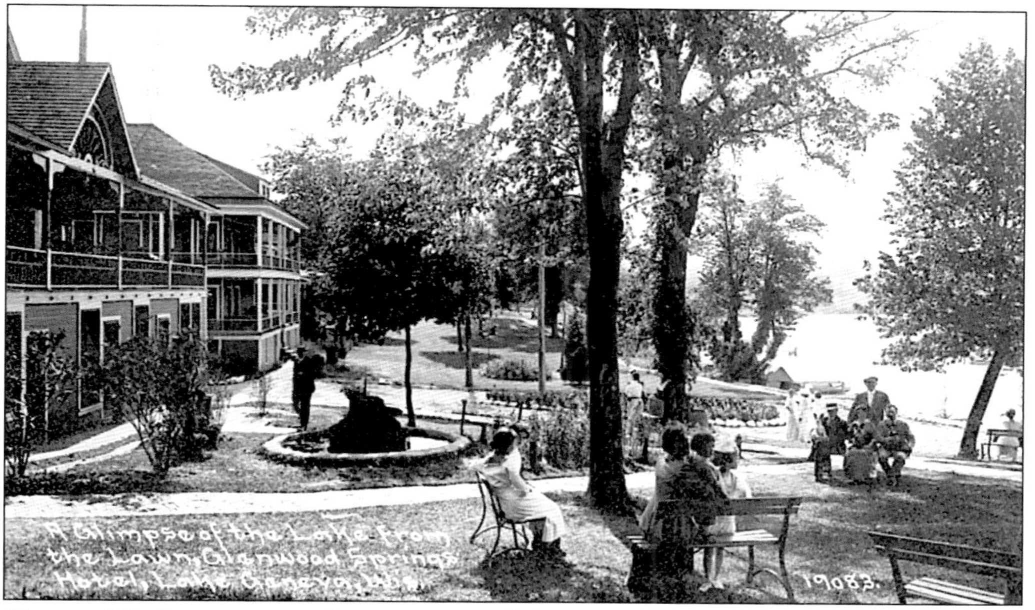

Glenwood Springs was a popular retreat around the turn of the century and was known for its therapeutic springs. (Courtesy of the Jerry Glass Collection.)

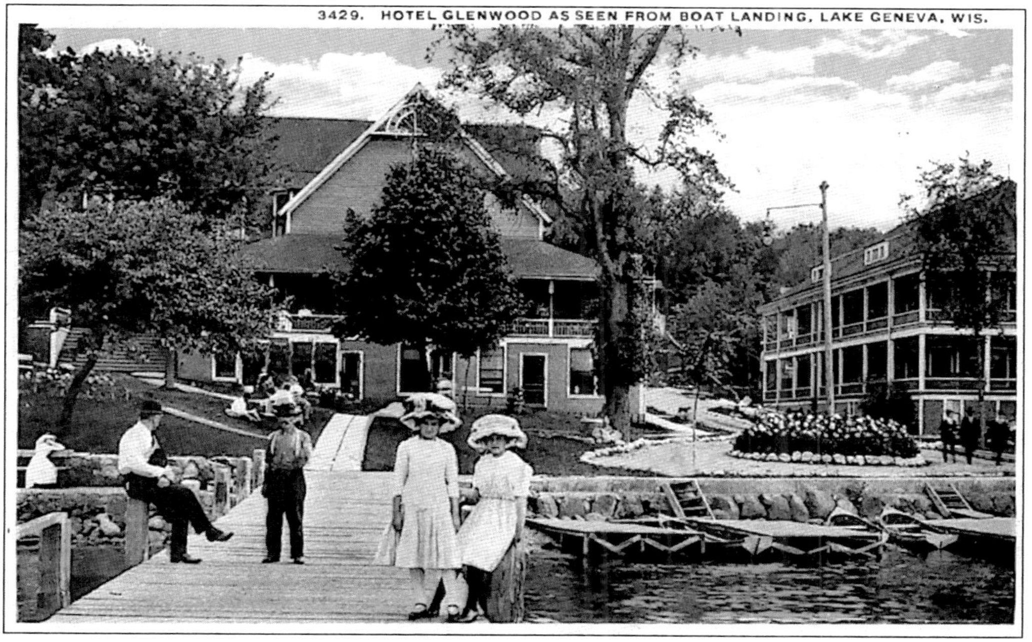

The Hotel Glenwood was built in 1902 by Robert J. Marshall of Harvard, Illinois. It was destroyed by fire in 1930; the building that stands today (now condominiums) is a replica of the original.

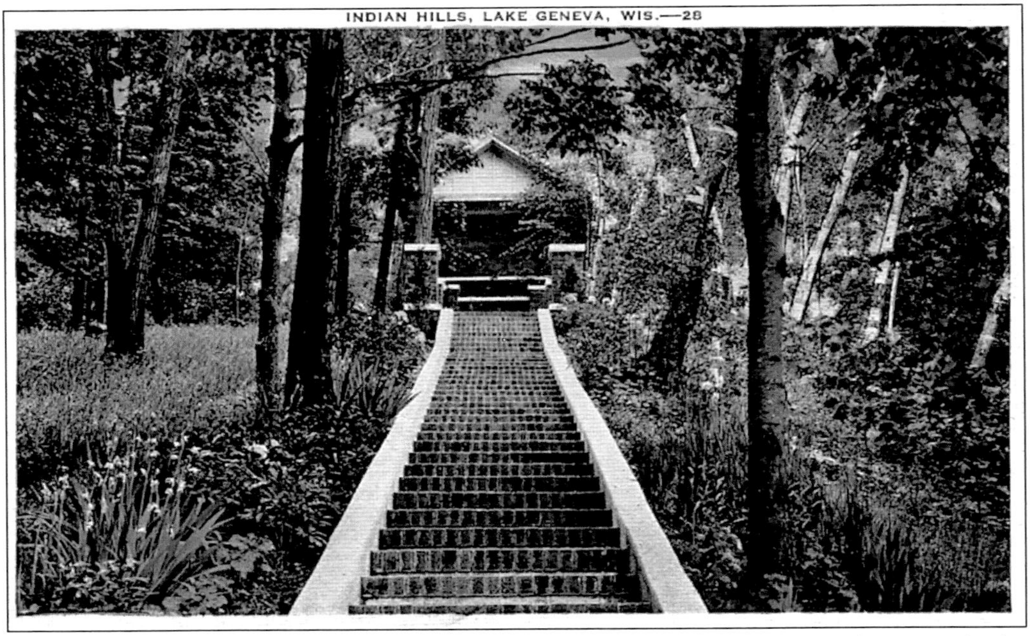

Indian Hills was developed in 1927 and was named for a large Indian mound just inside the west lakeside gate.

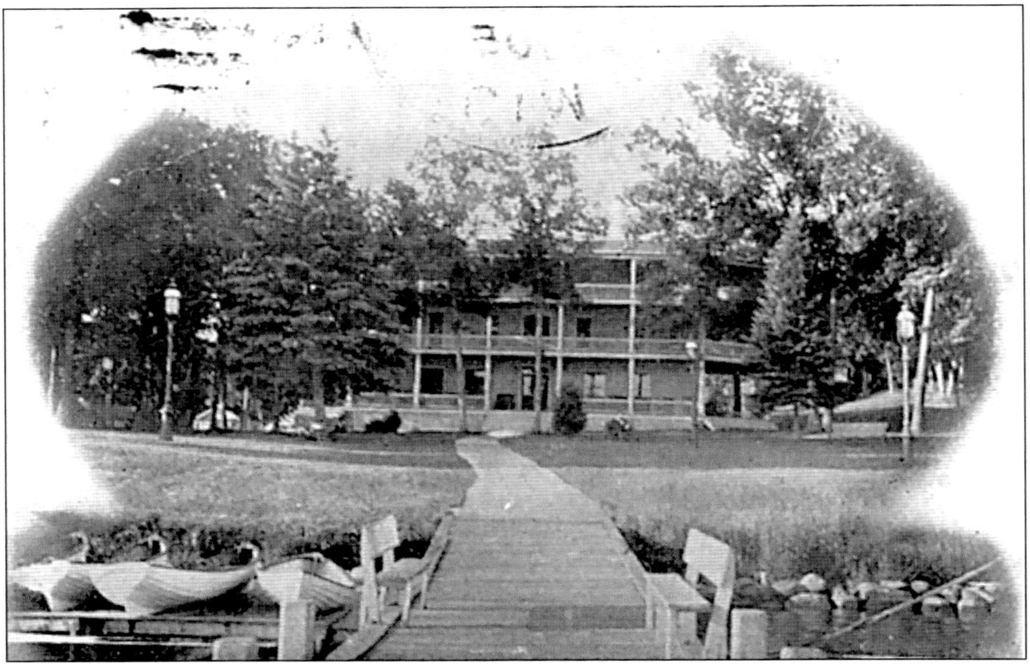

In the 1800s, the Hotel Green was located on what is now known as Club Unique. Sidney Middleton and U.S.G. Cherry Jr. developed this association in 1928 on land adjoining Indian Hills on the east. The main house, which was known as the Starck residence, was sold to Mr. and Mrs. George Kiefer Sr. in 1939. (Courtesy of the Jerry Glass Collection.)

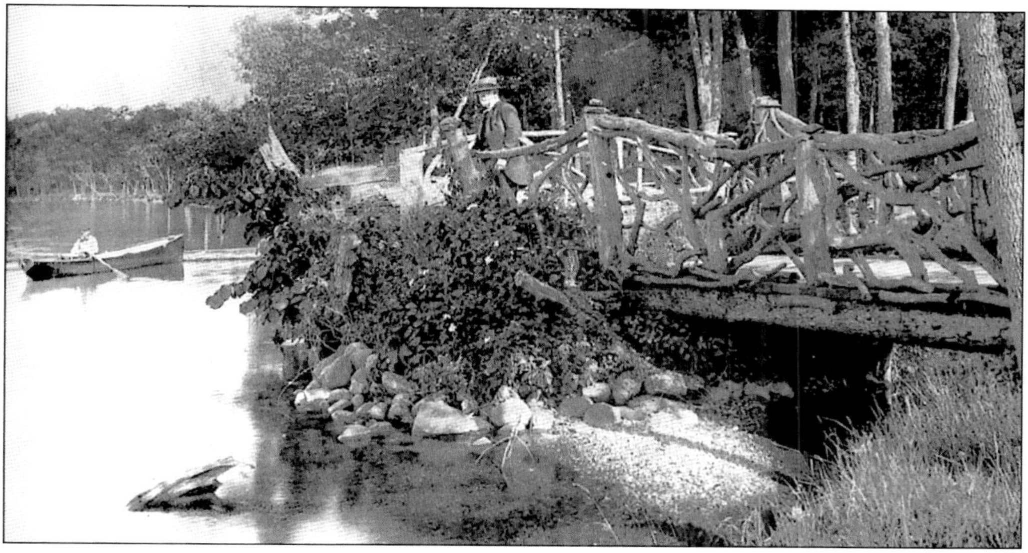

In 1875, the Edward G. Ayer estate was established here. It consisted of 1200 acres and was famous for its wildflowers and farmland. Mr. Ayer was co-owner of the Ayer and Lord Railroad Tie Company and was instrumental in the building of the Art Institute in Chicago. Today this area is known as Abbey Springs, and you can still see the stone wall that parallels South Shore Drive which was part of the Ayer estate. (Courtesy of the Geneva Lake Museum.)

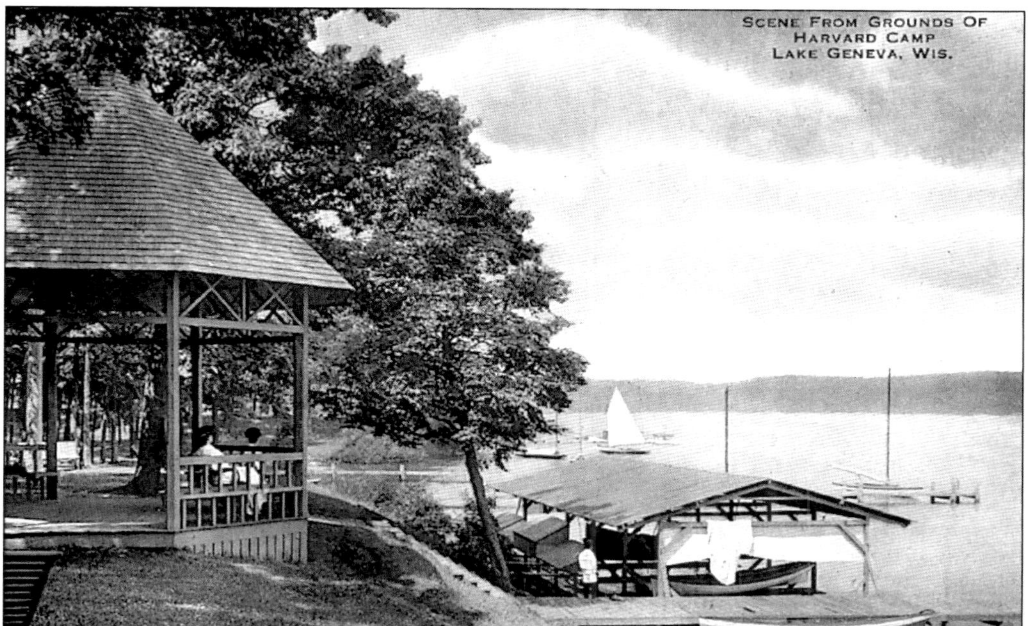

The Harvard Club was originally called Harvard Camp, and in 1875, it was only a tent camp. The early campers traveled the 12-mile dirt road from Harvard, Illinois by horse drawn wagons. Around 1880, the people decided to build their cottages and divided the property in 25 lots. In November 1963, a disastrous fire hit the club, and because of modern zoning laws, four of the seven homes destroyed were not allowed to be rebuilt.

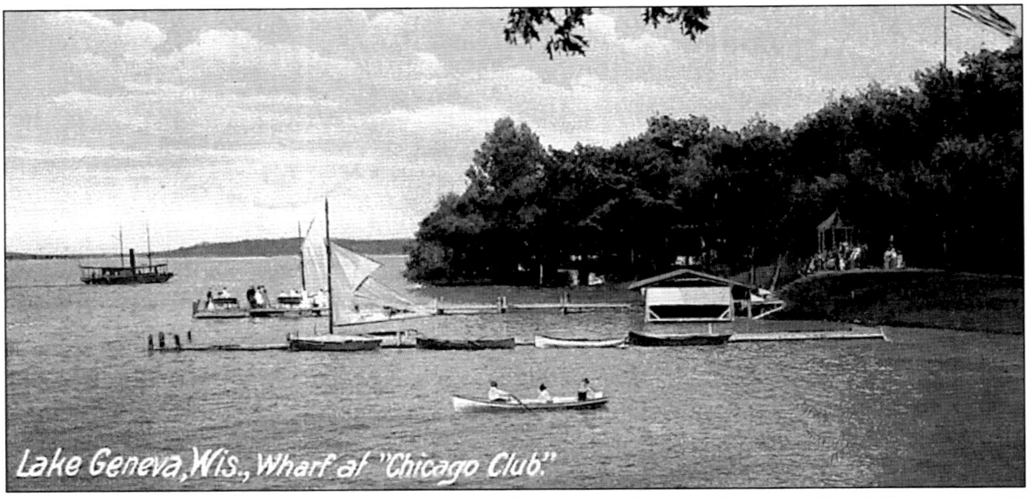

The Chicago Club was established in 1858 with the purcahse of 17 acres of land from the U.S. Government for $8 an acre. The poeple who purchased it at the time were from the Englewood area of Chicago, and it was originally called the Englewood Camp. They built a cookhouse and pitched large tents there every summer. The women would live there throughout the summer, while the gentlemen would visit most weekends. In 1886, the then owners of the property decided to build homes. There were six homes built, but none had kicthens. They still cooked their meals in the cookhouse, and at that time, many of the owners were not from the Englewood area, and chose a new name, the Chicago Club. Since then, the property has been inhabited by several generations of families. The homes have been considerably expanded, including the addition of kitchens. The cookhouse was taken down in the late 1920s.

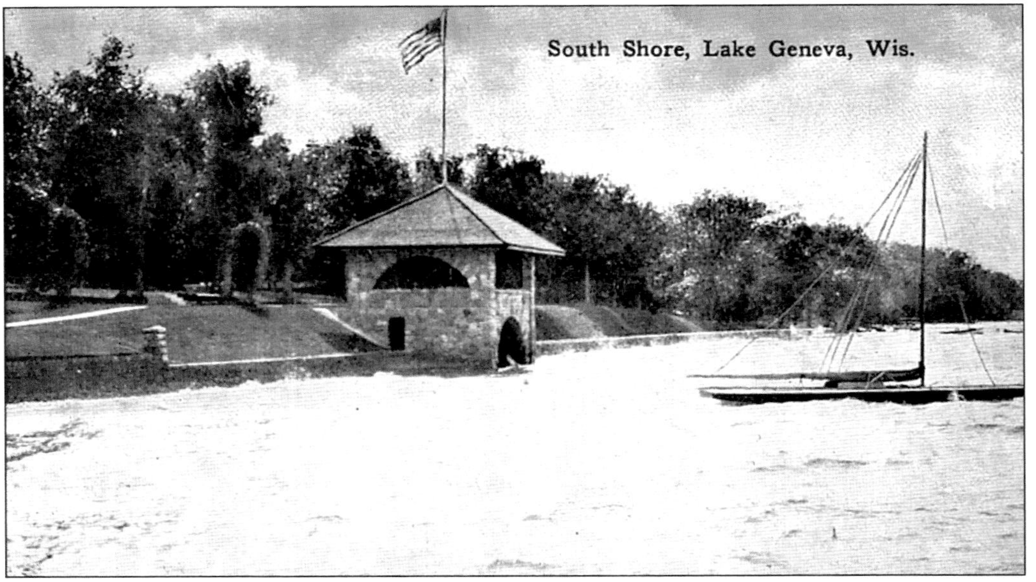

The Lake Geneva Club property was once a private estate owned by Edward Norton and called Our Home. The pavilion's stonework was echoed in the home's façade and, while the house no longer exists (it burned down in 1905), the pavilion anchors the Lake Geneva Club, which began in 1922. Most of the homes in this association were built between 1922 and 1930.

Two

The Beauty of the Lake . . . Moments in Time

Geneva Lake, referred to as Lake Geneva, or Kishwauketoe by the Indians, is surrounded by three towns: Lake Geneva, Williams Bay (the "Bay"), and Fontana (also known as "Fontana-on-Geneva-Lake"). Fontana's name was derived from the Italian and French words for a spring or fountain. The lake area boasts beaches, nature preserves, spring-fed streams, ponds, hills, and terrain well-suited for golf or skiing, as well as fields of farm land and abundant wildlife. Vintage postcards clearly depict the historic beauty and significance of the towns and lake.

The lake originated from the Michigan glacier; it is geologically known as a mountain lake due to its great depth, hard bottom, few shallow areas, and a very small drainage basin. Lake water comes from a combination of rainfall, springs, and streams. The outlet for Geneva Lake is the White River to the northeast.

Geneva Lake's beauty lies not only in the lake itself, but in the woods, flowers, and wildlife. Hawks, deer, birds, geese, swans, fish, cranes, and mink swim in the lake while herons, deer, turkey, fox, rabbits, and coyotes roam the properties. The farms and ranches in the Geneva Lake area are home to cows, pigs, horses, ponies, donkeys, and llama. All provide added beauty to the lake and the land surrounding it.

Each season, the lake offers its unique beauty. Summer, with the foliage in full green bloom, means colorful wild flowers, manicured flower gardens, and brightly colored birds. Farmers' fields add to the color with corn stalks, vegetable gardens, and sunflower fields. Bright stars and a full moon augment clear summer nights. Fall's vivid colors reflect on the clear blue water. In winter, the frozen lake looks like crystal glass, blanketed with snow. Green sprouts herald spring as yellow and white daffodils appear in unexpected places.

Each season offers its own smells and sounds, adding to the lake's beauty. Summer brings laughter echoing along the shores and the shouts of boaters on the lake. The smells of summer are productive farms lands and fresh-cut grass. In fall, leaves and acorns rustle as they fall and the smell of fresh crisp air and burning leaves fills the air. Winter brings the hush of snow fall and cracking ice on the lake, along with the scent of wood smoke. Spring offers the fresh smell of new life and the chirping of birds. Geneva Lake's beauty is a backdrop for the historic significance of the towns that surround it and the memories they provide.

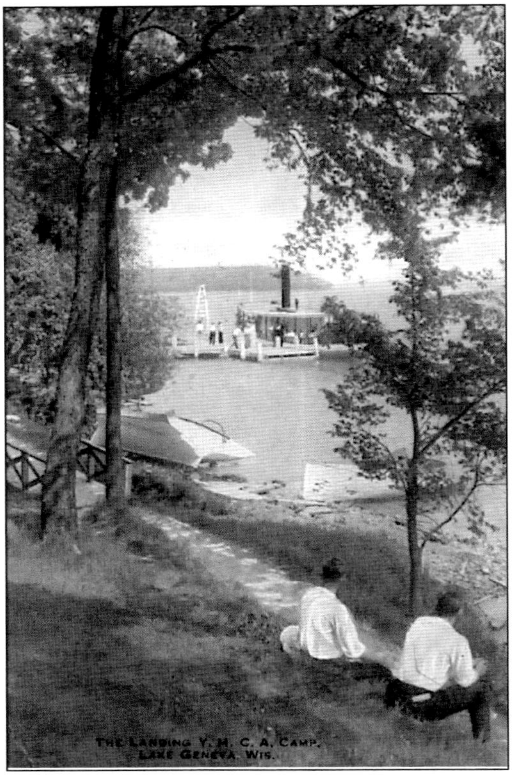

Taking you counterclockwise around the lake, the following historic postcard images begin in Williams Bay, continue in Fontana and along the southshore, and end up in the city of Lake Geneva.

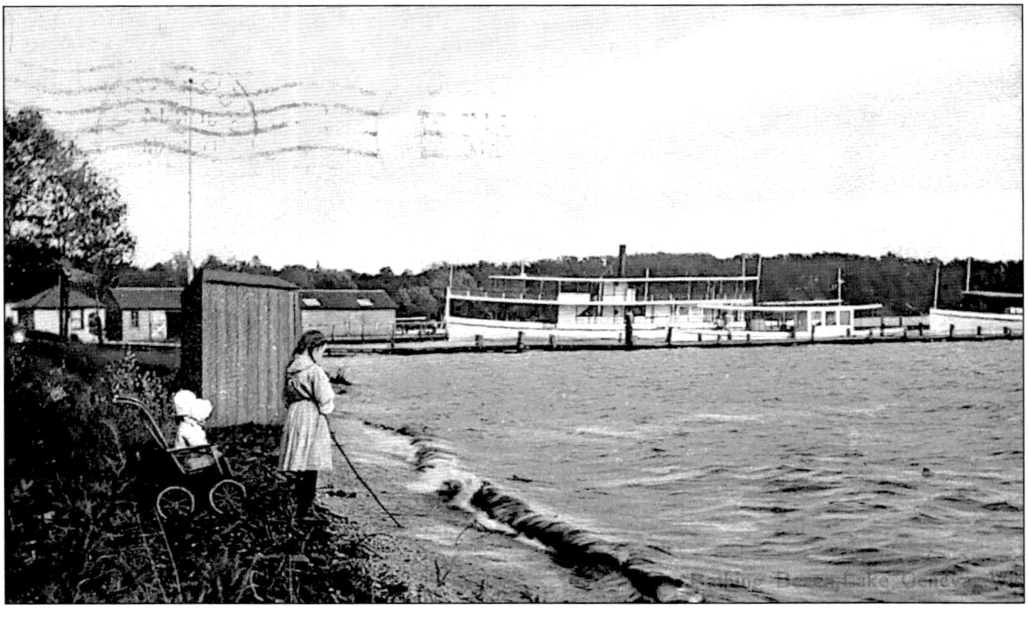

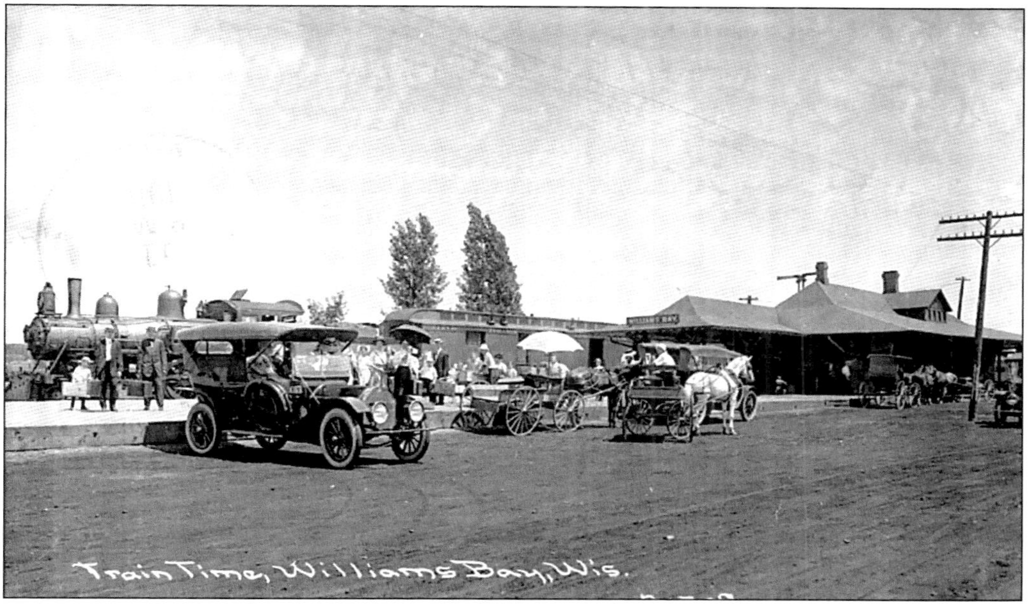

Though the railroad reached Williams Bay in 1887, the development of the village took almost 10 more years, aided greatly by the construction of Yerkes Observatory in 1895.

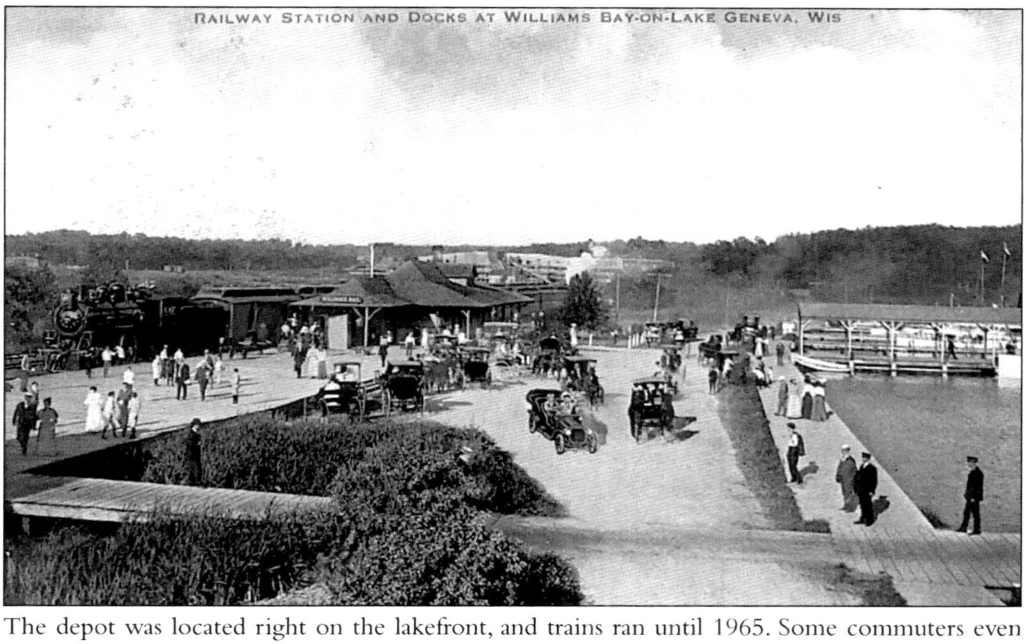

The depot was located right on the lakefront, and trains ran until 1965. Some commuters even docked their powerboats at the municipal pier and boarded the train for Chicago.

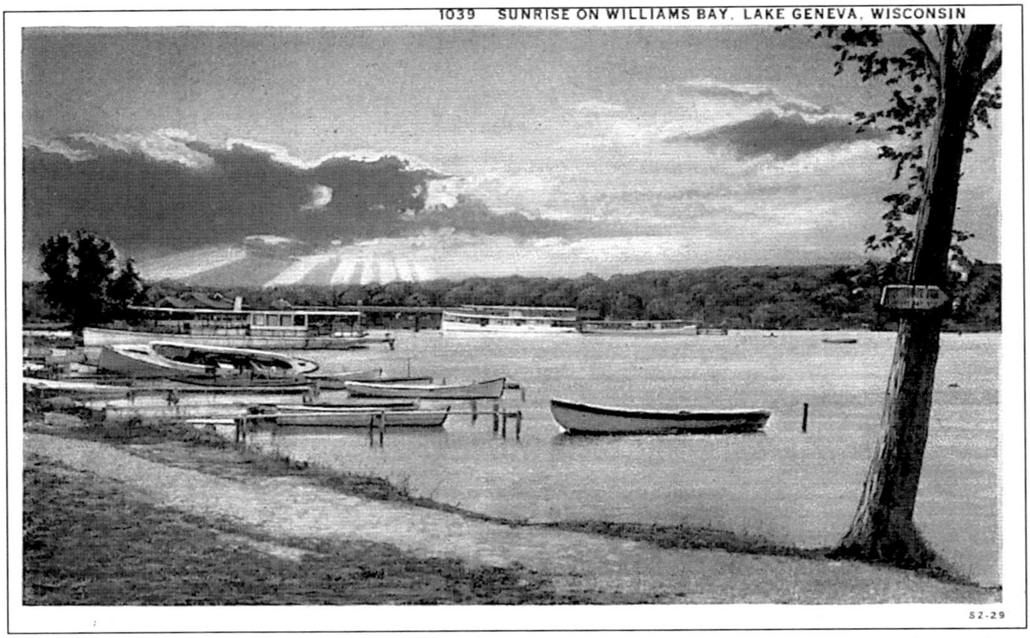

In early times, Geneva Lake residents would disembark from the train and immediately board their awaiting steamboats to take them to their grand estates. There was often a friendly competition to see which boat would deliver its passengers first.

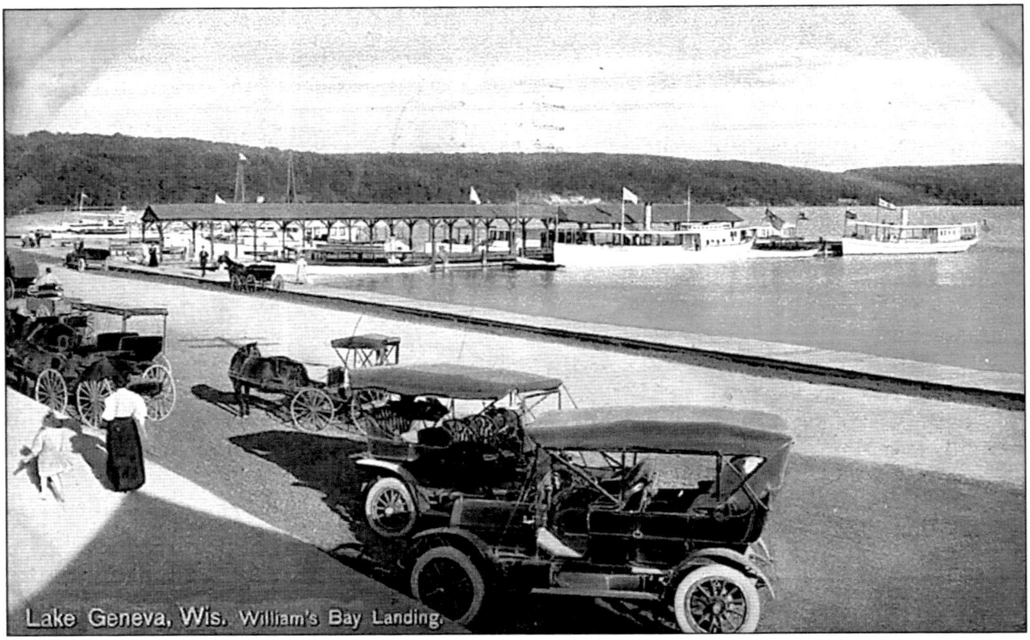

This card shows the dawning of the automobile age, with horse drawn buggies, cars, and steamers all awaiting their passengers. Postmarked in June of 1912, the author writes, "Dear Ma and Pa, We had a great time trying to stay out of the holes along the road to Lake Geneva, but all the same the trip was fun. Your loving daughter, Ethel."

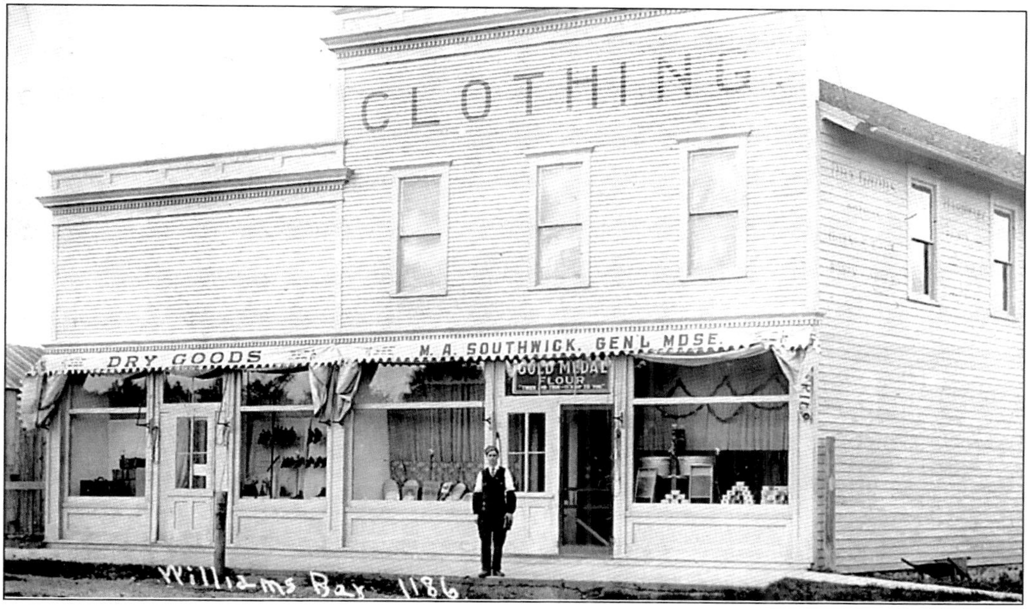

The quaint main street of Williams Bay still has storefronts with remembrances of the days of Southwick Dry Goods. Oliver P. Southwick built it on Geneva Street and operated a large general merchandise store there for many years with a sheet metal shop in the basement. (Courtesy of the John P. Urlakis Collection.)

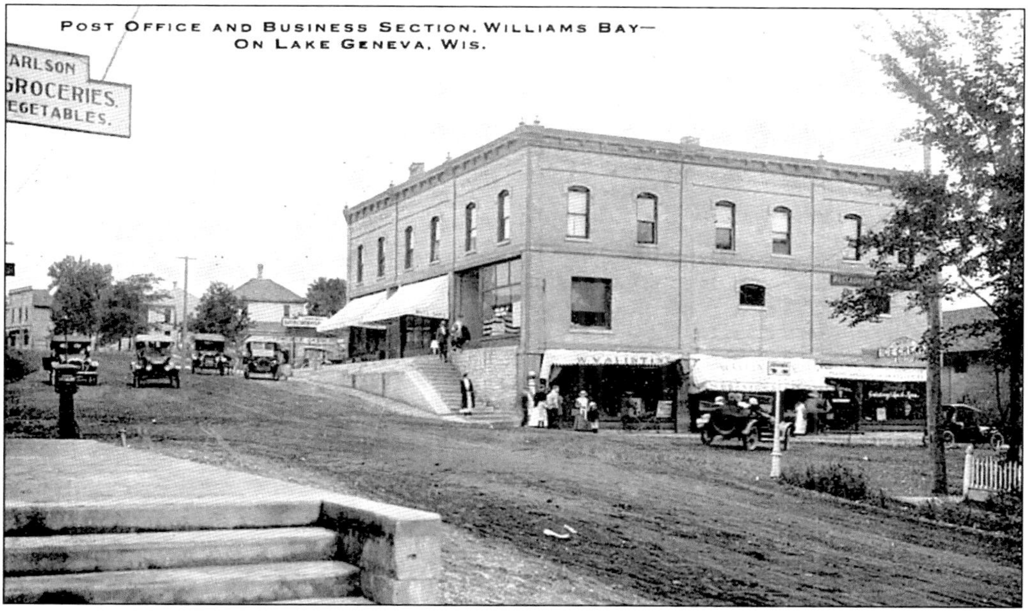

The Williams Bay Business District shows the Lackey Building (far right), which housed the new post office, clothing store, hardware, and a bakery. On the bottom left of the postcard are the stairs leading to the town grocery store, and on the horizon, along the road heading west, is the building that was Southwick's Dry Goods general store. The town still has several wonderful restaurants and charming shops for residents and visitors to enjoy. (Courtesy of the Jerry Glass Collection.)

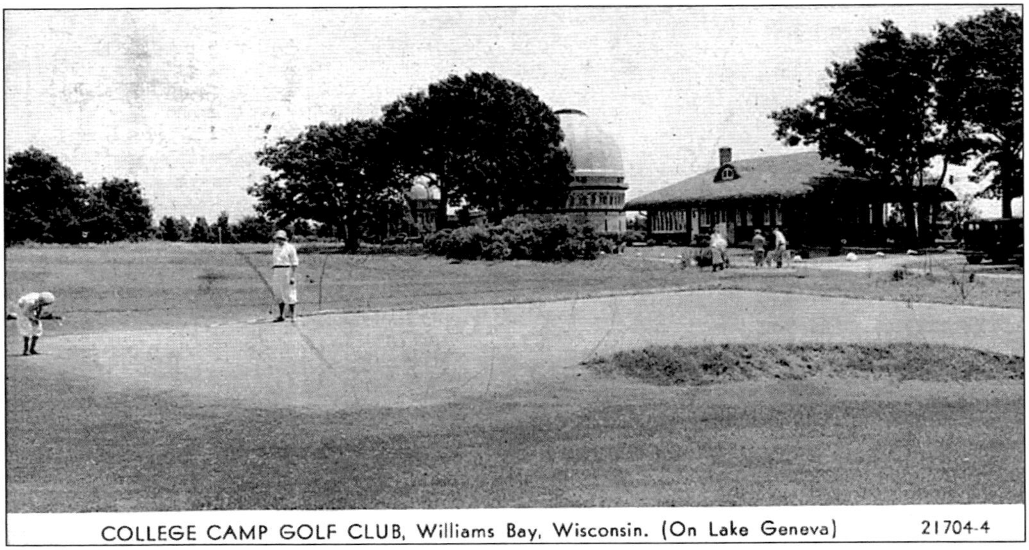

The George Williams College Camp Golf Club was a dream of a Yerkes professor and the Lake Geneva YMCA staff around the turn of the century. The six-hole golf course was laid out by Dr. James Naismith, the inventor of basketball. In 1906, the course was expanded to nine holes and opened to the public. In 1918, the course expanded to 18 holes through a gift of S.B. Chapin, and in 1929, the Gramley Clubhouse was built.

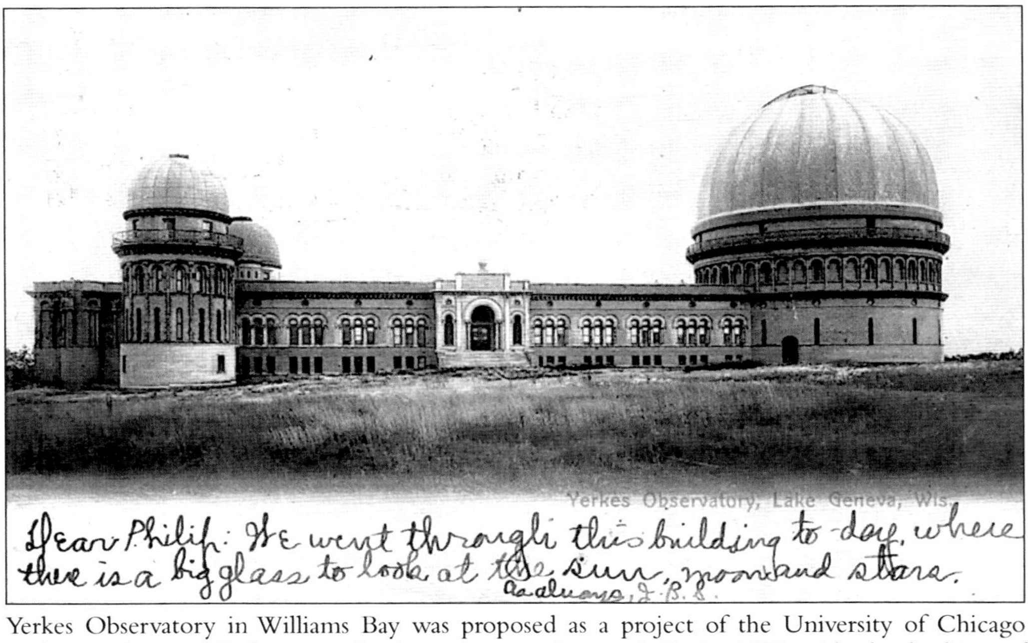

Yerkes Observatory in Williams Bay was proposed as a project of the University of Chicago to house the world's largest refracting telescope. It was built in 1895 with the backing of Charles T. Yerkes, the founder of the Chicago streetcar system.

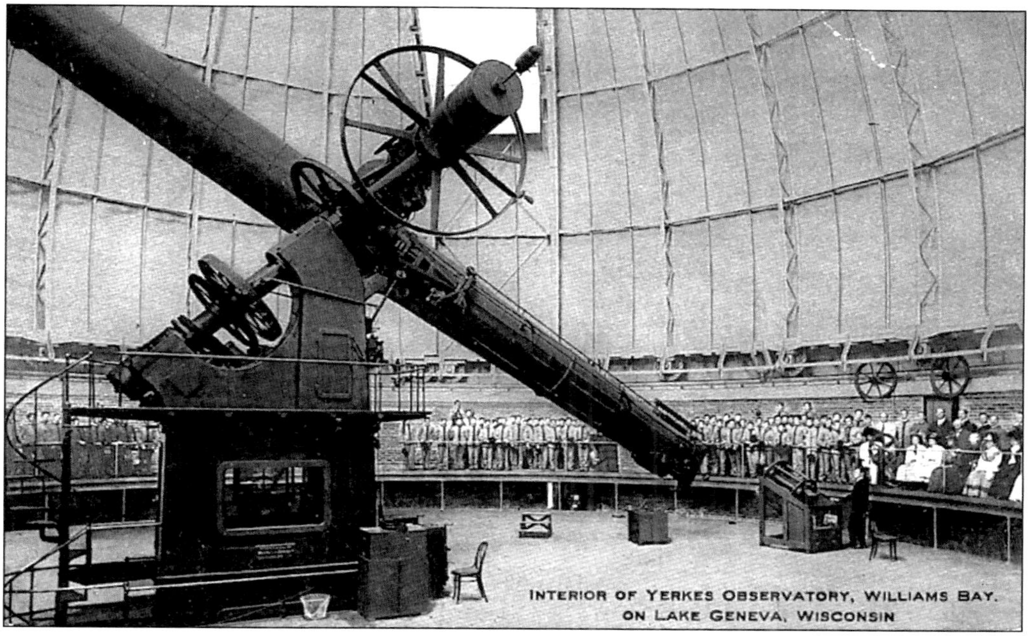

Pioneer work in photographing the moon and stars was achieved at the Yerkes Observatory between 1900 and 1905. Obtained from the Columbian Exposition, the main lens is 40 inches in diameter and is encased in a 64-foot long telescopic tube. The entire instrument weighs over 20 tons, and is still considered a valuable asset to astronomy because of the continuity of over 100 years of images from the same exact location.

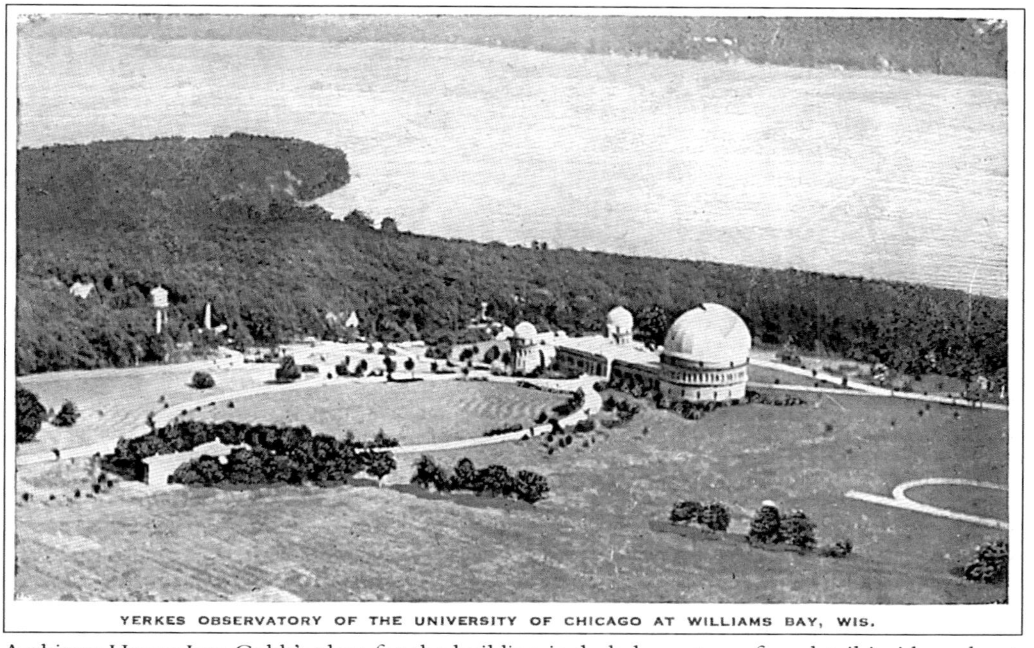

Architect Henry Ives Cobb's plans for the building included ornate surface detail inside and out. The smaller domed building was added in 1905 to house a horizontal telescope.

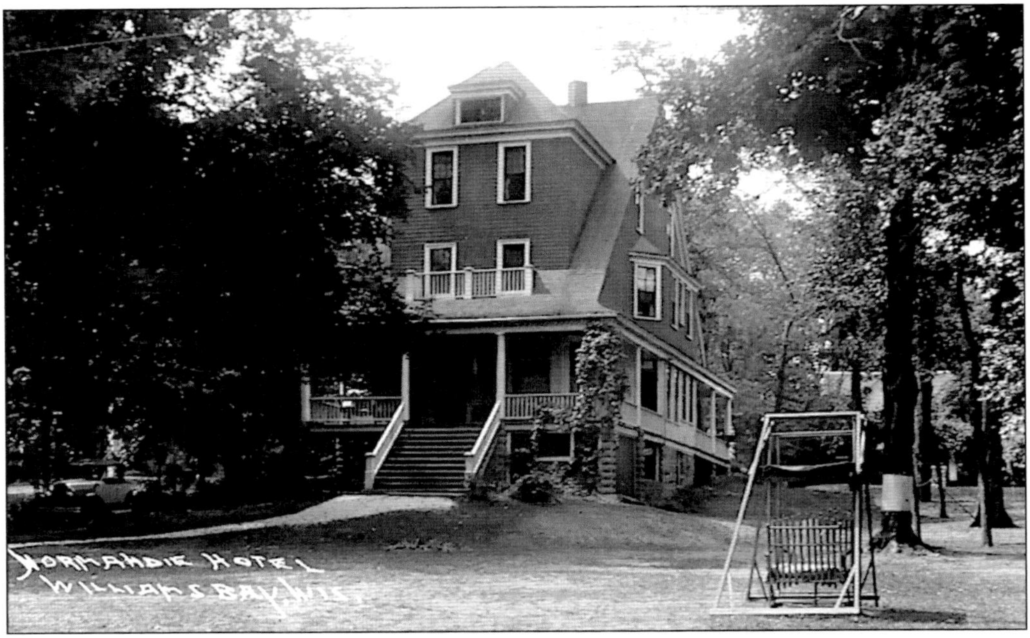

The Normandie Hotel was built during Williams Bay's boom of the early 1900s as a tourist hotel on Geneva Street. A private residence is now located in its place.

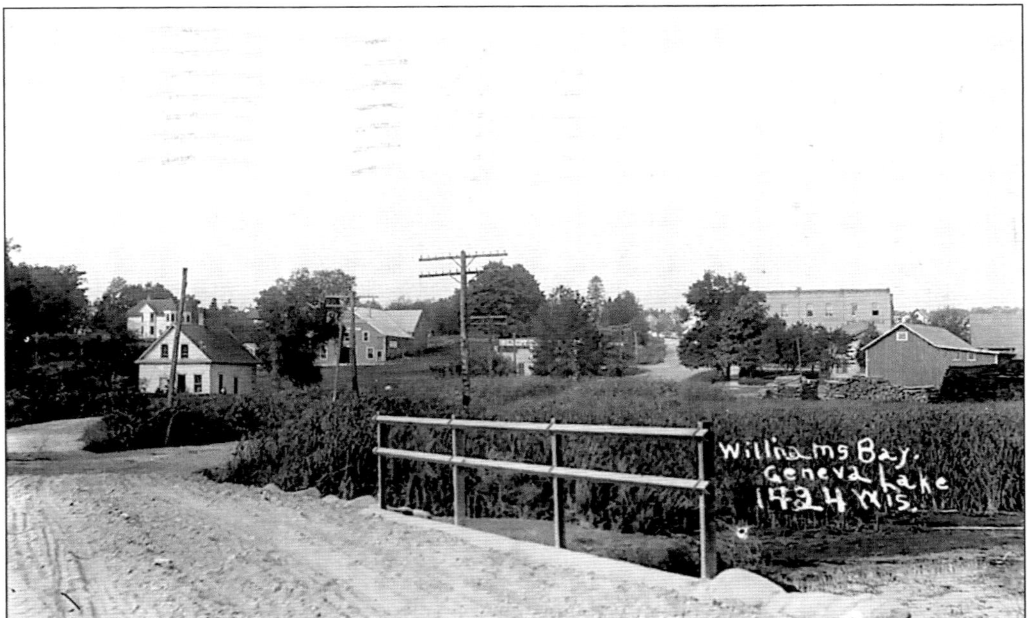

This antique postcard shows the bridge heading west into the town of Williams Bay with the Lackey Building on the far back right. Just in front of it is the old lumberyard, currently the location of Café Calamari. (Courtesy of the John P. Urlakis Collection.)

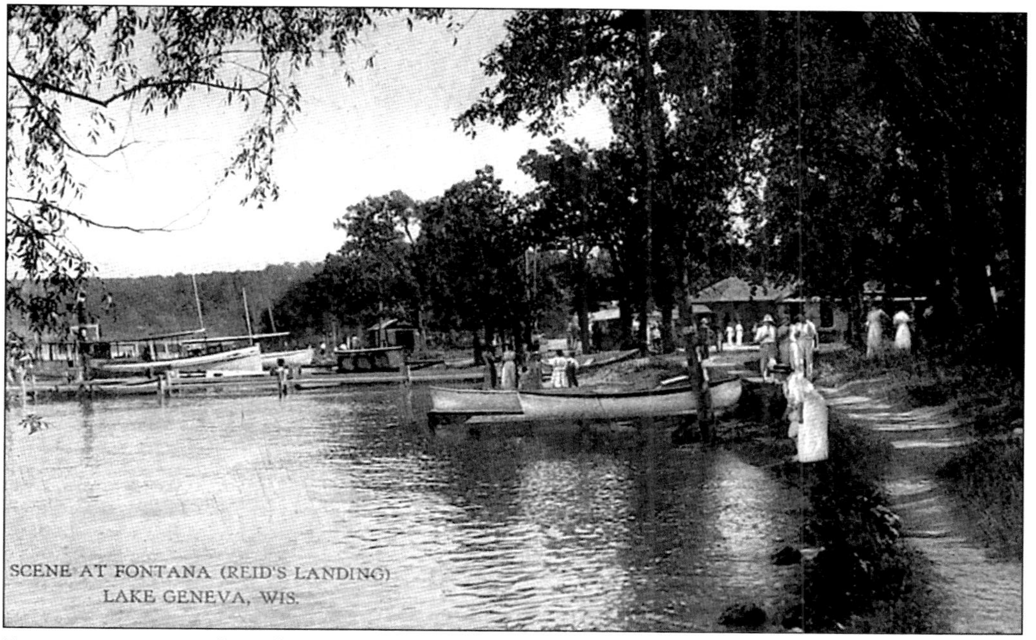

Fontana was originally called Reid's Landing, and even in 1901, the lakefront was a peaceful but very busy place.

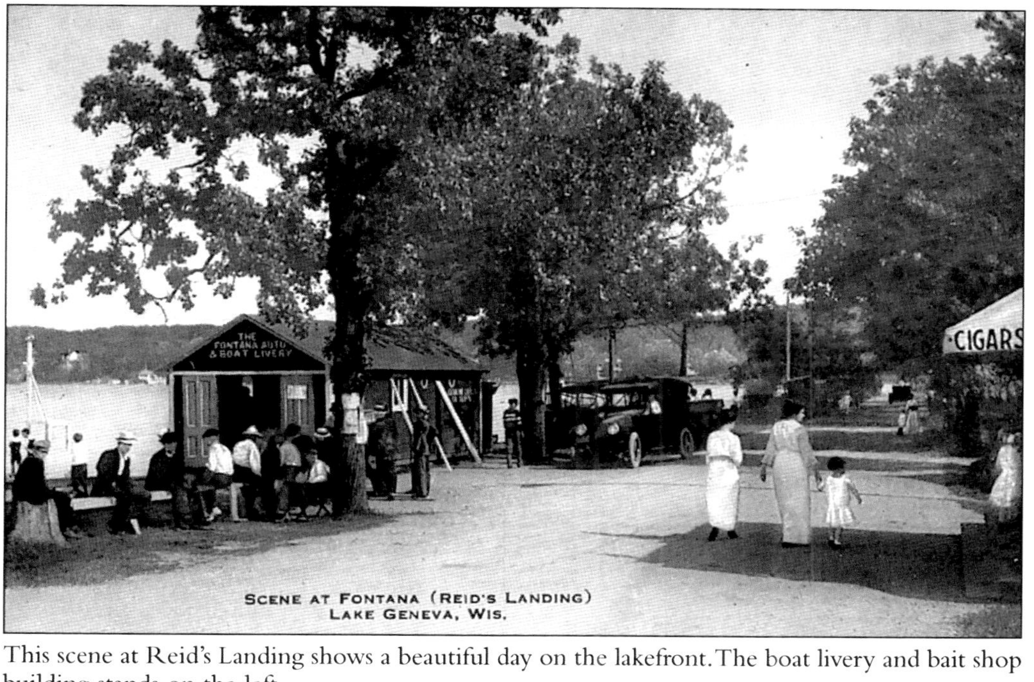

This scene at Reid's Landing shows a beautiful day on the lakefront. The boat livery and bait shop building stands on the left.

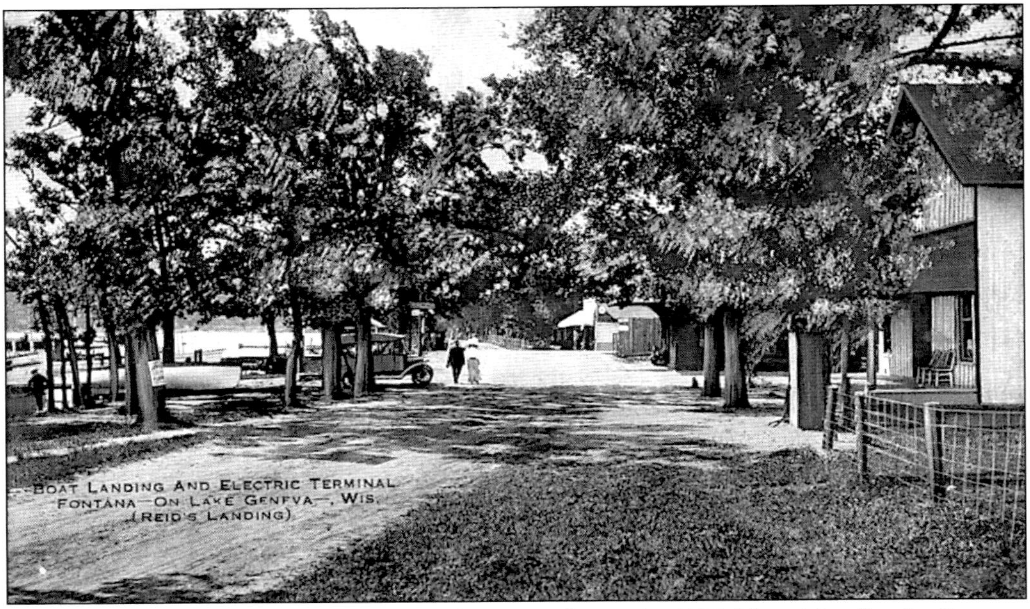

Rail service between Harvard, Illinois and Fontana began in 1898. Electricity for the line was supplied by a powerhouse in Walworth. The train carried gravel, coal, milk, and ice, as well as passengers, to Belvidere, Rockford, and Peoria. More of a trolley than a train, the 110-mile-long line claimed to be the longest of its kind at the time it was built. The electric line became obsolete as automobiles and trucks became popular, and service was discontinued in 1929.

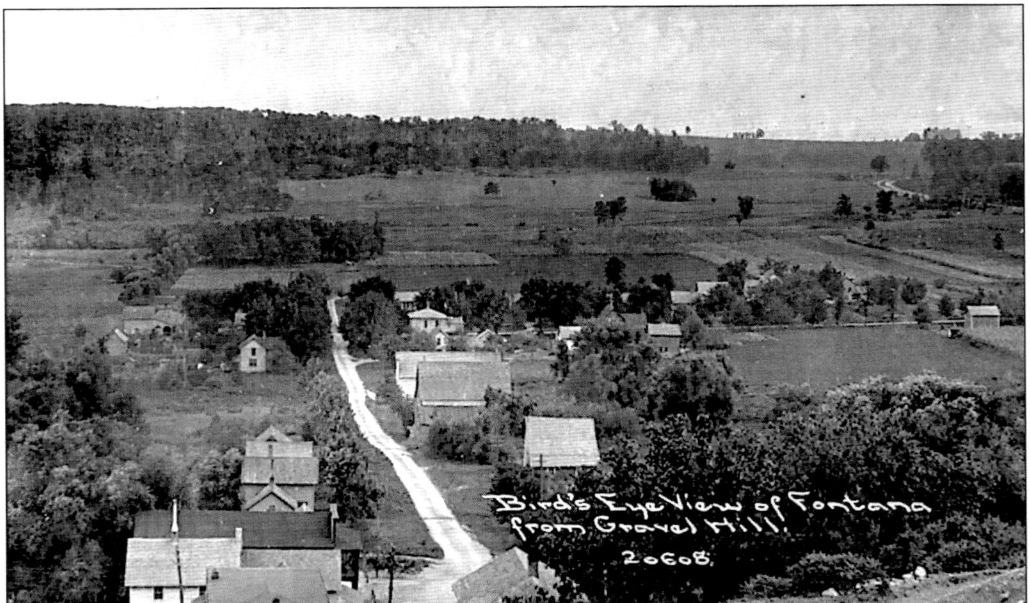

Postmarked 1914, this view is of Fontana's Mill Street from Gravel Hill. On the right side of the street you can see the roof of the Orcott home (now the Geneva Lake Conservancy), the old Douglas Mill, and the corner of the Woodman's Hall.

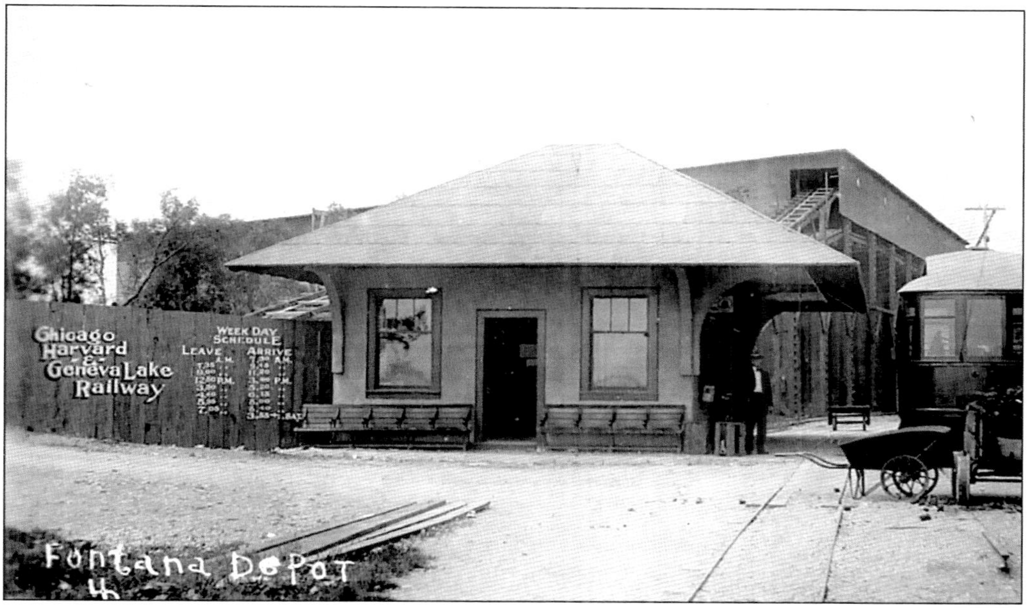

Here is a close up view of The Fontana Depot, a stop of the Chicago, Harvard, and Geneva Electric Railway. The building in this photo behind the depot was most probably the Boyle Ice Co. which employed 150–200 men during the season. It operated until 1915. (Courtesy of the Brown-Gabriel Collection.)

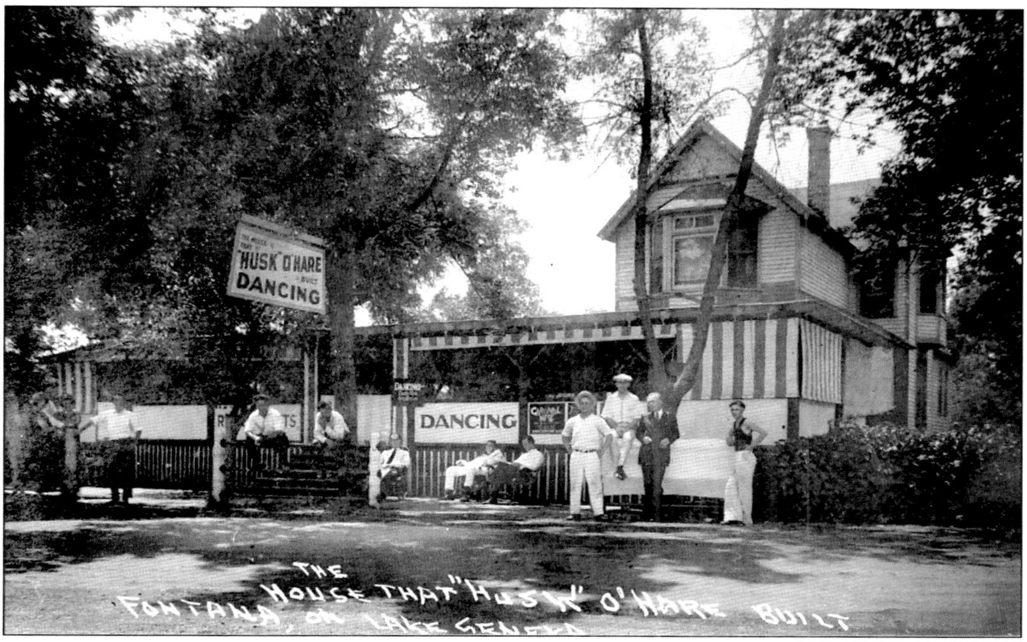

Husk O'Hare brought his band to Fontana from Chicago in the 1930s for summer entertainment. Prior to becoming an inn, the "house" was actually built by Dr. Pierce Tyrrell in the 1890s, and named Nirvana. It was the second lake house in Fontana after the Glenwood Hotel. Parts of the old house were hidden in the walls of the original "Chuck's." (Courtesy of the Brown-Gabriel Collection.)

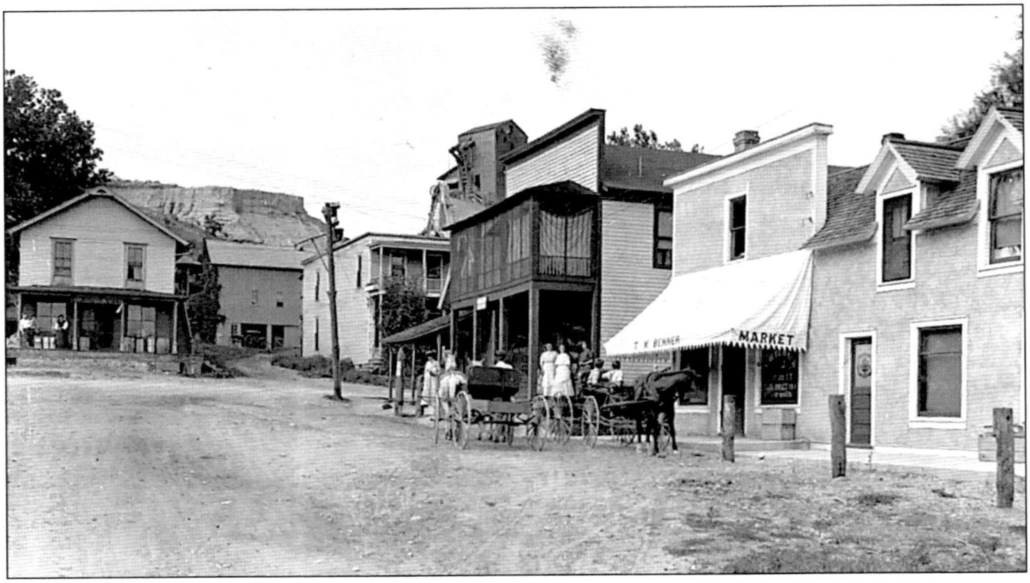

This Fontana scene shows Mill Street as it was in the early 1900s. Pictured are Benner's Meat Market as well as Porter's Store and the post office. At the end of the street is another market which housed the post office at one time. Note Gravel Hill in the background. (Courtesy of the Jerry Glass Collection.)

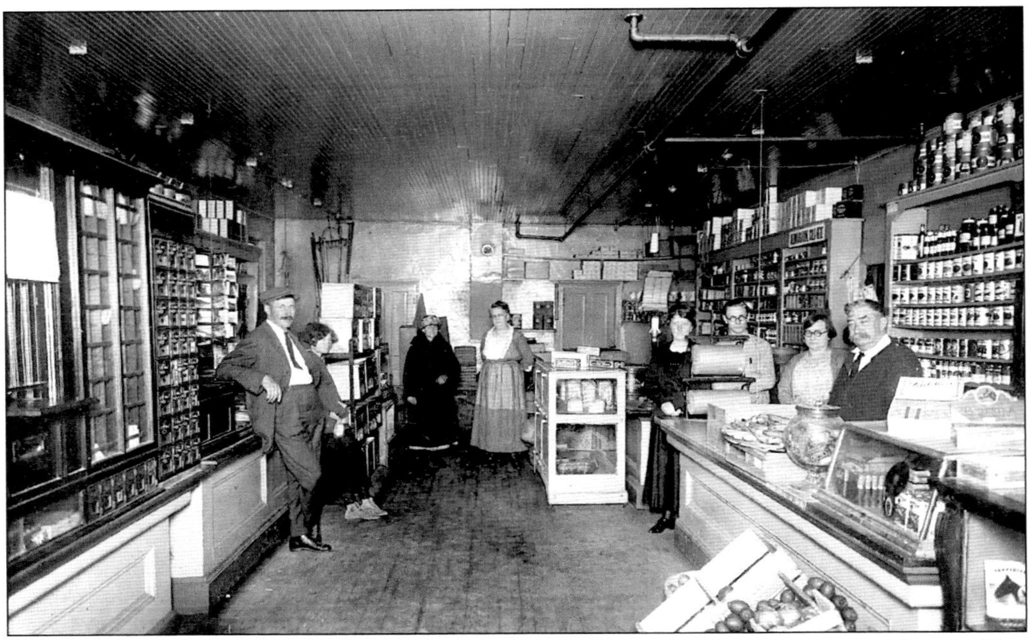

Porter's Store in Fontana was a true general store: a grocery, bakery, meat market, and post office. Shown on the far right is Mr. Porter with some of his children, who helped run the business: Irma, Doric, and Helen. Center, in the bakery department, is Mrs. Porter. At the far left are customers. The building was moved across the street in the 1960s to its present location on Main Street, where it is now Lucy's Coffee Shop. (Courtesy of the Brown-Gabriel Collection.)

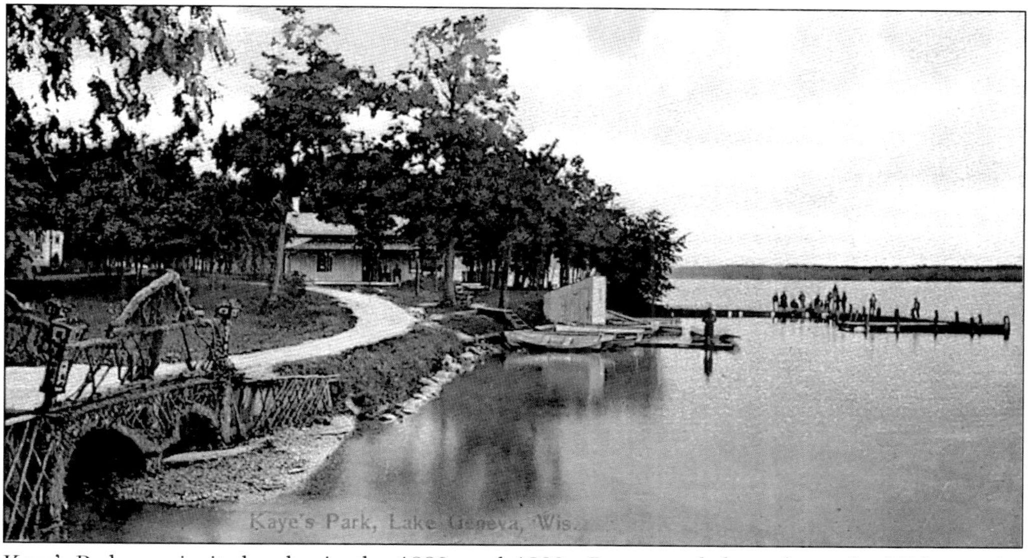

Kaye's Park was in its heyday in the 1880s and 1890s. Renowned throughout the Midwest, the resort was comprised of 300 acres of wooded land with a mile of lake shore picnic and camping grounds. Owned by Arthur Kaye, it featured a hotel and guest cottages. The dining hall, 40 by 80 feet and 50 feet high with black walnut and maple floors, was turned into a ball room for dancing every Saturday night. The park had a Russian sleigh for winter rides across fields and the frozen lake, as well as bowling, billiards, boating, lawn tennis, and croquet, along with a gift shop.

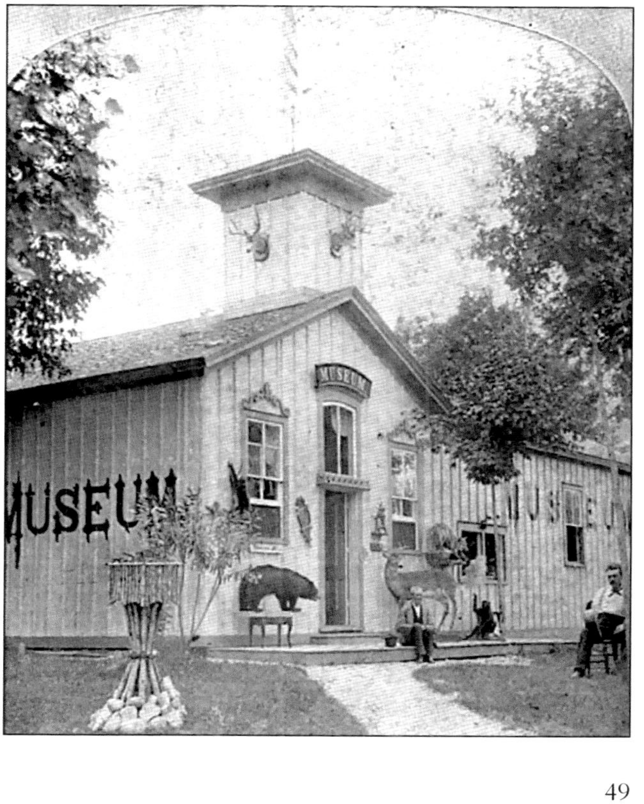

In addition to the recreational activities offered to visitors, Kaye's Park advertised mineral springs, fresh dairy products, and homegrown vegetables "for renewed strength." Another highlight was the Kaye's Park Museum, featuring a natural history collection of mammals, fish, birds, butterflies, shells, gemstones, coins, and artifacts from American Indians and the South Sea Islands. (Courtesy of the Brown-Gabriel Collection.)

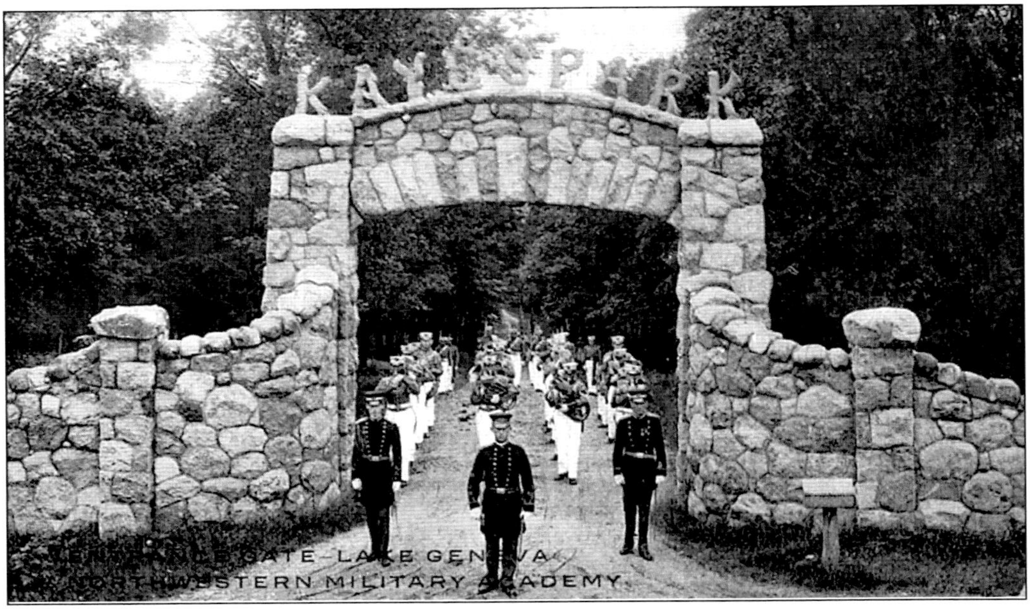

Cadets from the Northwestern Military and Naval Academy had used some of the land at Kaye's Park for camping and maneuvers. When the park closed in 1901 and the Kaye family offered the land for sale, the academy purchased it and moved to this site after fire destroyed its Highland Park, Illinois facility. (Courtesy of the Jerry Glass Collection.)

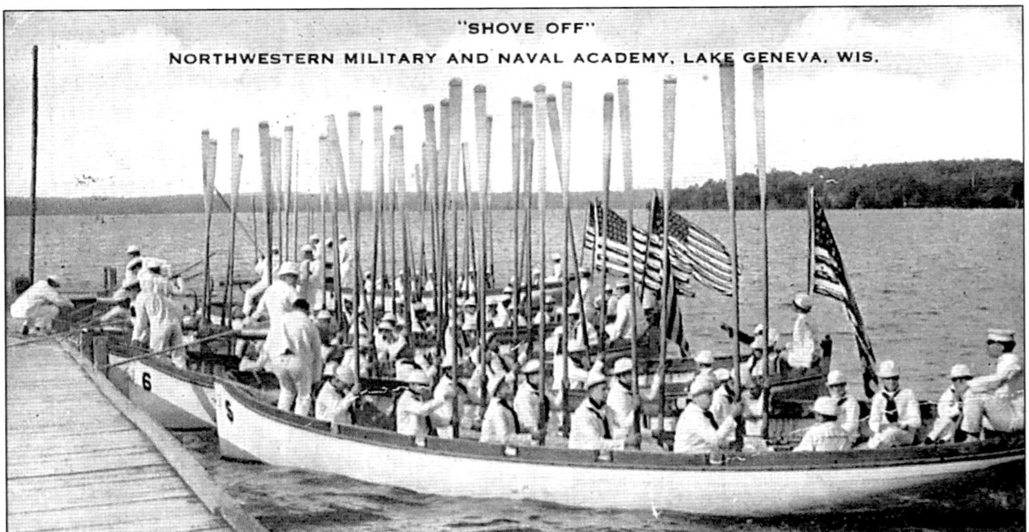

The Northwestern Military Academy in Highland Park was destroyed by fire on November 4, 1888 and then rebuilt. Colonel Davidson, one of the designers of the armored car, was seeking a new home for the academy near water so that the military training could include a naval program. Geneva Lake became their summer, spring, and fall location. In order to acclimate students to the outdoors, they slept in tents on the shore line and ate at the Kaye's Park dining hall. Again, in 1915, a fire struck the Highland Park Military Academy. The new school was built on the land of the lake's south shore.

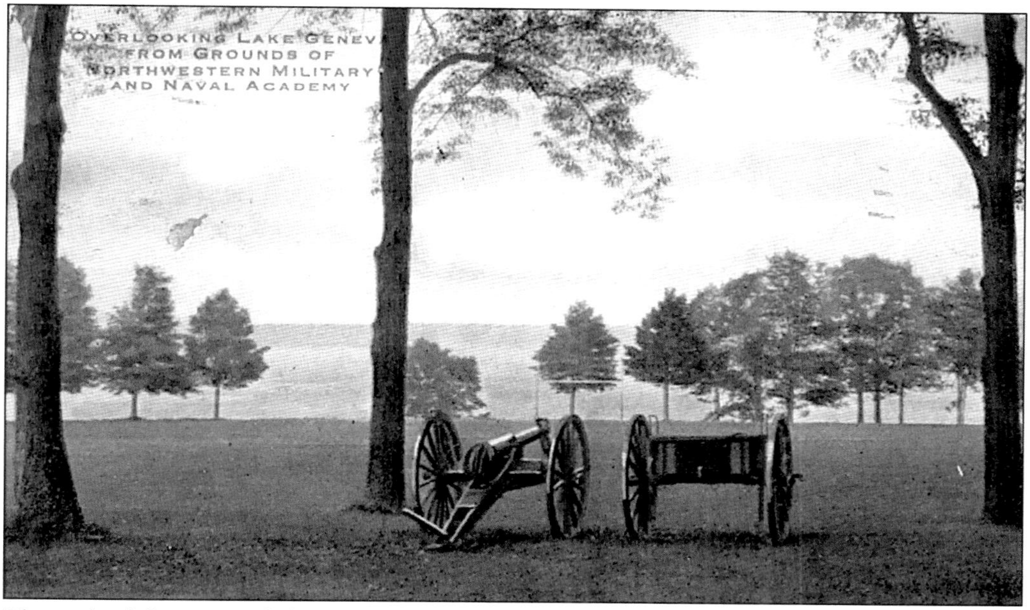

The end of the war and the peace conference in 1919 created the demobilization of part of the armed forces, which made available material no longer needed by the government. Colonel Davidson was successful in acquiring four small army tanks, Navy cutters, Gattling guns, and cannons to name a few. By the mid-1920s, Northwestern had an amazing arsenal of weaponry and equipment that the cadets used to practice their maneuvers.

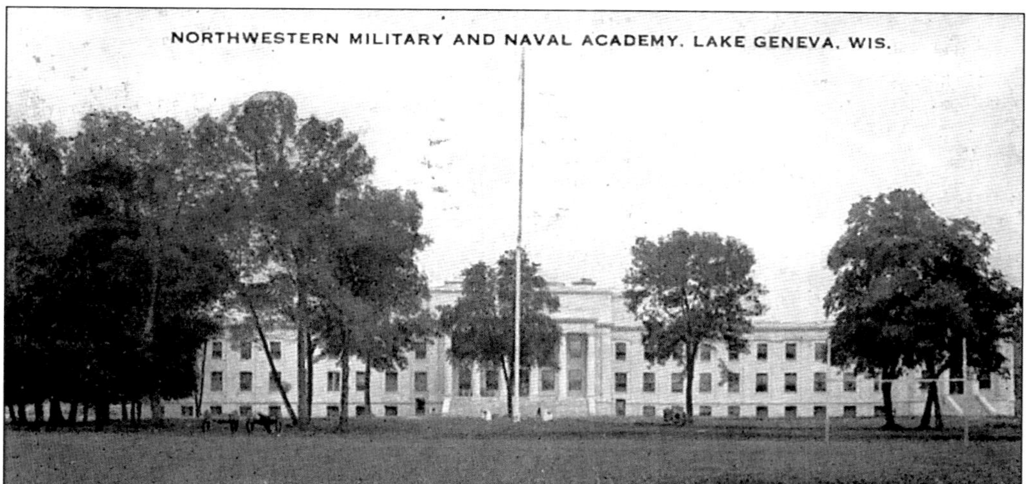

Northwestern Military Academy students' day began at 6:15 a.m. After dressing, they formed a double line in the hall, saluted the flag, and then marched to breakfast. Their quarters were inspected and lunch was accompanied by bagpipes, as the founders of the school were Scottish. Before dinner, there was retreat and inspection. After the meal, the senior cadets formed in the rotunda for precision marching practice. Study then began, and at ten p.m., taps could be heard. The school closed this facility in 1995 and merged with St. John's Academy in Delafield, Wisconsin. The building has since been razed, and the property is now known as The South Shore Club with beautiful single family residences.

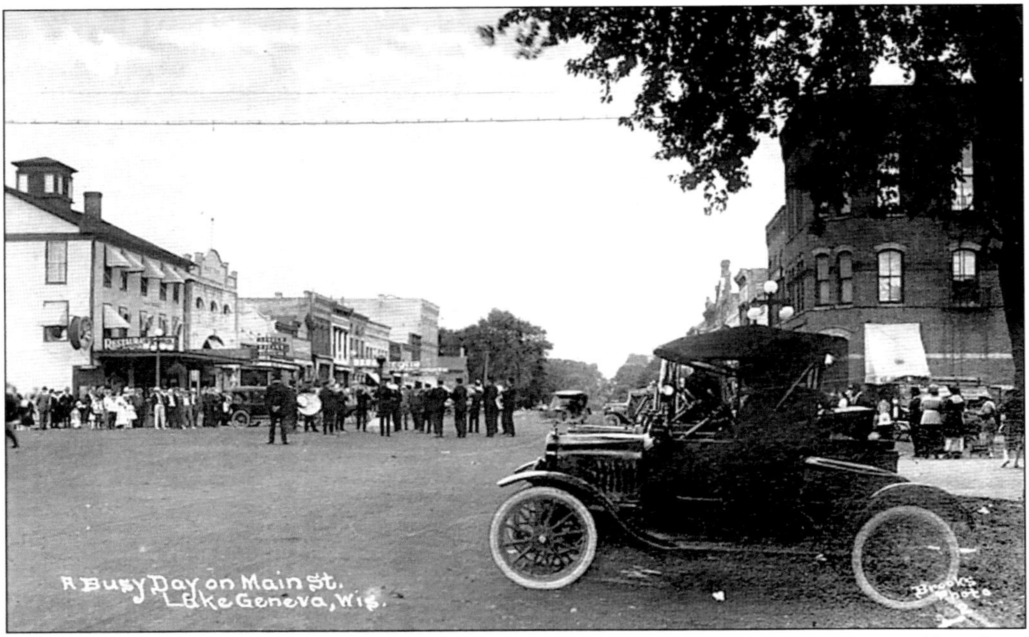

Lake Geneva's early settlers came from New England, New York, and Chicago as well as from communities like Harvard, Rockford, and Milwaukee. These early inhabitants made Lake Geneva their primary or secondary home. (Courtesy of the Brown-Gabriel Collection.)

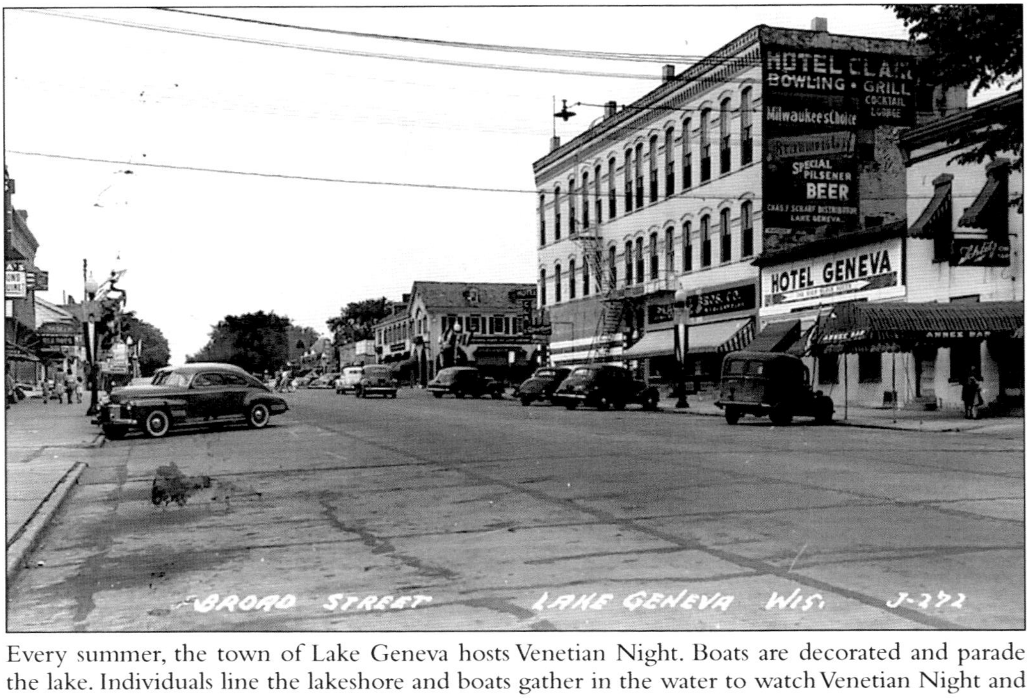

Every summer, the town of Lake Geneva hosts Venetian Night. Boats are decorated and parade the lake. Individuals line the lakeshore and boats gather in the water to watch Venetian Night and the fireworks display.

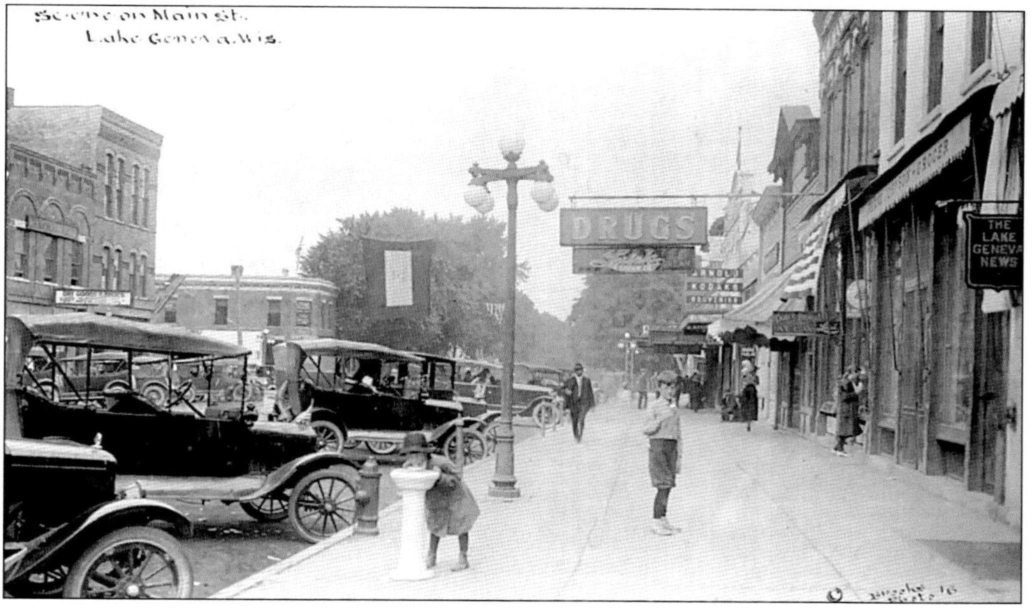

A little girl stops to get a drink on the north side of Main Street in front of Moore's Hardware store. The office of the Lake Geneva News was on the second floor of that building, now the home of a boutique shop. Other identifiable businesses include Frank Johnson Grocer, Chas. French at Law, Hammersley's Drugs and Ice Cream, Arnold's Drugs and Souvenirs, a hotel, and across the street, Allen Peacock's dry goods store. (Courtesy of the Brown-Gabriel Collection.)

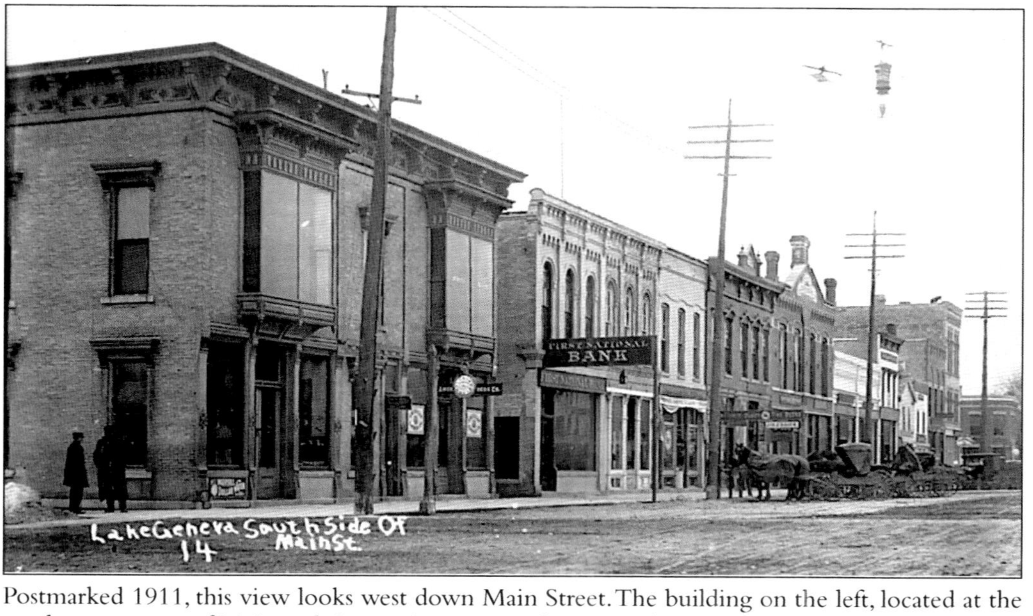

Postmarked 1911, this view looks west down Main Street. The building on the left, located at the southwest corner of Main and Center Streets, was the original site of the Bank of Geneva, which merged with the First National Bank in 1891. Robert Keefe began his real estate business in 1943 as a Farm Auction Service; this building was home to Keefe Real Estate from 1952 until 1997. (Courtesy of the John P. Urlakis Collection.)

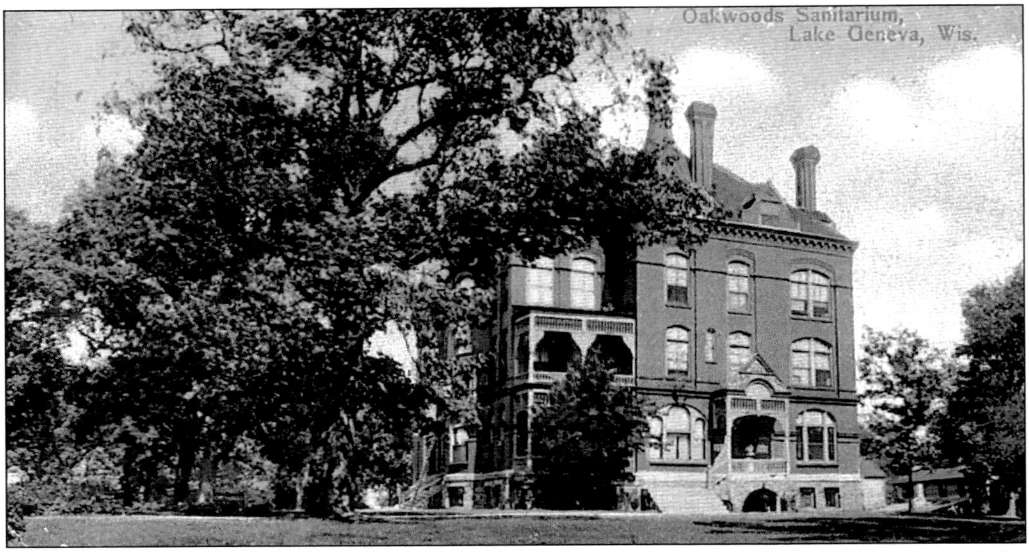

Oakwood Sanitarium, built around 1885, was an exclusive mental institution opened by Dr. Oscar A. King, a Chicago neurologist. This five-story, 50-room facility offered "retreat, therapy and some tight confinement." Its patients were of great wealth. It closed during the Depression, and as it stood empty, it was frequently vandalized. Two fires in the 1950s gave it a dangerous and spooky atmosphere. Thrill seeking tourists and townspeople spread rumors that the building was haunted, it stood vacant and in disrepair until it was razed in 1959. It was located on Highway 50 across from St. Francis de Sales Catholic Church.

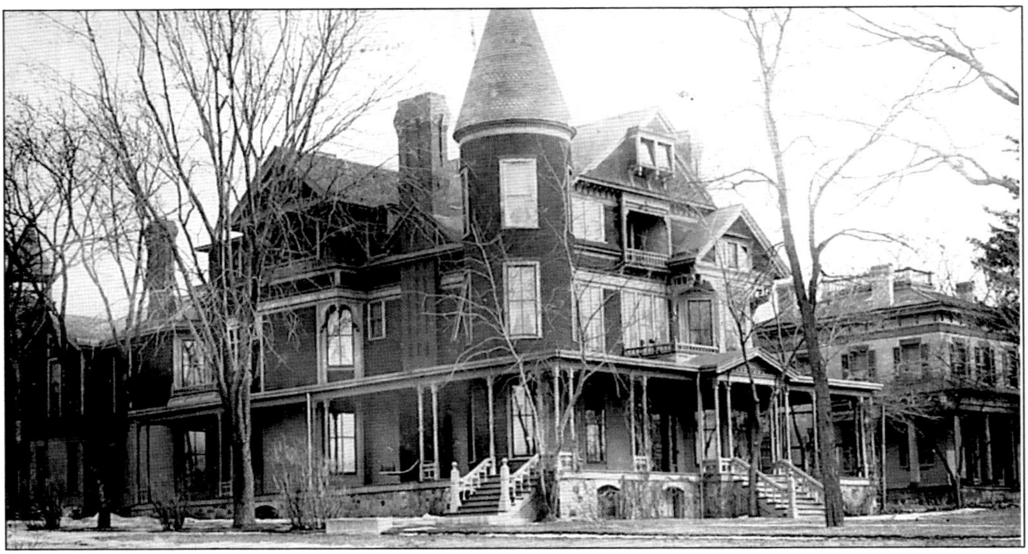

Lakeside Cottage, above, was used briefly as a ward for Oakwood Sanitarium, reportedly for "lighter nervous disorders." Acquired around 1896, it was originally the Emily Baker house, used as a dorm for the Lake Geneva Seminary for Young Ladies. It closed in the 1930s, and was eventually known as the St. Moritz, now Gilbert's Restaurant. Next door was the Lakeside, also used as a ward of the Lake Geneva Sanitarium Complex. This became the Lucerne Hotel, but was torn down to make way for the Hilton Hotel, currently the site of the Harbor Shores Hotel.

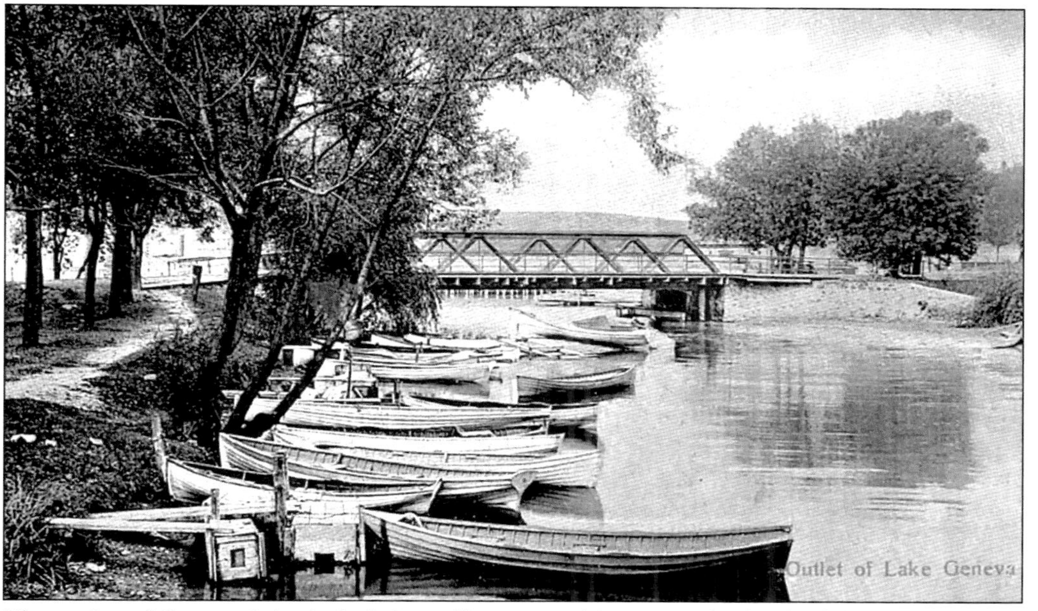

The outlet of Geneva Lake included a mill race pond in 1904. The level of the lake has been controlled to some extent by the same outlet since then, although the pond is no longer needed to produce power. (Courtesy of the Robert Webster Sr. Collection.)

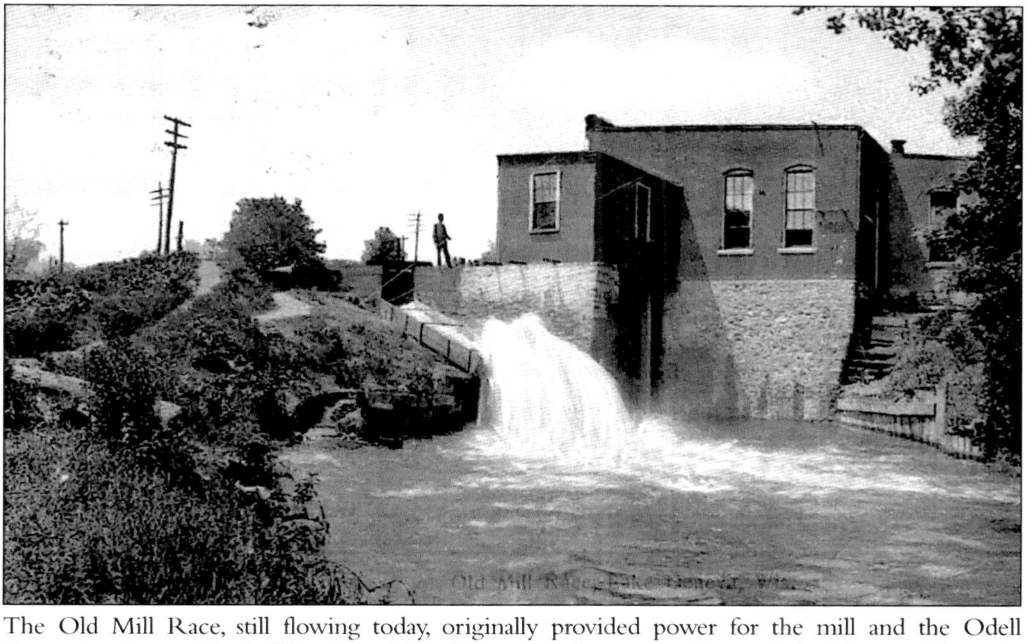
The Old Mill Race, still flowing today, originally provided power for the mill and the Odell Typewriter factory. The building is on Main Street, next door to the Geneva Lake Museum (formerly the Wisconsin Power and Light Company). Located at 225 Mill Street in downtown Lake Geneva, the museum is open to the public and is a great place to explore the area's colorful past.

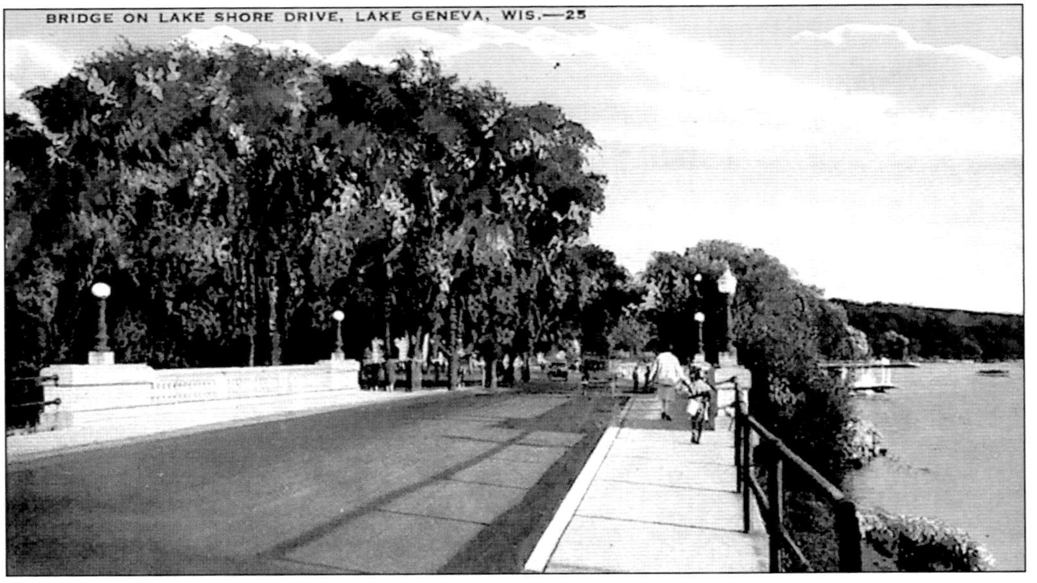

John Brink, a government surveyor in the mid-1800s, renamed the lake "Geneva," after his New York hometown. Today, there are least four other communities in the world called Lake Geneva: Seneca, Lake Geneva in New York State, Geneva-on-the-Lake in Ohio, Lake Geneva in Florida and of course Lac Leman of Lac Geneva in Switzerland.

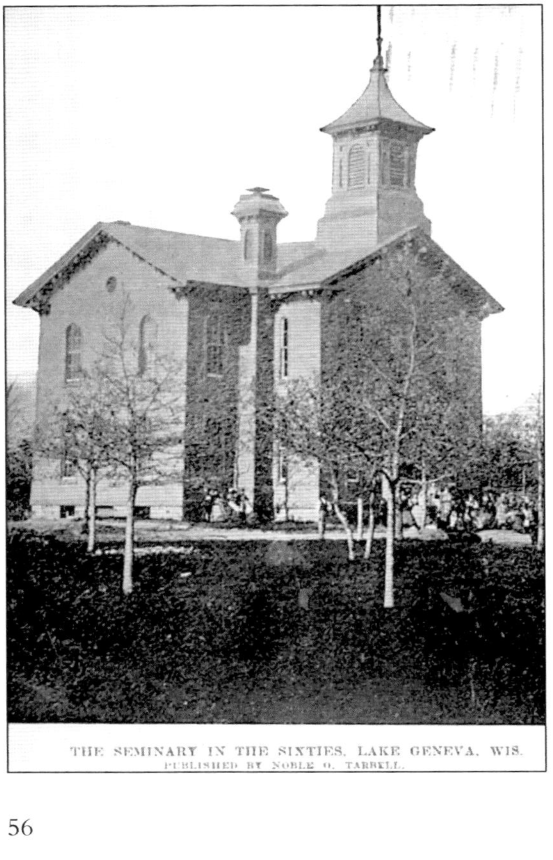

The Lake Geneva Seminary for Young Ladies was the first private school in the region. The curriculum included many art classes, and many of their students were trained in painting on china and velvet. Pictured here in the 1860s, it was located on Willow and Baker Streets, and while it was razed in 1901, the area today is known as Seminary Park. (Courtesy of the Jerry Glass Collection.)

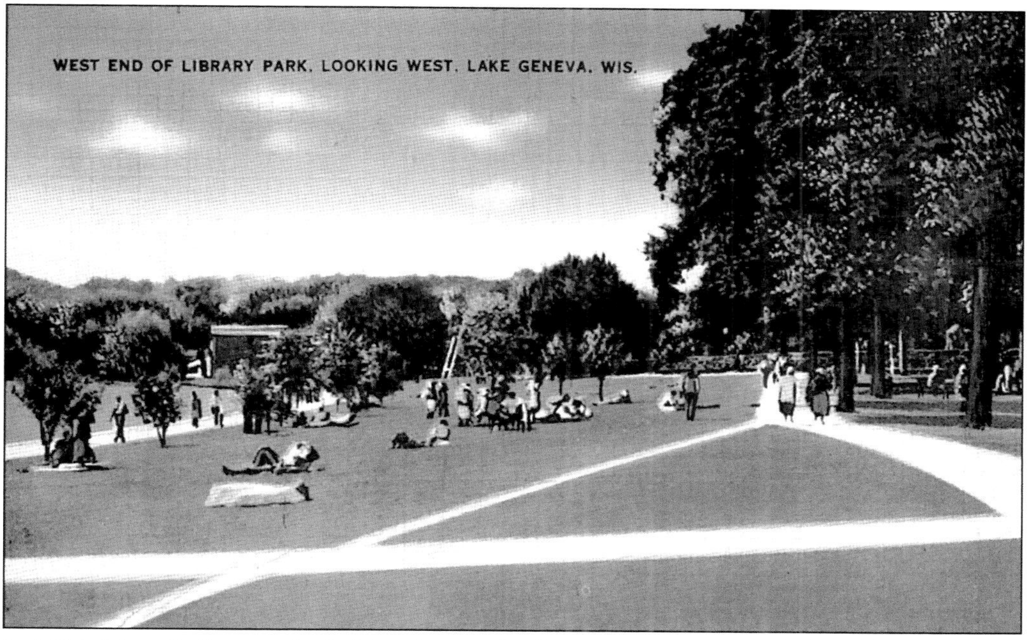

In 1894, Mary D. Sturges deeded the Sturges family summer cottage and three blocks of Main Street to the City of Lake Geneva. The land was to be forever devoted for the sole uses of a public park and public library. The park was once known as Elm Park, but after the elm trees died of disease, it was renamed Library Park.

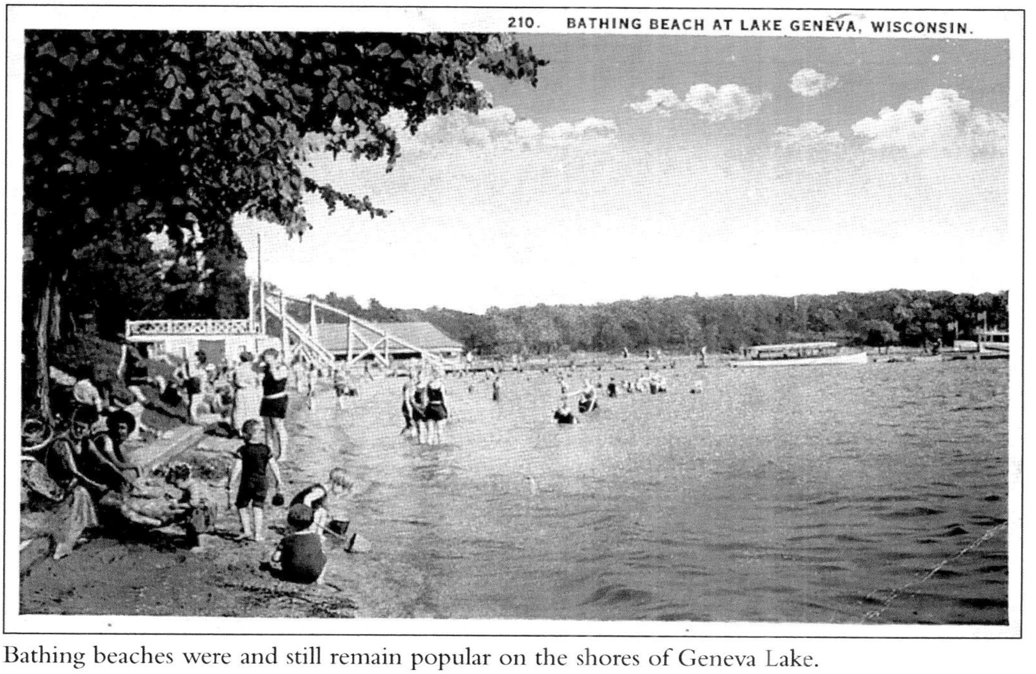

Bathing beaches were and still remain popular on the shores of Geneva Lake.

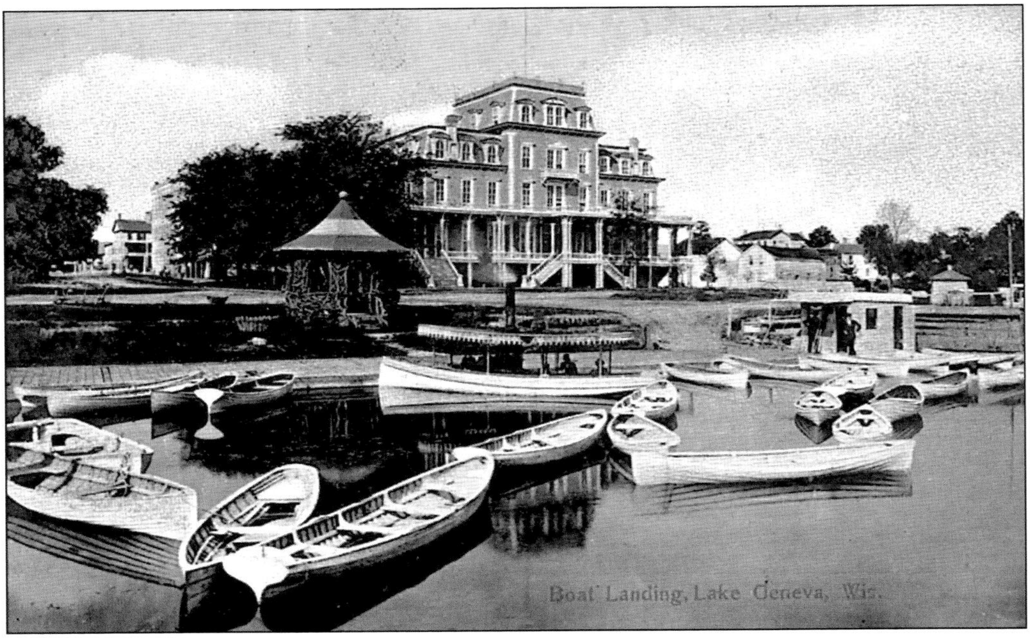

In 1873, David T. Whiting built the luxurious Whiting House Hotel at the foot of Broad Street. Four stories high, it boasted accommodations for 200 guests. It featured a ballroom on the top floor, large verandas, and was the site of many elegant social events. The hotel, which graced the lakeshore between Broad and Center Streets, was destroyed by fire in 1894. It was eventually replaced by another hotel, The Hotel Geneva, in 1911.

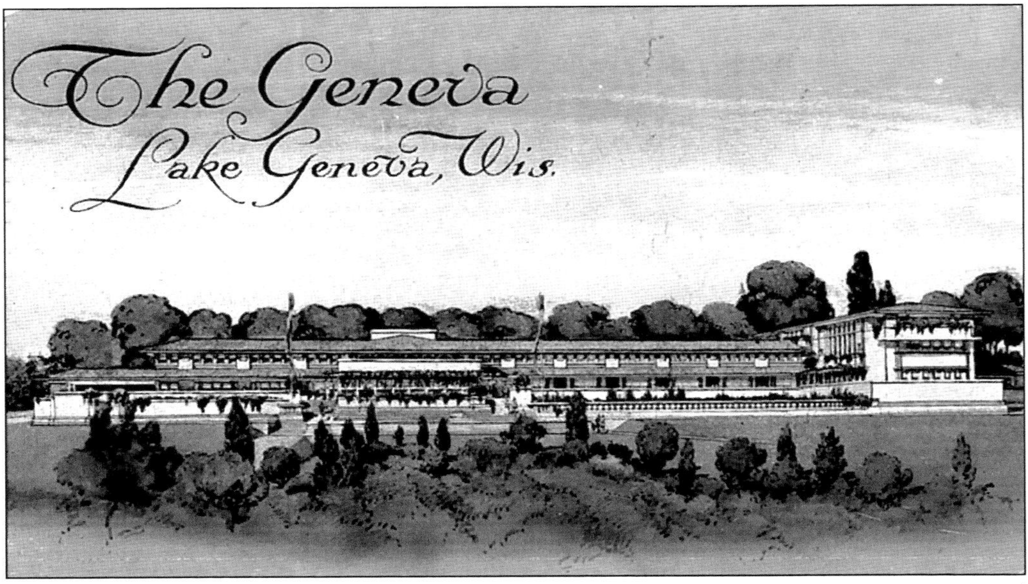

The Hotel Geneva was built on the former grounds of the old Whiting House in 1912. Designed by famous architect Frank Lloyd Wright, this ornate hotel was "the place to stay" when visiting Lake Geneva. The hotel fell into disrepair and was razed in 1969–1970. The Geneva Towers Condominiums are on this location today.

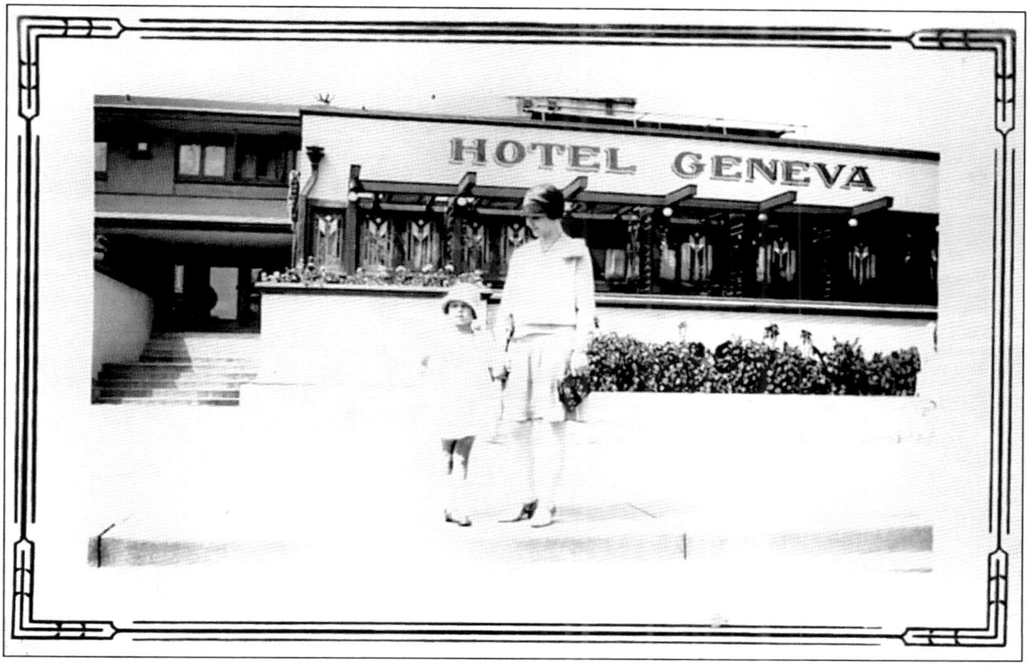

This mother and daughter visited the Hotel Geneva in 1927. (Courtesy of the Brown-Gabriel Collection.)

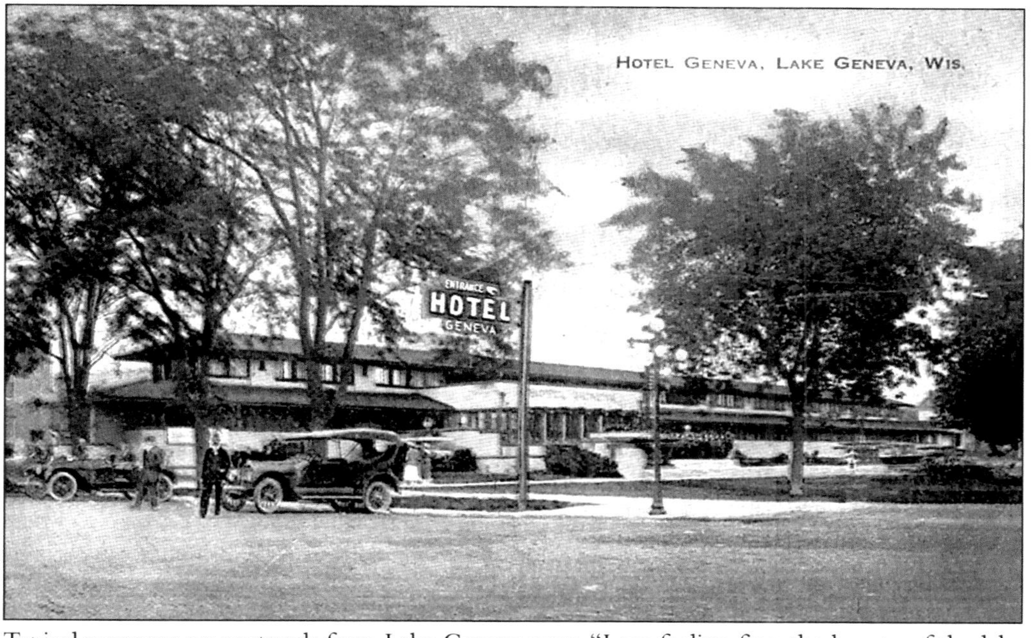

Typical messages on postcards from Lake Geneva were, "I am feeling fine, the beauty of the lake is relaxing, I wish you were here, I will be home in a couple of days. . . ." This postcard is a view of the Hotel Geneva from Broad Street. Postcards became more popular as the rail system was created, providing transportation of the postcards cross county. Postcards were also used more in the "motor era," as families could "hit the road" and send messages to friends back home.

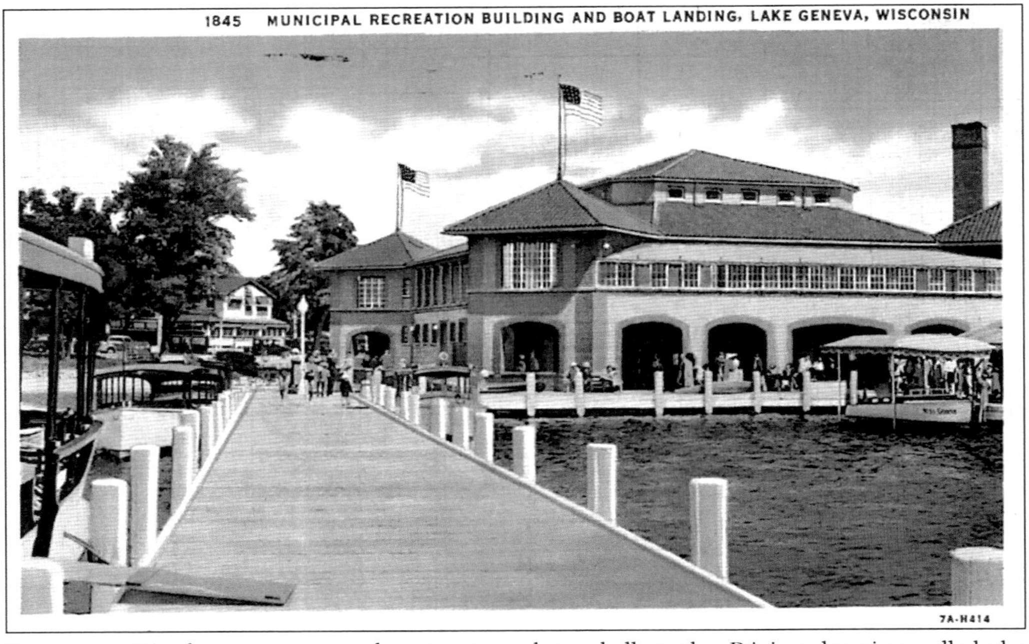

Prior to 1932, there was a wooden structure dance hall at the Riviera location called the Northport Ballroom. Also located in the same area were a merry-go-round, water slides, and hydro-plane rides. The Italian-renaissance Revival structure, the Riviera, was built by the Works Public Administration during the Great Depression.

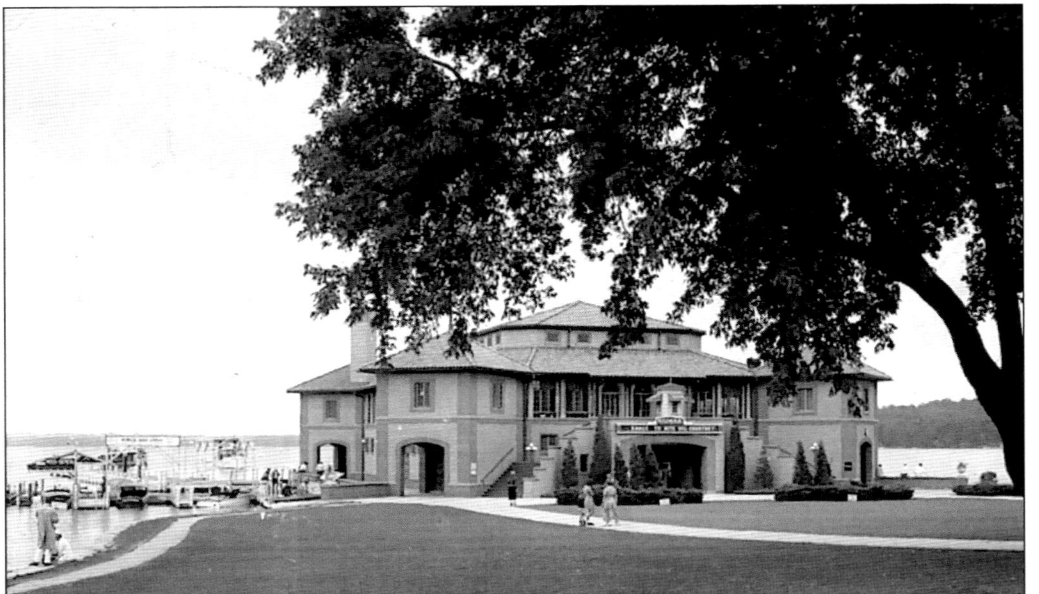

Wayne King and his Orchestra was the entertainment for the grand opening of the Riviera in 1932. Other big bands, including Tommy Dorsey, Paul Whitman, and Louis Armstrong, provided Riviera entertainment in the 1930s and 1940s.

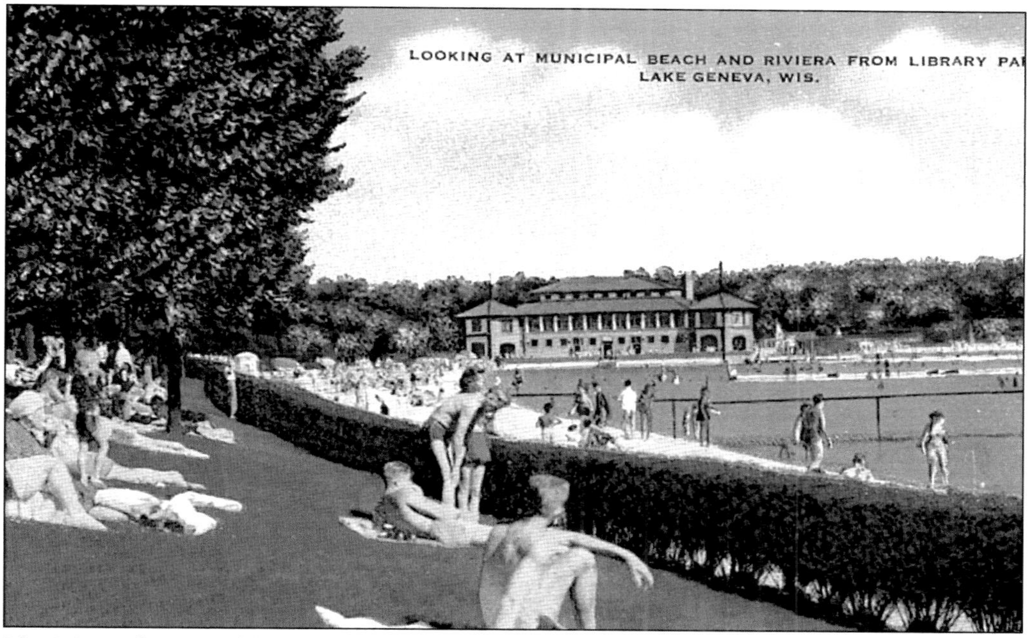

The Riviera has graceful arches, 32 Doric columns, a parquet dance floor and a mirror-faceted ball chandelier. It is both a marina and recreational facility. The City of Lake Geneva had a contest in 1932 to name the structure, and Mrs. Hobart Smith won the contest, thus naming the Riviera.

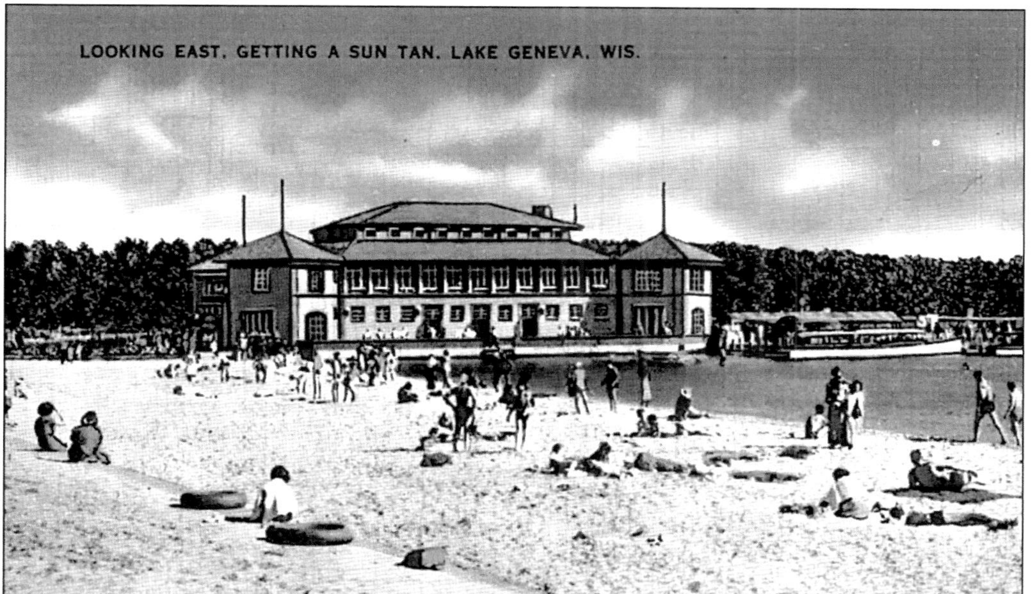

By the 1980s, the historic building had fallen into disrepair from years of neglect and abuse. An appointed citizen's committee outlined an extensive renovation, and the Riviera was restored to its original grandeur. Now listed in the National Register of Historic Places, this vintage structure is host to countless weddings and social events, and the Riviera docks are the seasonal home of excursion boats.

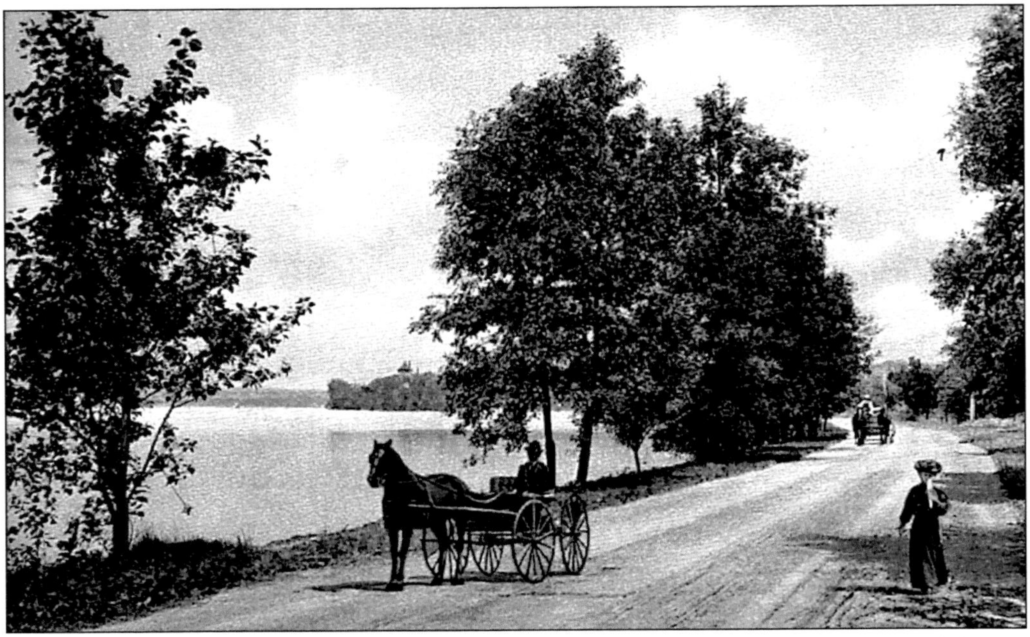

This was a typical view of Button's Bay along Lake Shore Drive before the automobile age, with horse and buggy riders or walkers traveling along the bumpy dirt road. Many preferred the steamboat for transportation to their lake estates.

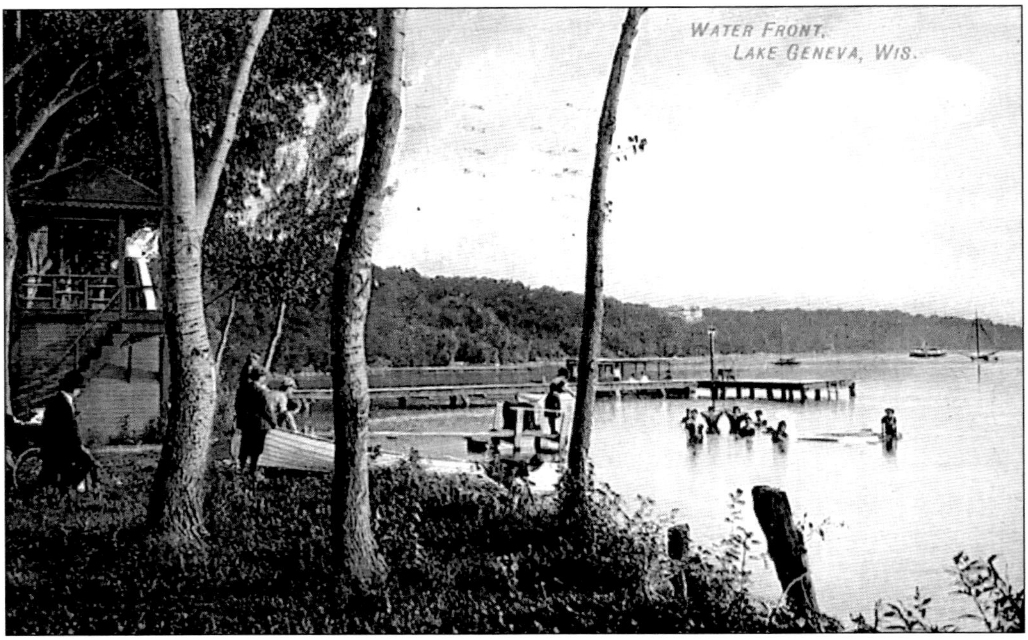

This crystal clear sparking lake, at maximum, is 142 feet deep. Geneva Lake is nine miles long with a width ranging from .5 to 1.5 miles. The lake is surrounded by 21 miles of shore line with a public walking path for all to enjoy.

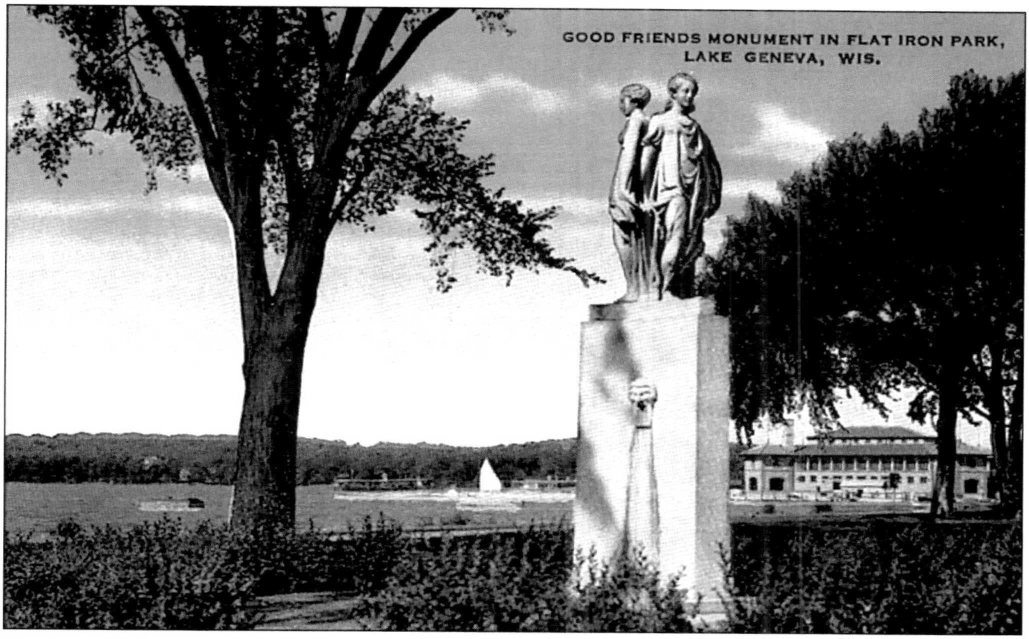

Flat Iron Park was originally known as Willow Park and is located on Wrigley Drive. Flat Iron Park is also the home of a statue with a fountain, known by three different names: the Three Sisters, The Good Friends, and the Three Graces statue. The monument was willed to the city in 1916 by Mrs. Reinette M. McCrea (one of the charter members of the Lake Geneva Garden Club). Also in Flat Iron Park are the Gump statue and a white, octagonal-shaped gazebo.

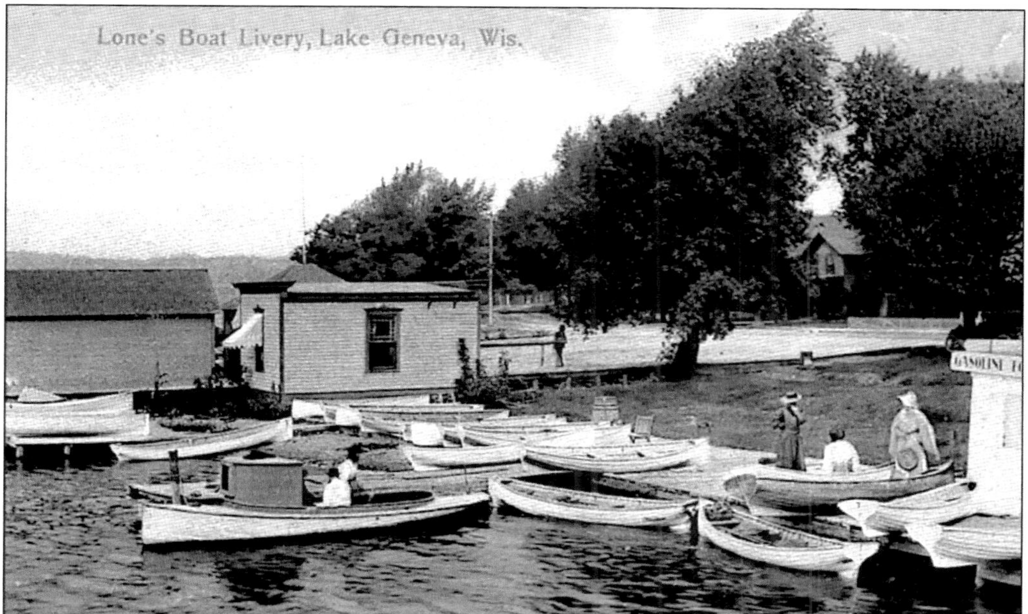

John Lone came to Lake Geneva in 1893 and bought this boat livery from Ephraim Sanford. It was across Wrigley Drive and later became the site of the Riviera.

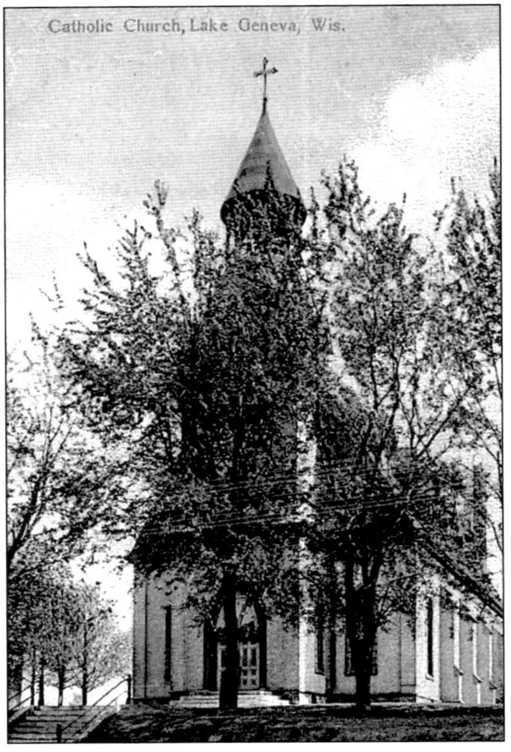

St. Francis de Sales Church is sometimes referred to as "Catholic Hill." As early as the late 1830s, Father Kundig from Milwaukee would minister to the Lake Geneva Catholic families. In 1844–1847, the church community was known as St.Martin's Parish. In 1844, the rectory building was constructed, where Mass was said on the second floor until the first church was built in 1852. The original church building was a frame structure located on the southeast area of the property. The present church was built in 1889 at a cost of $16,000. The modified gothic structure was designed and built by William Brady. Patrick Healy, founder of the Lyon & Healy Music Publishing Co. in Chicago, donated the large pipe organ.

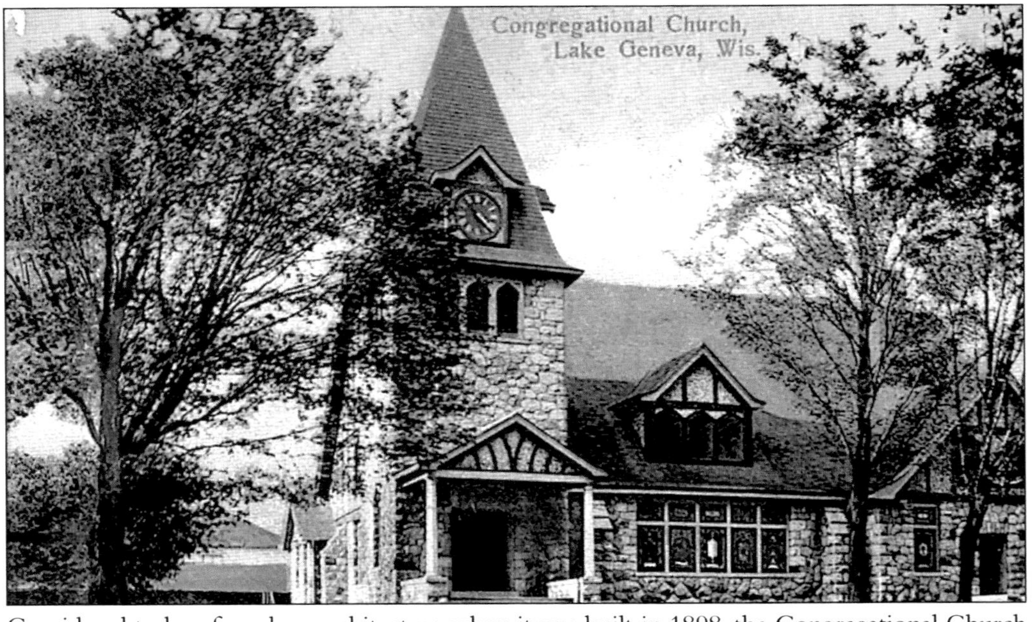

Considered to be of modern architecture when it was built in 1898, the Congregational Church still stands on Wisconsin Avenue in Lake Geneva. Now called the First Congregational United Church of Christ, it was the third church building on that site.

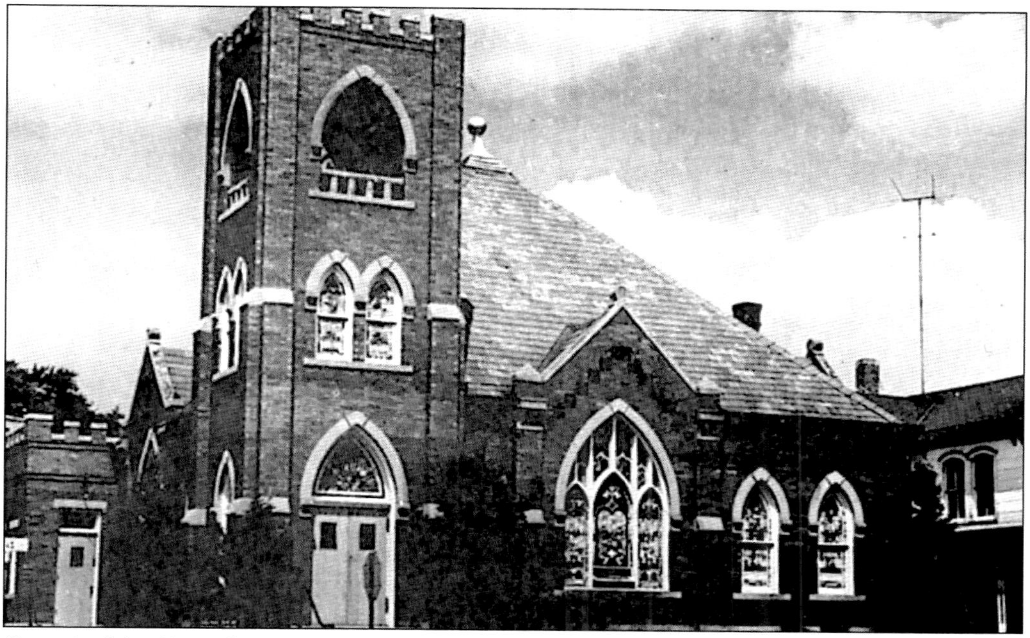

Organized in 1840, the Baptists were the third denomination established in Lake Geneva. The original church, built in 1847, was razed in 1910 to make room for the church shown here that still stands on the corner of Broad and Geneva Streets. Designed in a brick gothic-revival style with a square-corner bell tower, paired arch openings, and cut-stone window hoods, the chiming of its bells could be heard all over downtown Lake Geneva. Today it houses boutique shops.

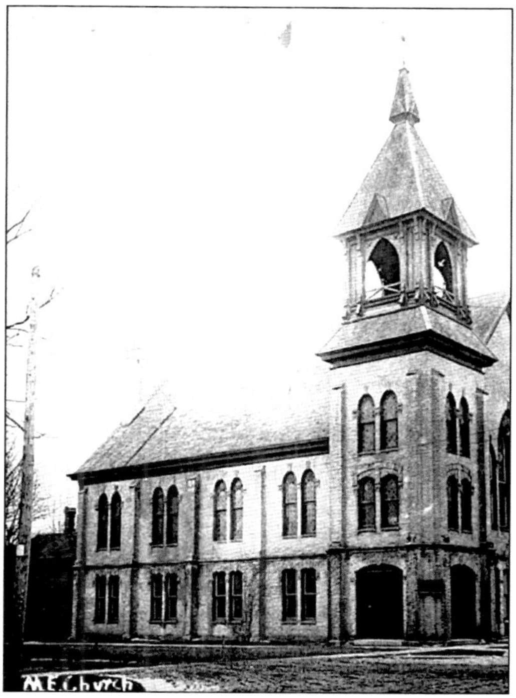

The United Methodist Church is the oldest organized church in Lake Geneva. It dates back to 1837, when the church services were held in a school house. The structure was built in 1877–1878 for $10,000 on the corner of Cook and Geneva Streets. The church was remodeled in 1944 and in the 1960s. In 1965, a new parish hall was constructed.

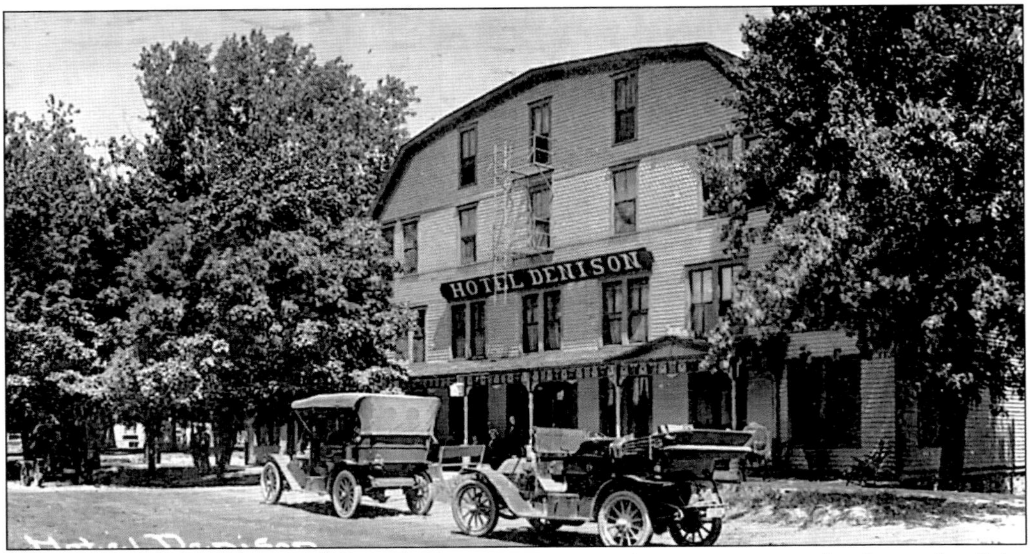

In 1870, Benjamin Fish built the Union House on Broad Street to meet the demands of the anticipated tourist trade upon completion of the railway in 1871. The hotel was enlarged in 1892 by adding on a store building moved from Main Street. The building has been known as the Garrison House, the Hotel Denison and later, the Traver Hotel. Its façade is easily recognized today on Broad Street. Mrs. Traver was reportedly famous for her homemade pies. (Courtesy of the Jerry Glass Collection.)

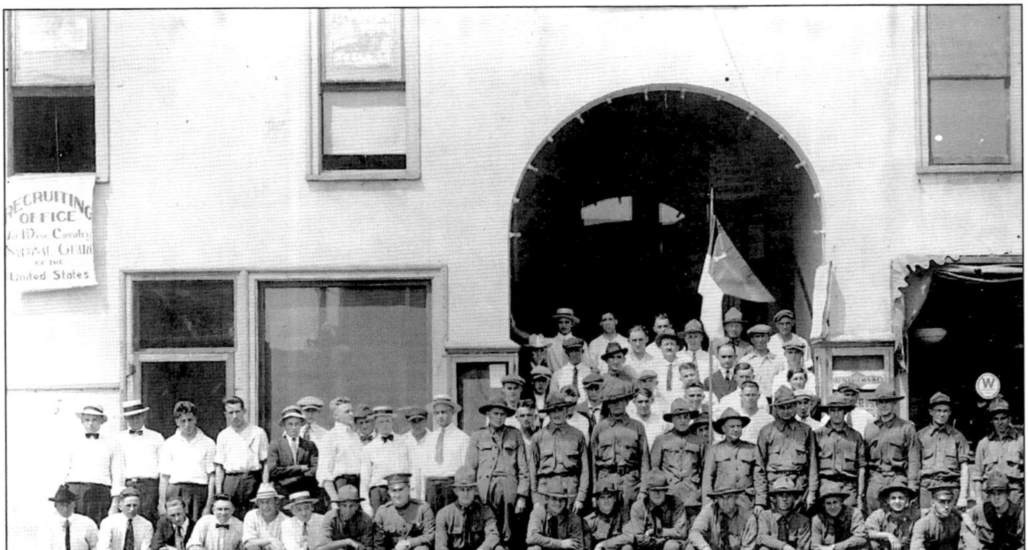

This Broad Street building was constructed in 1876 as Centennial Hall and rechristened Ford's Opera House after it was purchased by Miss Cornelia L. Ford. It served a wide variety of needs for over 50 years, including a roller rink and a high school gymnasium for basketball games. It was also used as a screening center for army recruits at the outbreak of World War I. It was razed in 1927 to make way for the red brick Mediterranean-style building that replaced it, now known as the Geneva Theatre. (Courtesy of the Brown-Gabriel Collection.)

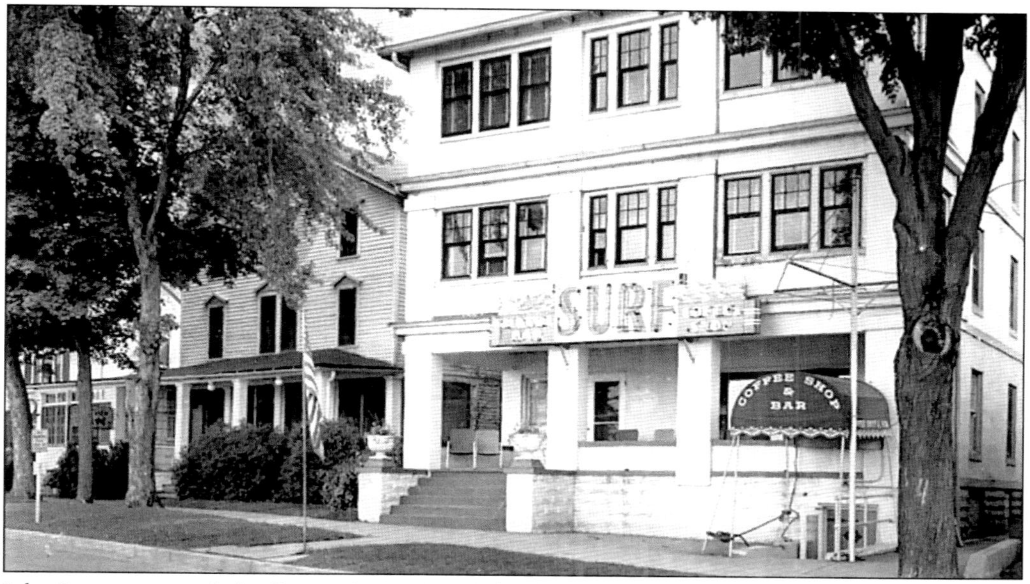

John Lone came to Lake Geneva in 1893, and the first of his Lake Geneva businesses was the boat livery. Later, around 1914, he bought the Stafford residence on Lake Street (now called Wrigley Drive) where he built The Surf Hotel. (Courtesy of the Jerry Glass Collection.)

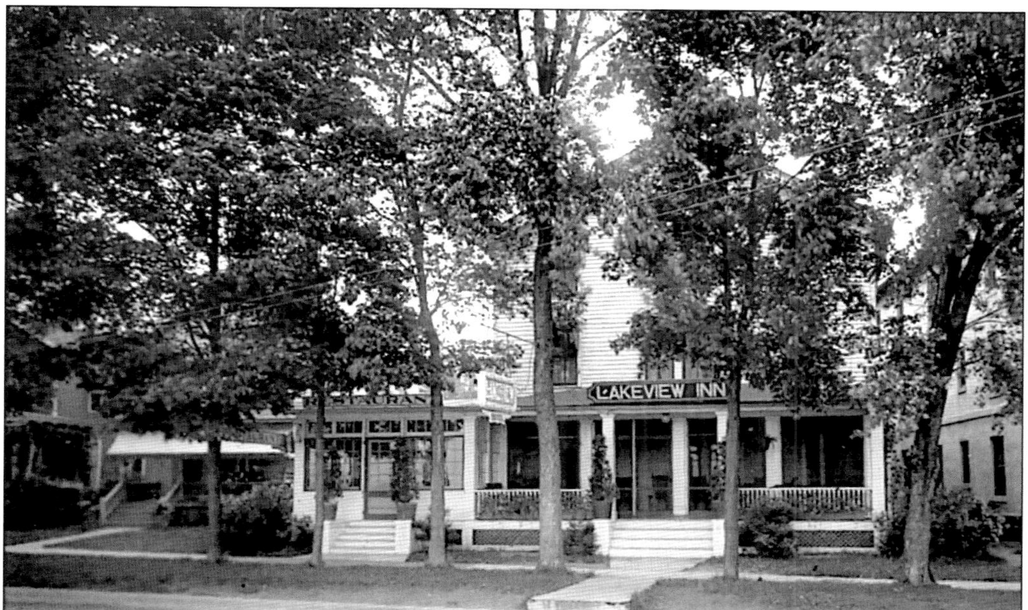

Mrs. Watson was the proprietor of the Lakeview Inn, also located on Lake Street. (Courtesy of the Jerry Glass Collection.)

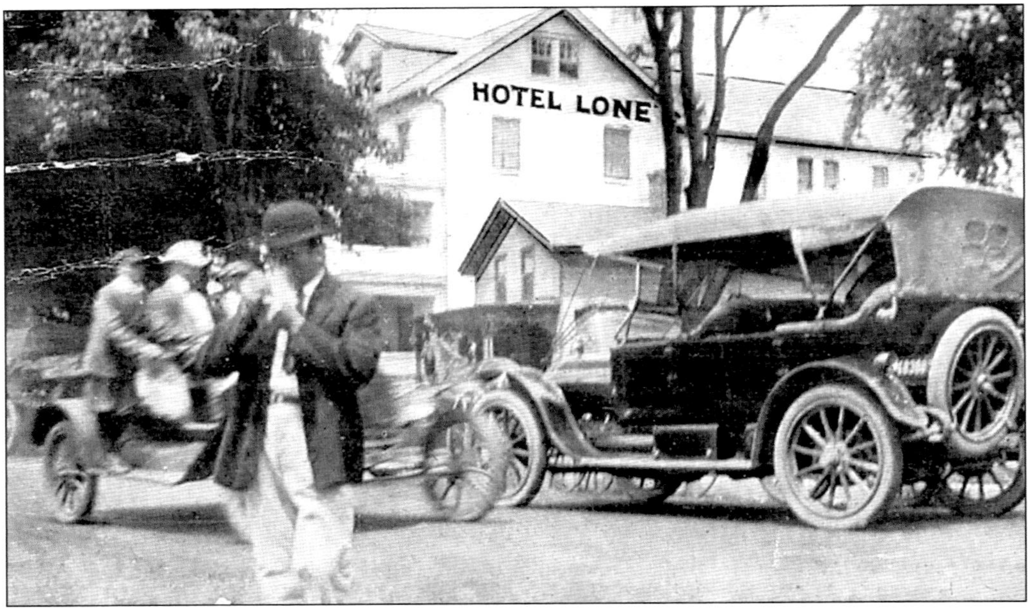

The Hotel Lone was on Wrigley Drive, right across from the Lake. Today, the Popeye's Restaurant parking lot fills its place. (Courtesy of the Jerry Glass Collection.)

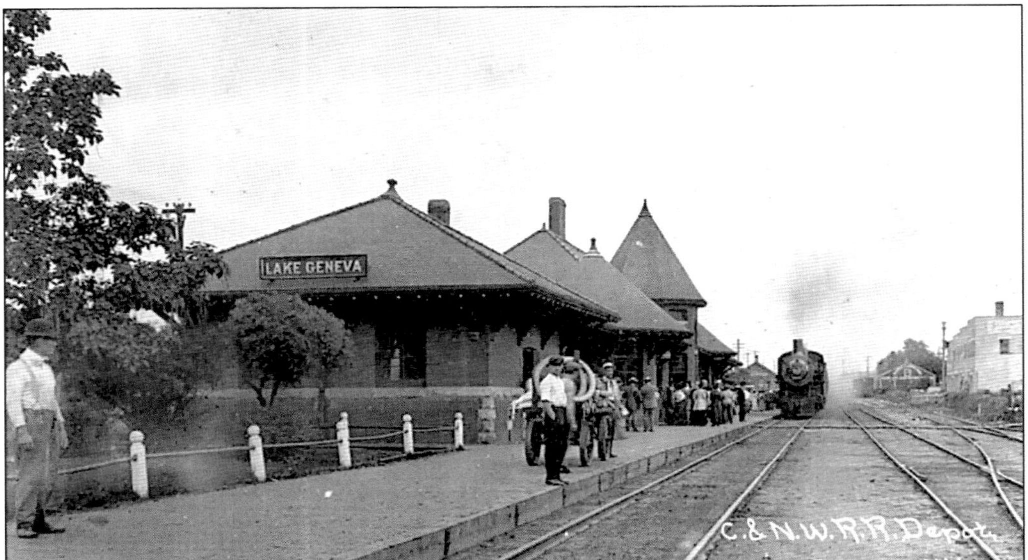

The Chicago Northwestern Depot was once the grand scene of tallyhos, with coachmen awaiting the commuter train to take lakeshore residents to their homes. Later, fancy automobiles would meet the passengers and drive them to their lakefront estates, either via Lake Shore Drive or to the steamboat docks, where they would conclude their journey by yacht. The last train ran on August 11, 1975, and despite campaigns to save the structure, it was razed in the 1980s. The Geneva Family Practice Building opened on this site in 1986.

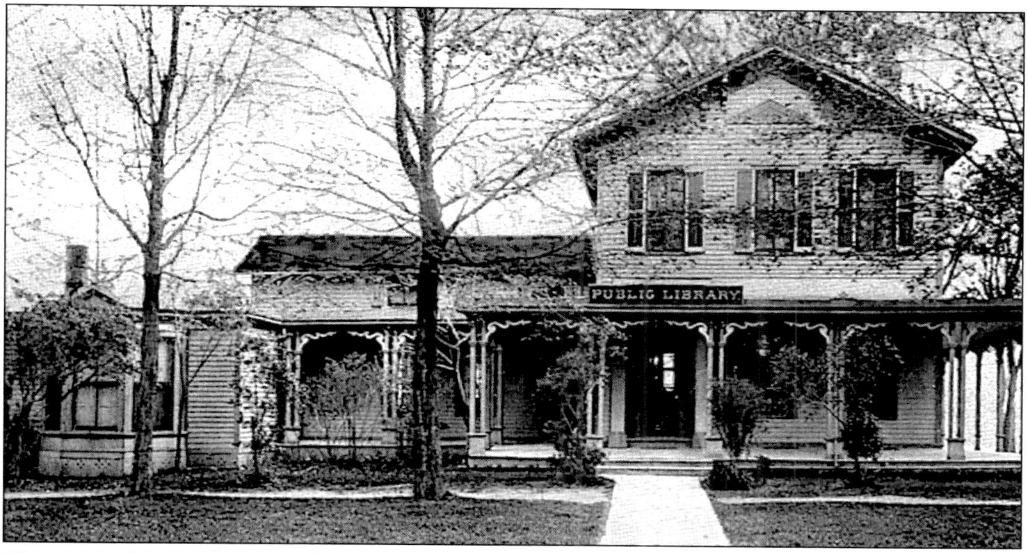

The original Lake Geneva Library was willed to the City of Lake Geneva by Mary D. Sturges. Built by A.W. Farr in 1859, it was the Sturges family cottage for many years. Prior to the gift of this site, the public read books in a reading room of the local YMCA. By 1953, the old Sturges building was nearly 100 years old and was no longer structurally sound or adequate in size for the library. The present library is on this very site. Designed by a Frank Lloyd Wright protégé, James P. Dresser, the new building was dedicated in December 1954. The interior is open and windows face the lake, providing the perfect environment to read, write, study, or reflect.

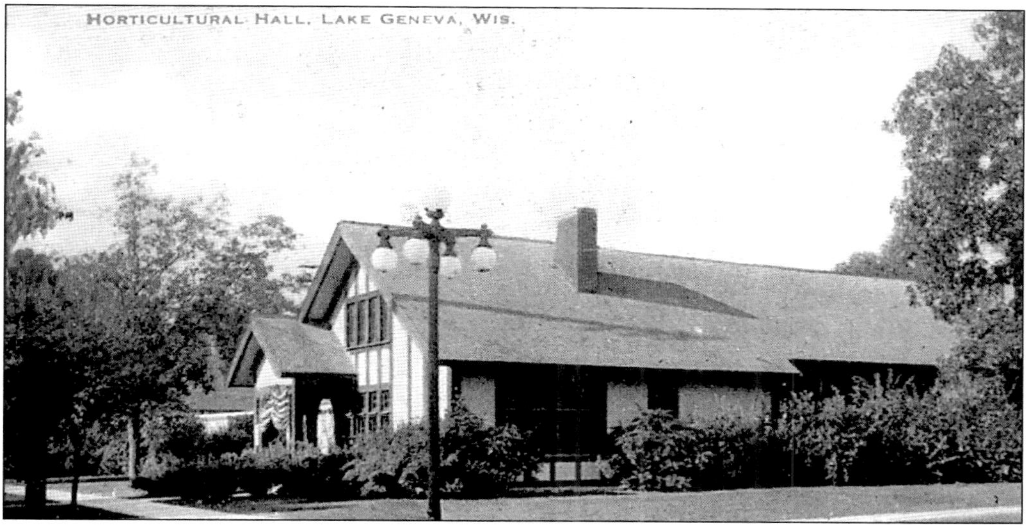

Simeon B. Chapin, owner of Flowerside Inn and Farms, founded the Lake Geneva Horticultural Society in 1911. Horticultural Hall, designed by Robert B. Spencer Jr., was built in 1912, thanks to the generosity of Mr. Chapin and other lake estate owners. It was used by Holiday Home as a site for fundraising activities, by the Lake Geneva Garden Club for meetings and hosting flower shows, and as a meeting place by the Gardener and Foreman's Association, an organization of the estate managers on the lake. It is used today by not-for-profit organizations, weddings, and a weekly farmer's market in the summer months.

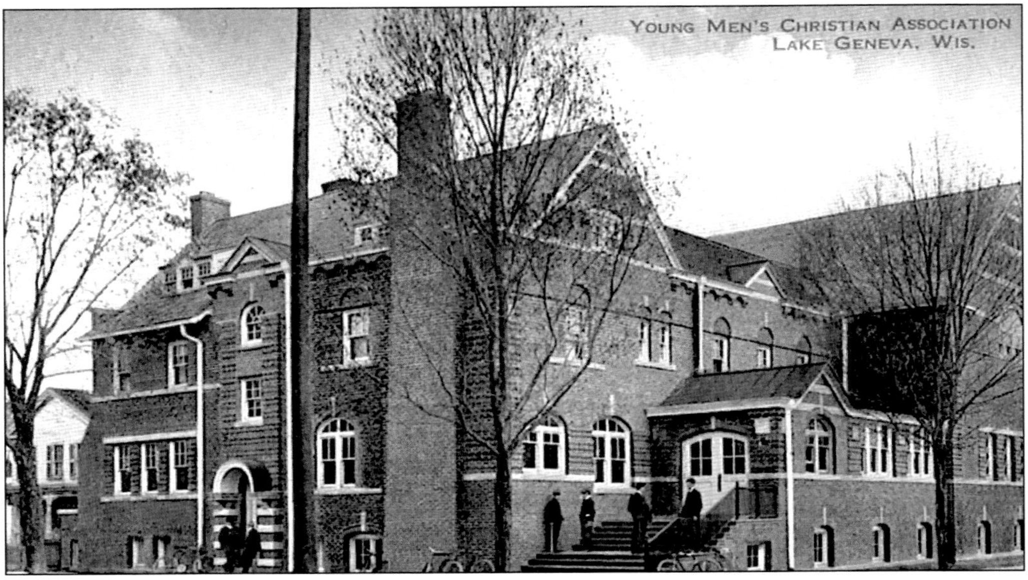

The Lake Geneva YMCA was organized in 1883 and met in churches and private homes. By 1890, they were meeting frequently in the old Sturges family cottage (which eventually became the public library). In 1902, Mrs. Sarah M. Reed bequeathed $10,000, and other citizens joined with philanthropist Simeon Chapin to support a building. The new YMCA was constructed at the southeast corner of Main Street and Wrigley Drive at the site of what is currently the Lakeside Market.

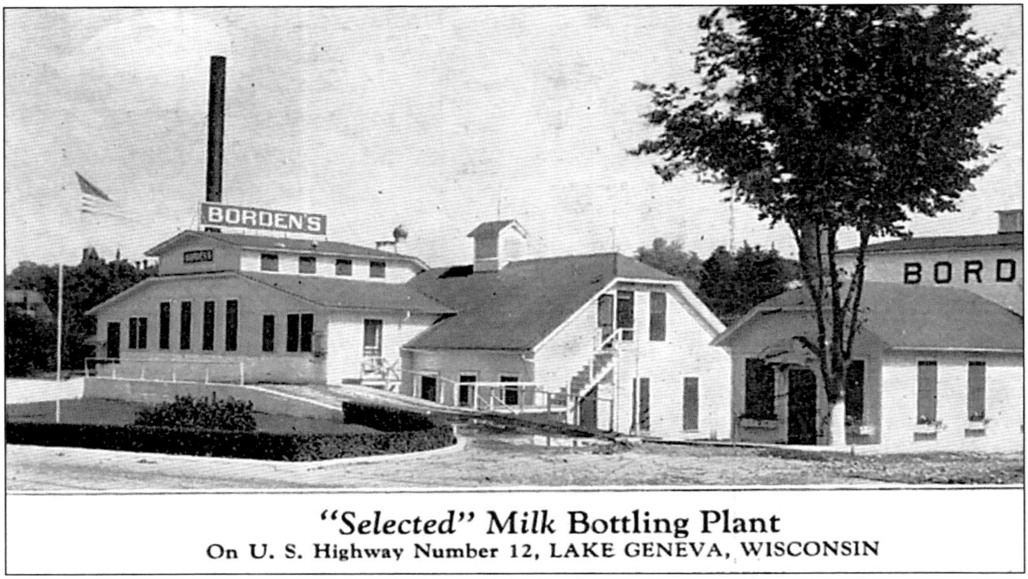

"*Selected*" *Milk* Bottling Plant
On U. S. Highway Number 12, LAKE GENEVA, WISCONSIN

Borden's Milk Bottling Plant provided chocolate milk, butter, cream, ice cream, and many other food products. Other Lake Geneva dairies included Mariondale (begun in 1920), the Modern Dairy, Maple Leaf, Hawthorne Melody, Carlson, and Pet. Later, the Piggly Wiggly was built on this site; since 1965 it has been the home of the Lake Geneva YMCA. (Courtesy of the Jerry Glass Collection.)

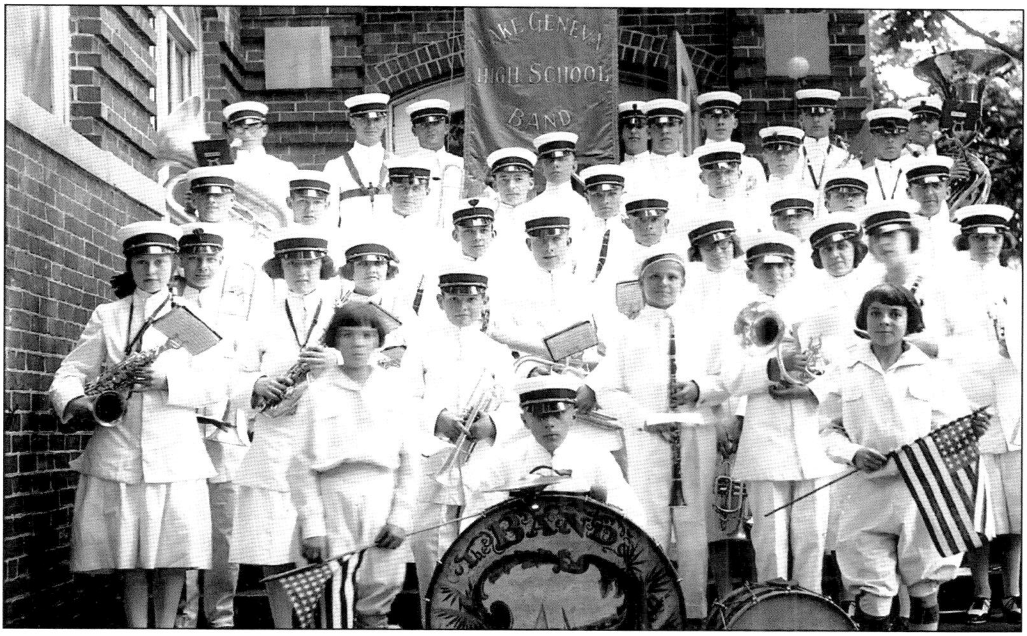

Lake Geneva High School officially began in 1895. High school classes were held at various places around Lake Geneva as early as 1865, but records from that time are not clear on the locations. The city purchased the former Young Women's Seminary as a temporary building while the new high school was being constructed next to Central School; classes were held there from the turn of the century. In 1958, Badger High School was built, and the old red-brick high school building was connected to the elementary school and became Denison Junior High School. This photo of the high school band was taken around 1923; the band was directed by music teacher Helen McDonald. (Courtesy of the Brown-Gabriel Collection.)

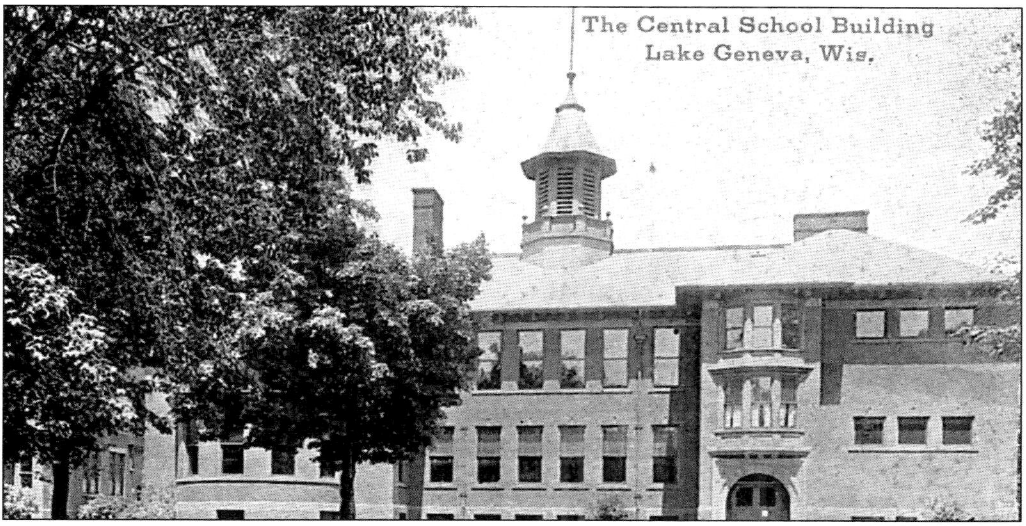

The Central School building, built in 1867 (replacing the first small school built in 1847), was destroyed by a disastrous Christmas Day fire in 1903. The "new" building, shown in this postcard, was constructed in 1904 and recently celebrated its 100th anniversary.

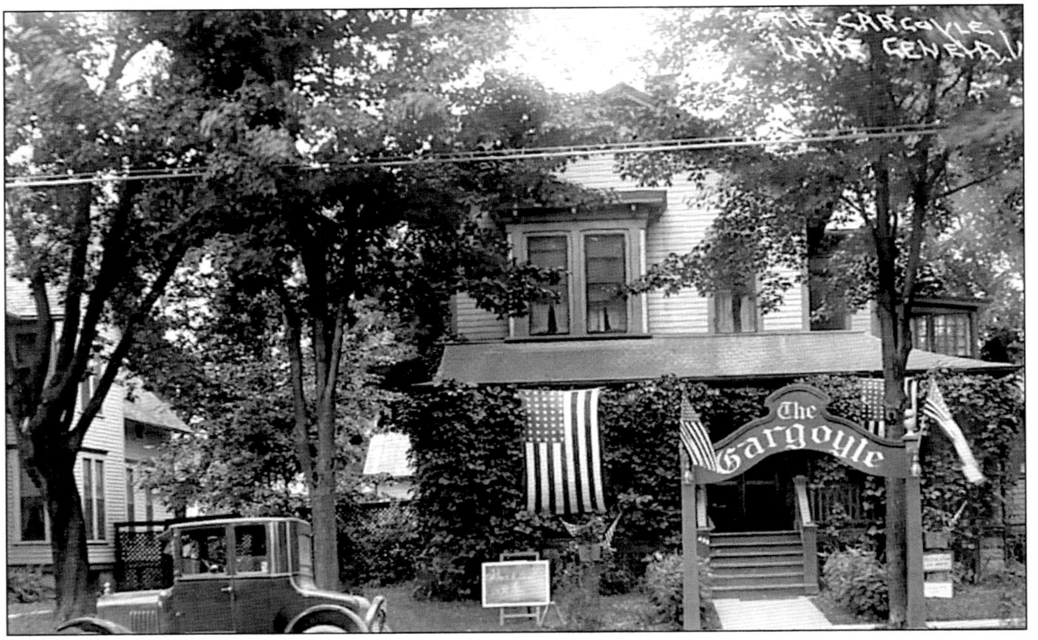

The Gargoyle Restaurant opened 1921 and became one of Lake Geneva's favorite spots during the Depression, as it featured live radio broadcasts. Boasting many interesting architectural features, it showcased Tiffany windows as well as an iron fence from the John Burton home. It later became Dana's, then Augie's, and today is the Cactus Club restaurant.

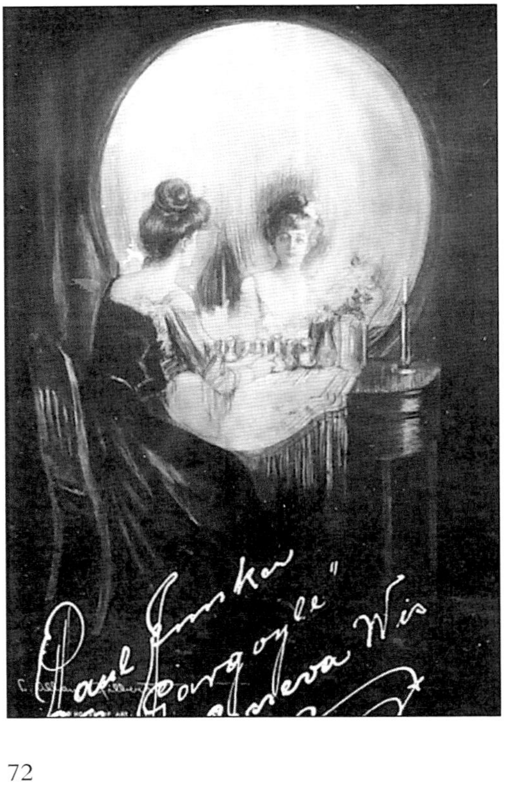

This very interesting postcard was given out by Paul Junker, owner of Gargoyle's, to advertise his establishment. Look closely—do you see a skull? Or an elegant lady looking in the mirror of her dressing table? (Courtesy of the Brown-Gabriel Collection.)

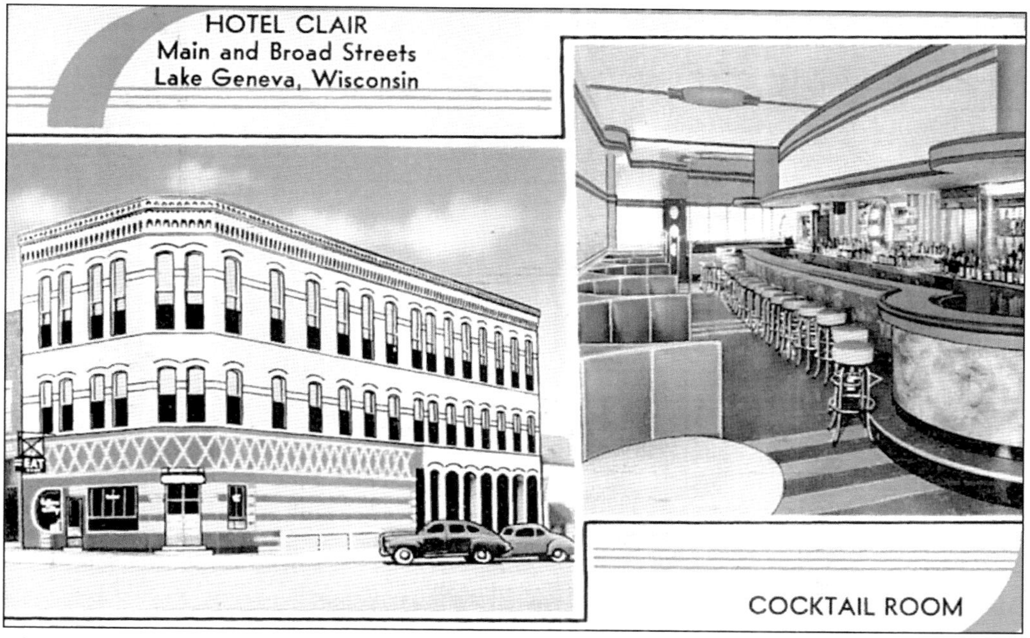

This 1950s-era postcard shows the lounge in the Hotel Clair. Established in 1920 at Main and Broad Streets in downtown Lake Geneva, the hotel included two bowling alleys and six pool tables in the basement. This historical building, constructed in 1874, has been carefully restored and is now known as the Landmark Building. (Courtesy of the Patti Black Collection.)

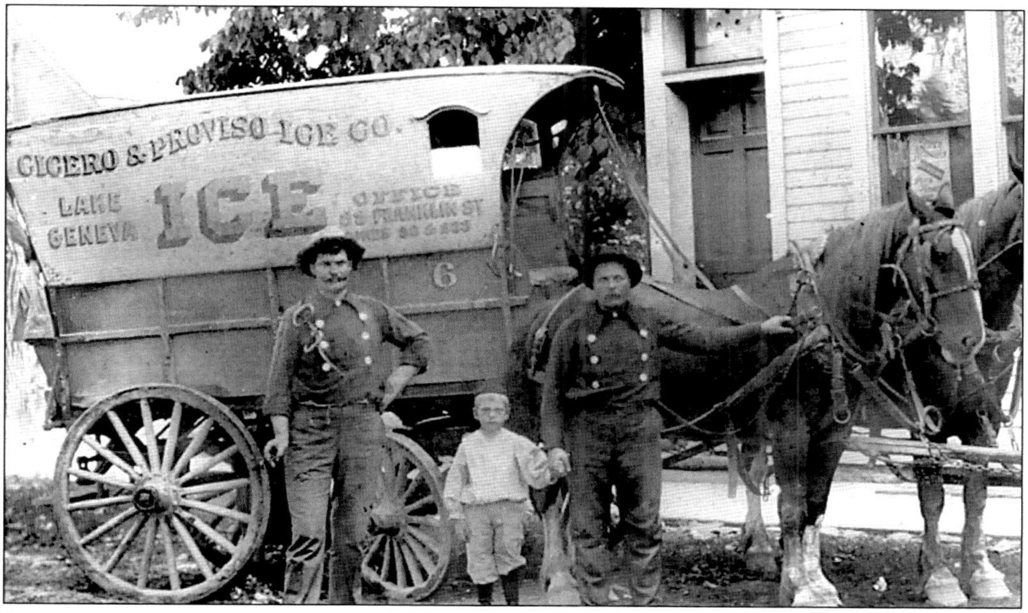

Ice-cutting was a major local industry for many decades. The deep, spring-fed, crystal-clear lake water was cut into blocks by hard workers using special tools and wearing leather aprons. Ice was delivered to local citizens by horse and buggy. Chicagoans also eagerly awaited their Lake Geneva ice delivery, which came via railroad cars. (Courtesy of the Brown-Gabriel Collection.)

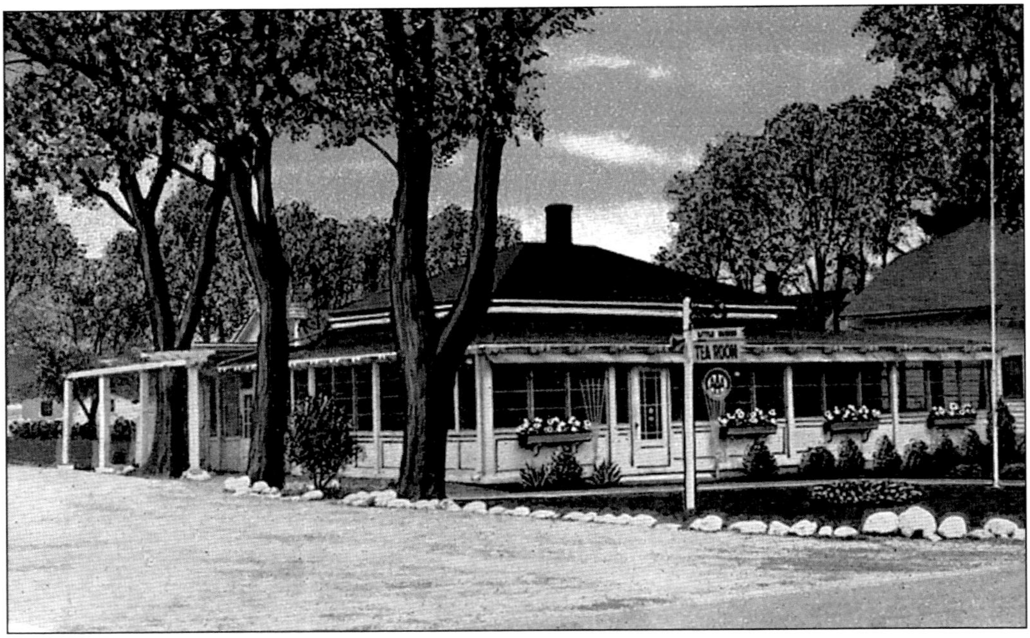

The Little Danish Tea Room was opened in 1933 by the Houlbergs, who came to the United States from Denmark. Initially, they served only tea and sandwiches, but the menu was expanded and the tea room became well known for its Danish specialties. Later, this restaurant became the Danish Tea Room, Great Dane Restaurant, Fazio's, The Excalibur, and is now Celebrations on Wells Street.

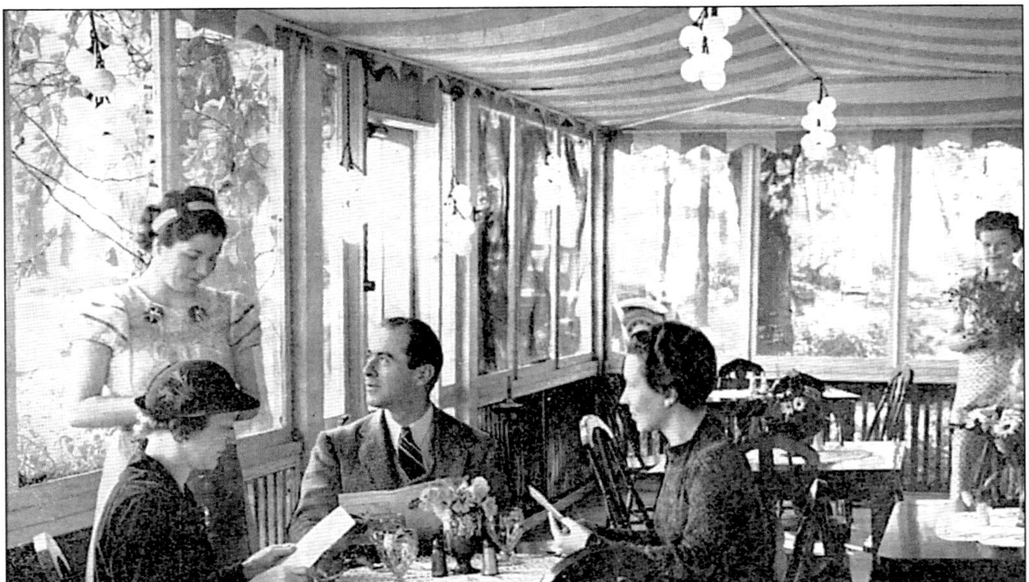

Shown here is the dining room of the Little Danish Tea Room where many people over the years met for an elegant meal. (Courtesy of the Patti Black Collection.)

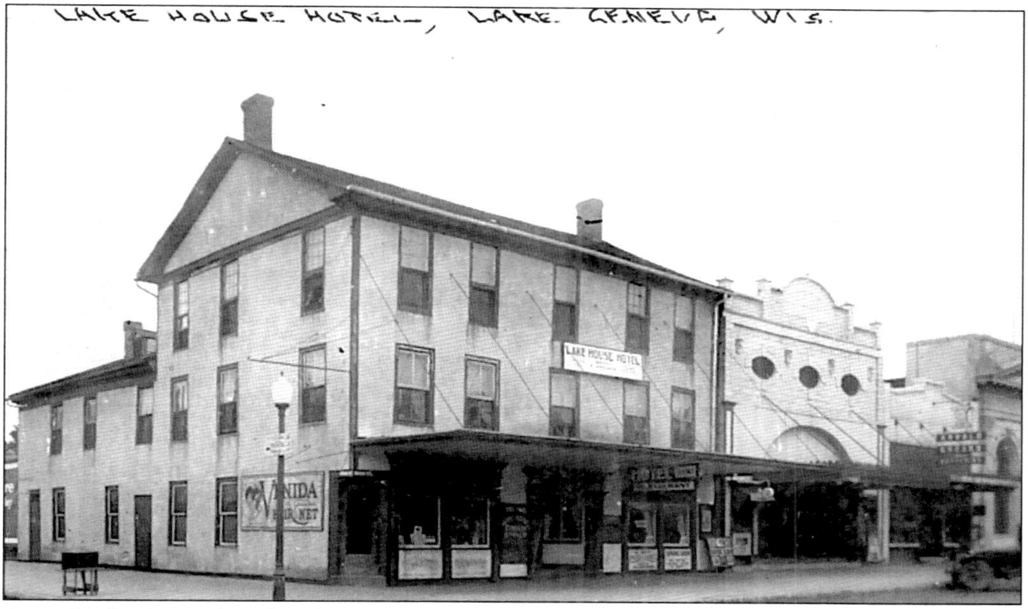

One of Lake Geneva's earliest hotels, the Lake House, was established in 1837 by Greenleaf Warren. Through the years, it was also known as the Stafford House, and later the Hotel Florence. Located at the northeast corner of Broad and Main Streets, it was demolished in the 1920s to make room for the Wisconsin Power and Light headquarters, which occupied the site until about 1927. Much of the interior woodwork was retained when the building was remodeled for its modern day uses. Currently, it houses several shops and offices. (Courtesy of the John P. Urlakis Collection.)

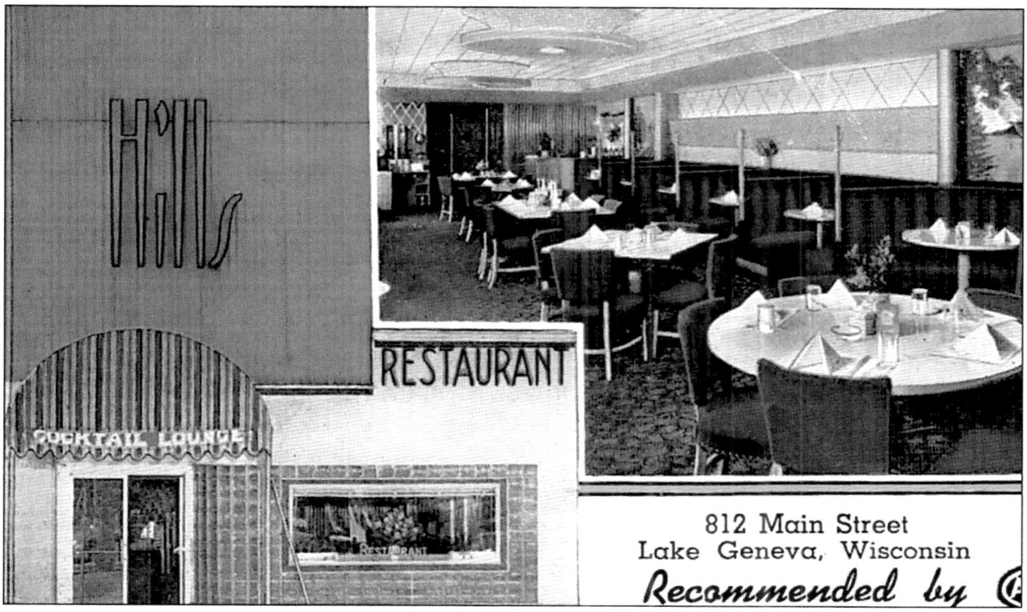

Hill's Restaurant on Main Street was later known as Glen Nelson's, Chuckle's, and Le Gournet.

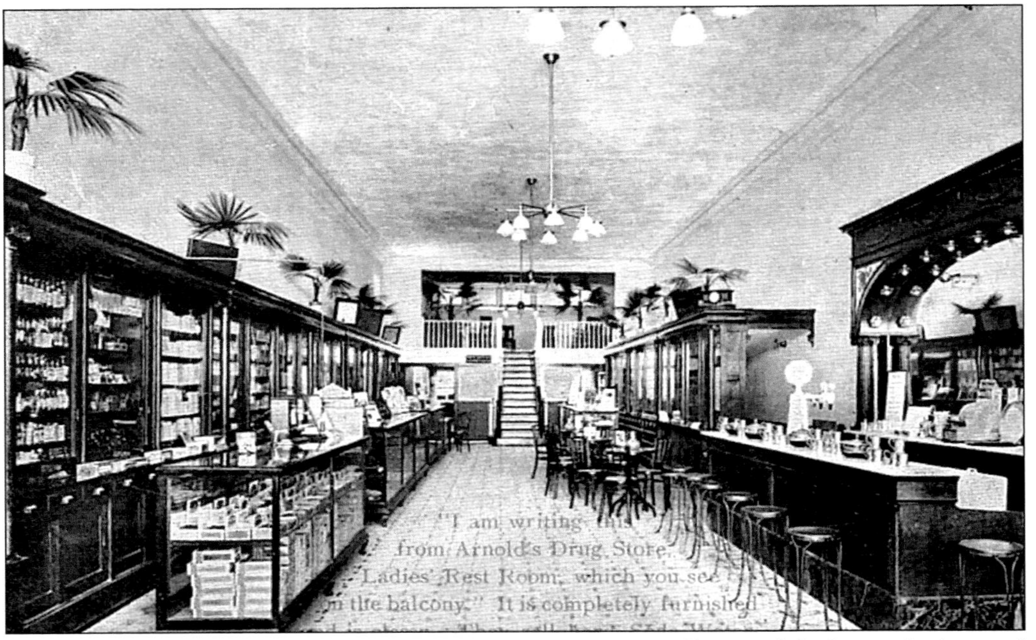

In 1905, Arnold's Drugs was located on Broad Street and reportedly served the best sodas in town! The building now houses a restaurant, and the interior is still very recognizable. (Courtesy of the Joy Peterkin Rasin Collection.)

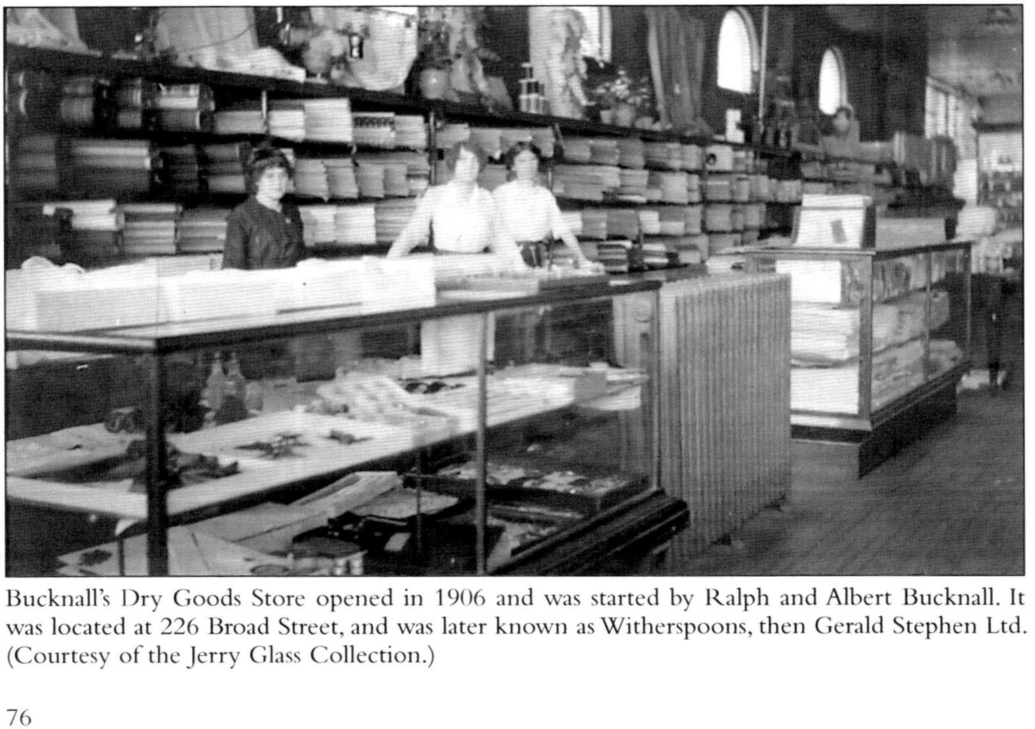

Bucknall's Dry Goods Store opened in 1906 and was started by Ralph and Albert Bucknall. It was located at 226 Broad Street, and was later known as Witherspoons, then Gerald Stephen Ltd. (Courtesy of the Jerry Glass Collection.)

Three

The Joy of Opportunities at lake Camps

Camps have been an important part of the Geneva Lake culture, heritage, and environment. The camps comprise over 100 acres of land, with many having lake frontages. They serve as conference centers, retreats, educational programs, and specialized summer programs like camps for children with cancer. The Geneva Lake camps allow visitors a chance to enjoy living on the lake and experience all the recreational activities. All the camps are unique and have rich histories. The following postcard images highlight the history of some of these camps, encouraging an appreciation of their mission, their significance, and the opportunities they offer.

In 1886, the YMCA purchased four acres of Geneva Lake land as a summer retreat and educational facility for teaching leadership skills. The YMCA Chicago Training School merged with the Institute at Lake Geneva in 1896, and the Lake Geneva campus hosted human services education for leaders. In 1933, the institute was renamed after the founder of the YMCA movement, George Williams.

In 1992, the George Williams College, in cooperation with Aurora University, reestablished the human service educational programs. The following year, Aurora University established the George Williams College of Aurora University as a separate school housing the Schools for Social Work, Education, Physical Education, and Recreation Administration. The camp merged with Aurora University in 2001. Today, it is dedicated to carrying on the tradition and legacy of the human service mission, the heritage of the George Williams College, specialty camps, and the preservation of the arts.

The Eleanor Association of Chicago, a club for young working women, had no place for the women to vacation. In 1909, it initiated a summer camp as an experiment. Their first campsite was just east of Black Point on Geneva Lake and immediately proved successful.

Once the Eleanor Association had begun the tradition of sending young women to the lake for their summer vacations, it pursued camp ownership. In 1912, the group discovered the Rockford Camp, which housed "stand-alone family cottages." Those cottages began to disappear after the Eleanor Association purchased the land and created its own Eleanor Camp.

Society was changing, and in 1953, it was determined that the Eleanor Camp for Women was no longer vital. The Eleanor Record commented that, "The life of the camp and the camp itself have become very dear to many of us but, like many good things in this life, in time something comes to supplant them, and the need for this sort of summer vacation for the business girls seems to have passed, at least for the time. New opportunities for her vacation period have opened up to her, with the development of greater ease in the travel and new knowledge and new curiosity about the many points of interest, historic and scenic, that this world of ours possesses." (Excerpts courtesy of the Eleanor Foundation Website.)

Some camps have continued traditional activities dating back to their origins, like big dining halls or ice cream shops. Other camps, like Aurora University (previously the YMCA Camp), have returned to some of their traditions. In 2001, the university recreated "Music by the Lake," a traditional George Williams College music concert from the 1950s and 1960s.

Other Geneva Lake camps include the Geneva Bay Center at Covenant Harbor Bible Camp and Retreat Center, Holiday Home, Lake Geneva Youth Camp and Conference Center, a year-round Christian Retreat Center and summer Bible camp, the YMCA's Camp Nawakwa, and the Norman B. Barr Camp, which has been a summer retreat and conference center for church groups since the early 1900s. The camps have given and continue to provide learning opportunities and lake joy to many visitors.

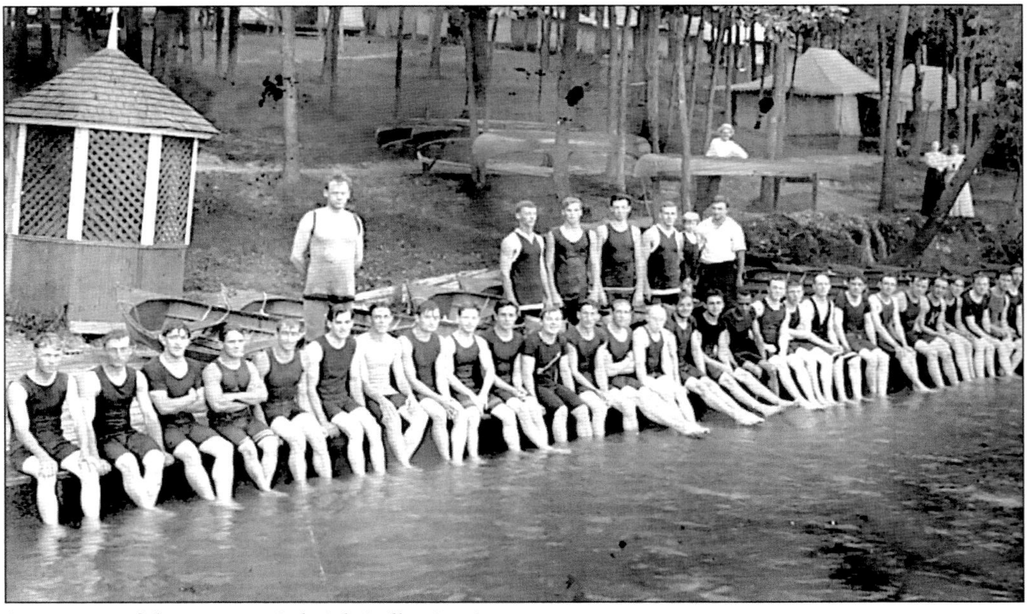

(Courtesy of the Brown-Gabriel Collection.)

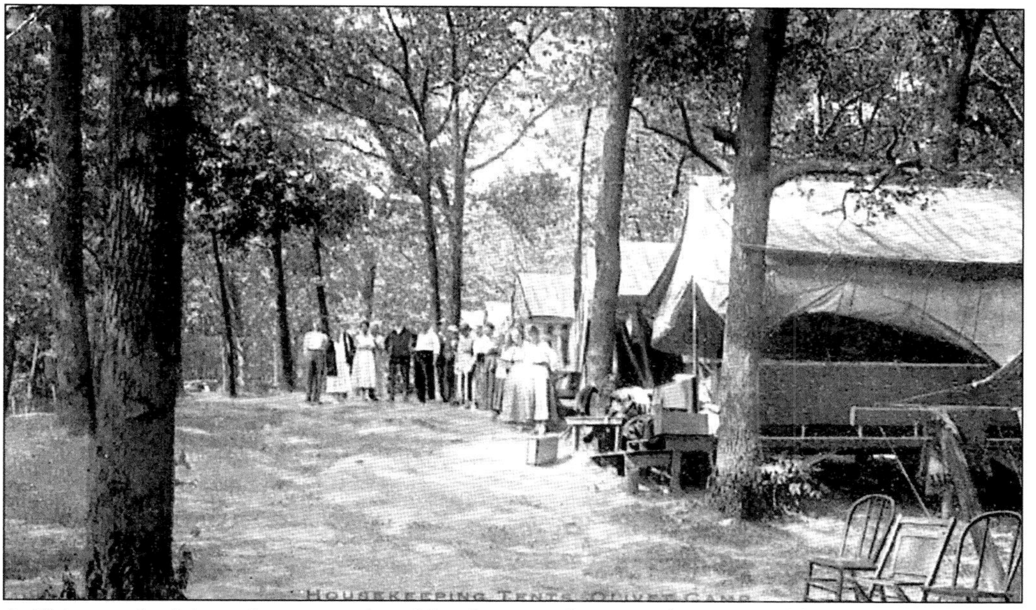

A Chicago physician, educator, and social reform worker, Dr. Alice B. Stockham was the founder of this camp. Frequently involved in intellectual discussions held around Geneva Lake, she took it upon herself to initiate and provide a site for further forums, and purchased the property in 1898. She built a home and school which she called Vralia Heights; for eight years, she held conferences and ran the Vralia Camp and Summer School of Nature Study and Philosophy.

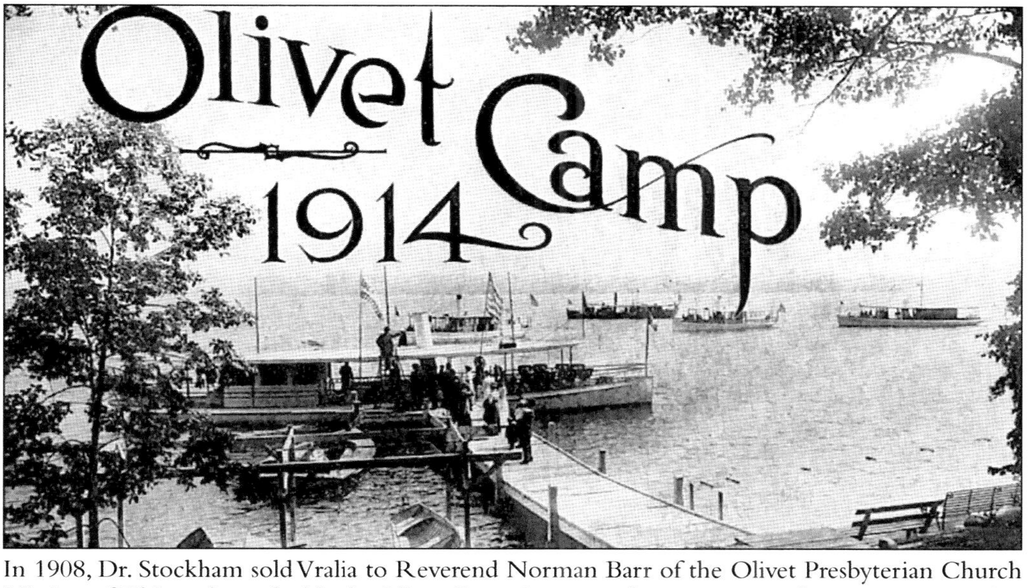

In 1908, Dr. Stockham sold Vralia to Reverend Norman Barr of the Olivet Presbyterian Church Mission of Chicago's north side. As Olivet Camp, it operated as an expense-free summer camping experience for children whose parents could not otherwise afford it. After Reverend Barr's death in 1943, the camp was renamed Norman Barr Camp in his honor. Today it is supported by several church organizations and continues to operate in the same manner. (Courtesy of the Brown-Gabriel Collection .)

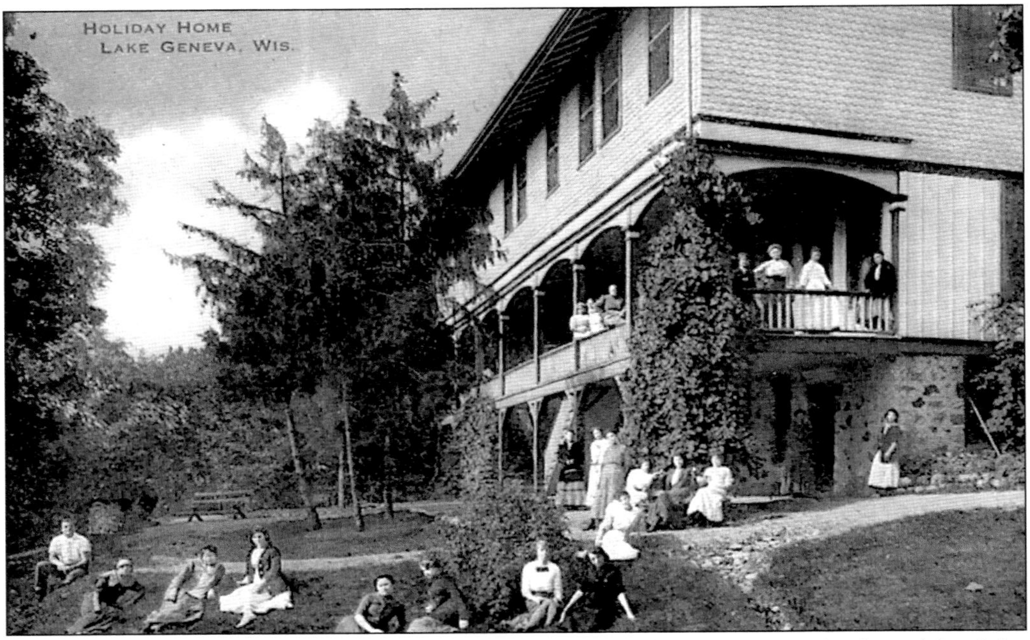

Holiday Home was founded in 1887 by a group of philanthropic women in the spirit of the Fresh Air Movement that was spreading throughout the country at that time. The objective was to provide an opportunity for lake enjoyment and relaxation for the less fortunate children and youth of industrialized urban communities in and around the Chicago area. Today, it is run with the same philosophy and is partially supported by donations and volunteers of people from the lake community.

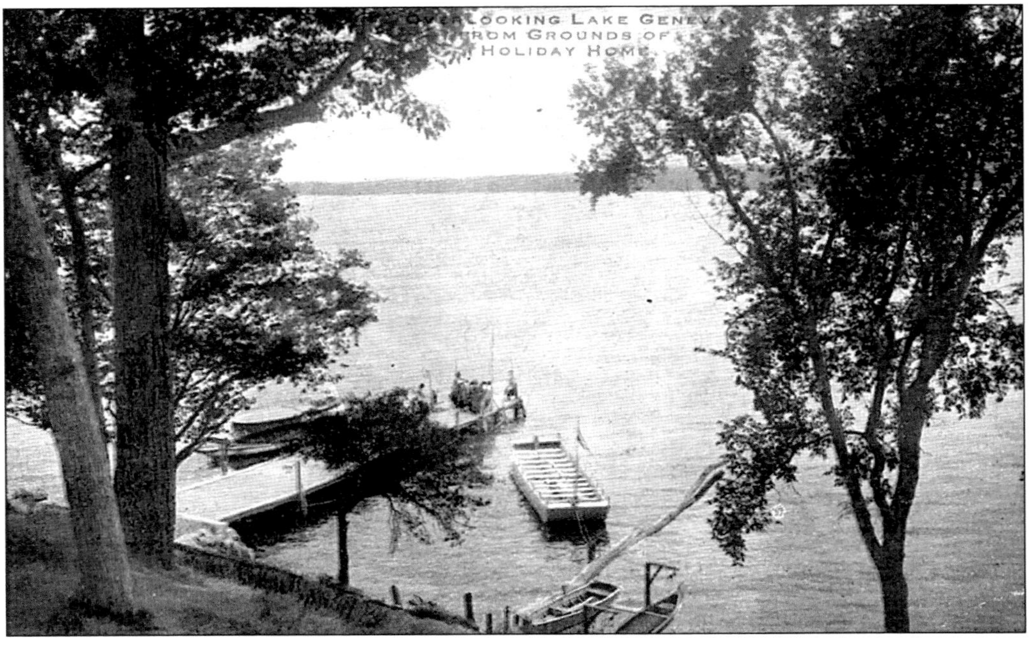

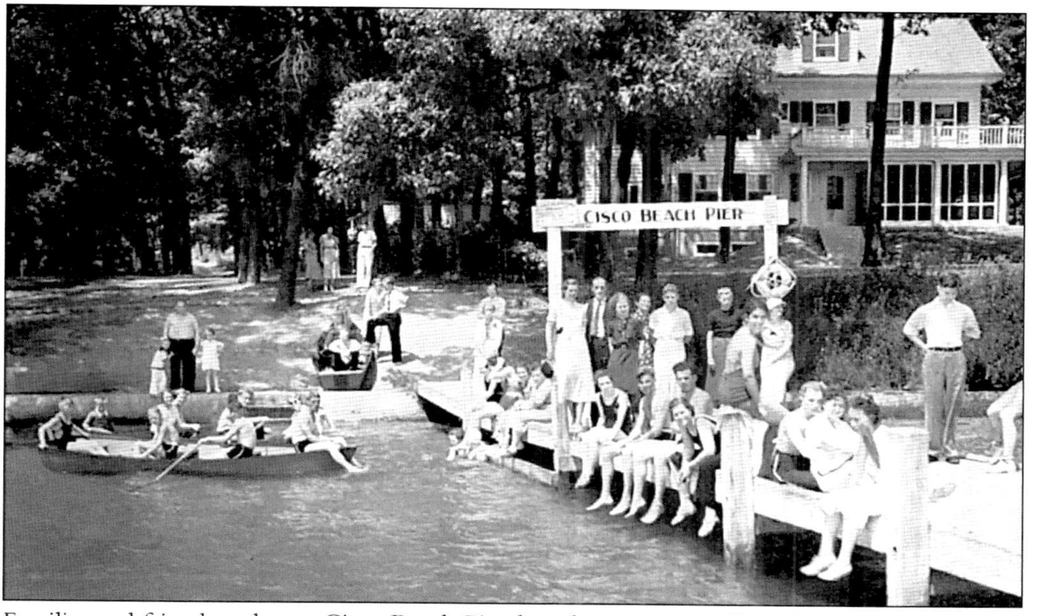

Families and friends gather at Cisco Beach Pier, later known as Knollwood Association, adjacent to then Camp Augustana. (Courtesy of the Jerry Glass Collection.)

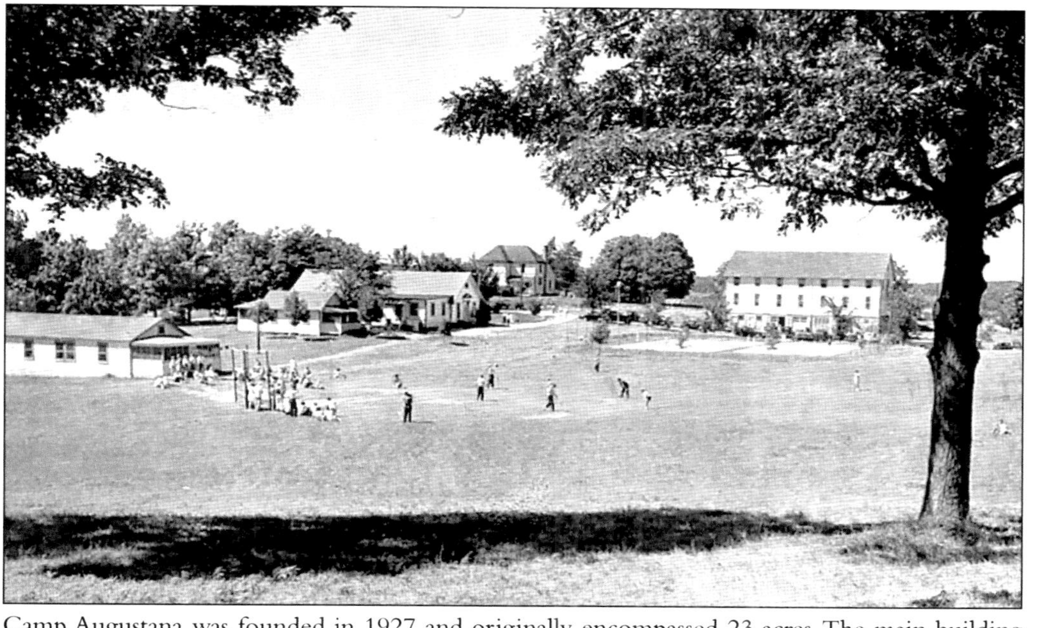

Camp Augustana was founded in 1927 and originally encompassed 23 acres. The main building on the lake used for the camp was Ara Glen. It was operated by the Illinois Lutheran Synod, which moved to Oregon, Illinois when the property was sold to developers in 1977. Some of the property is now the subdivision Ara Glen, while part is now Chapel on the Hill, and the remainder is the Knollwood Association. (Courtesy of the Joy Grossman Collection.)

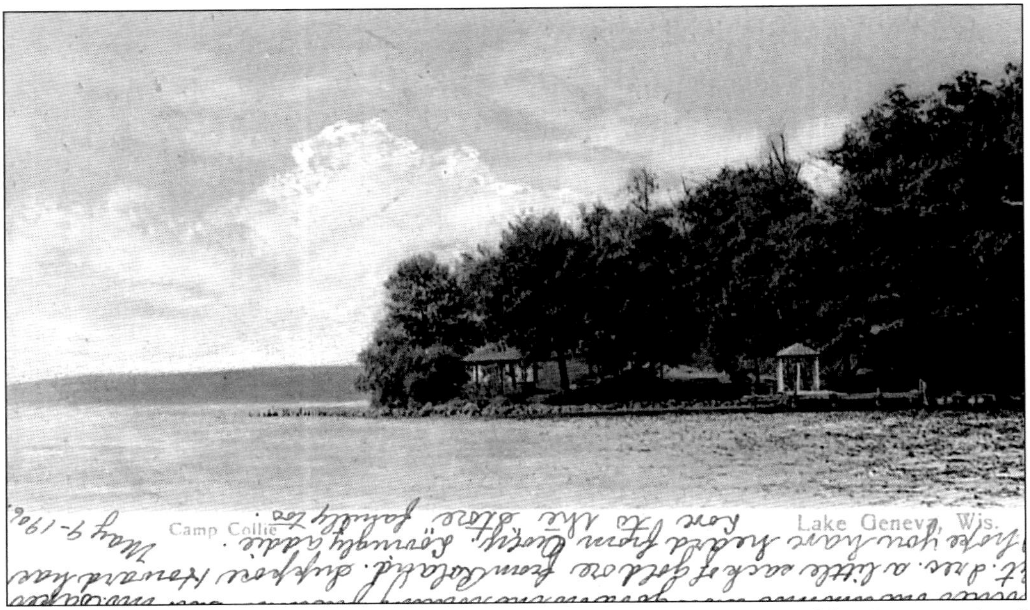

Camp Collie was owned and operated by Reverend Collie, who was pastor of the Congregational Church of Delavan for 40 years. Created in 1874, the camp offered programs devoted to religious and intellectual issues.

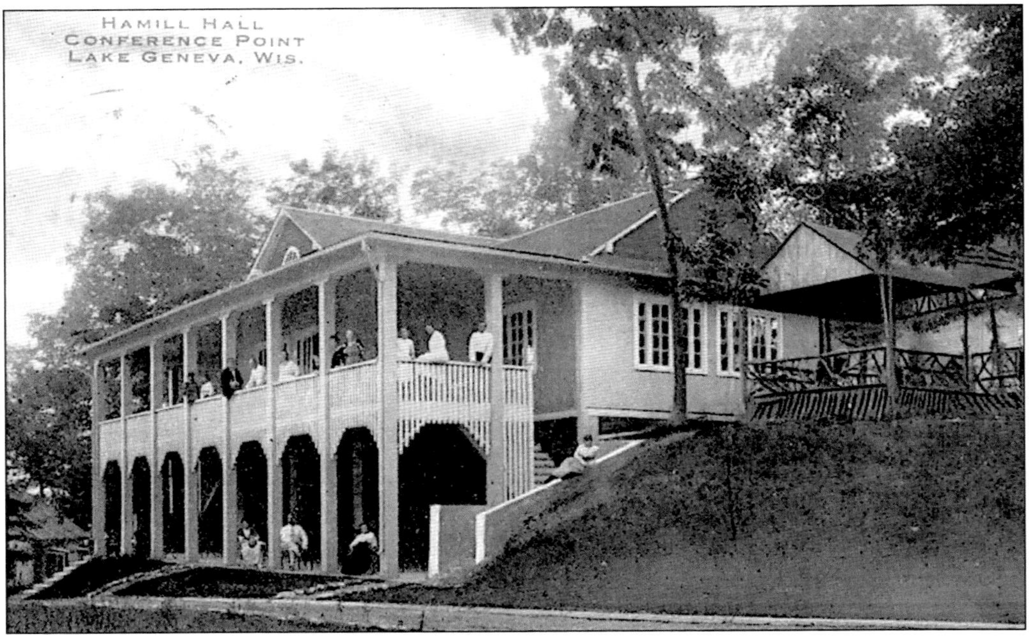

Camp Collie was sold to Mr. Nichols, who formed a corporation named The Lake Geneva Sunday School Association; this property was deeded to the association in 1907. The International Sunday School Association sponsored their first organized training school for Sunday School leaders in 1907. In 1908, the name of the property was changed from Camp Collie to Conference Point Camp.

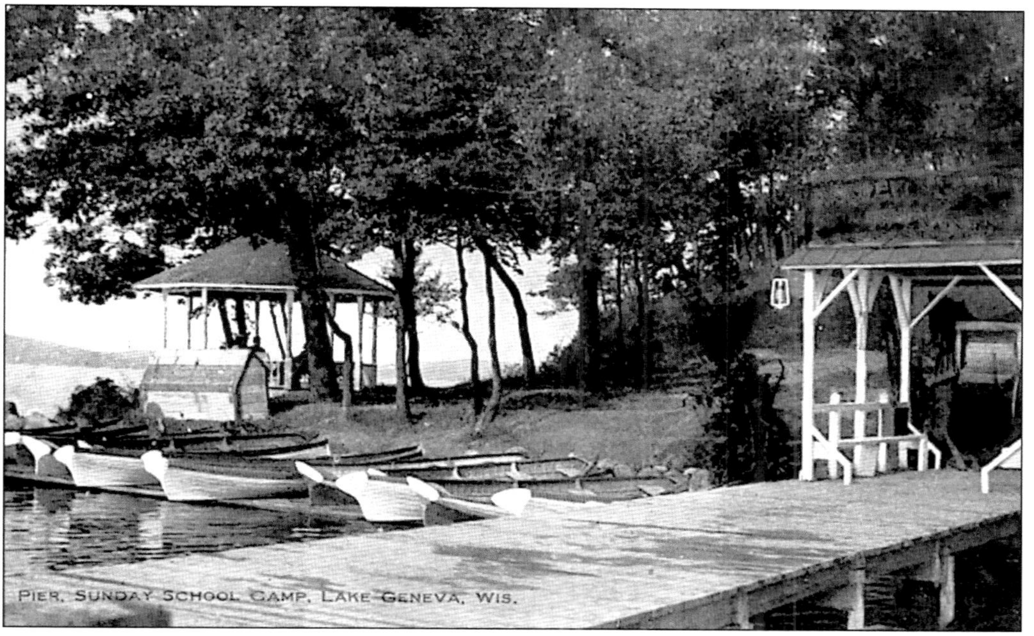

The beautiful setting of Conference Point Camp has made it an ideal retreat center for church groups for over 125 years. The serenity of the lakefront lends itself to reflection and meditation. The sports and activities provide socialization and team building. In the summer, the camp fires blaze while singing and laughter echo around the lake, creating lifetime friendships.

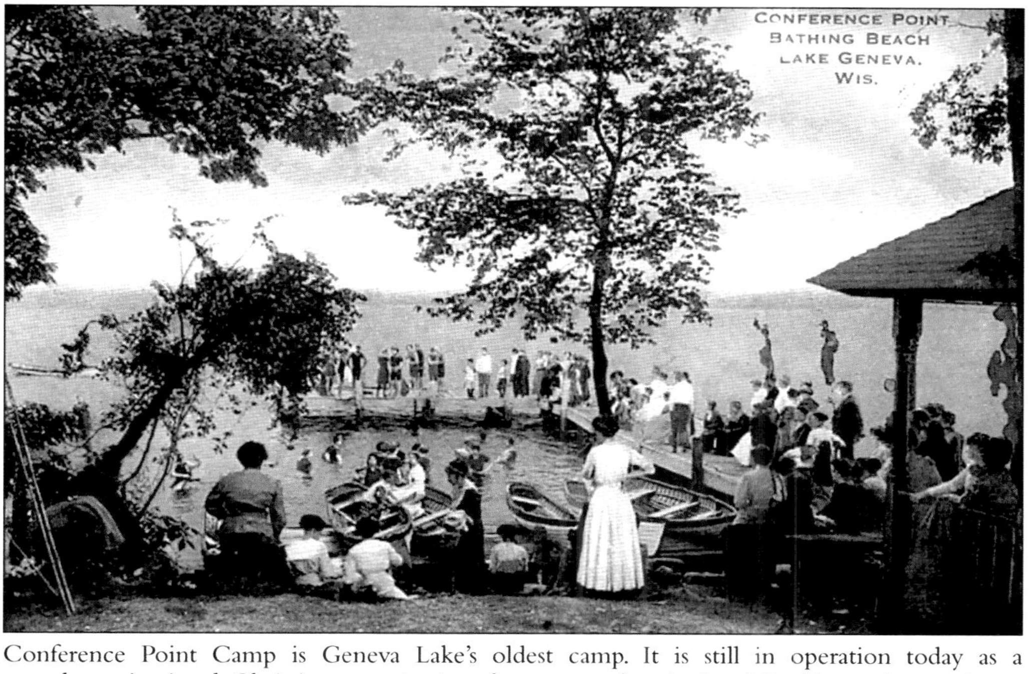

Conference Point Camp is Geneva Lake's oldest camp. It is still in operation today as a non-denominational Christian organization that attracts hundreds of families and participants from all over the United States.

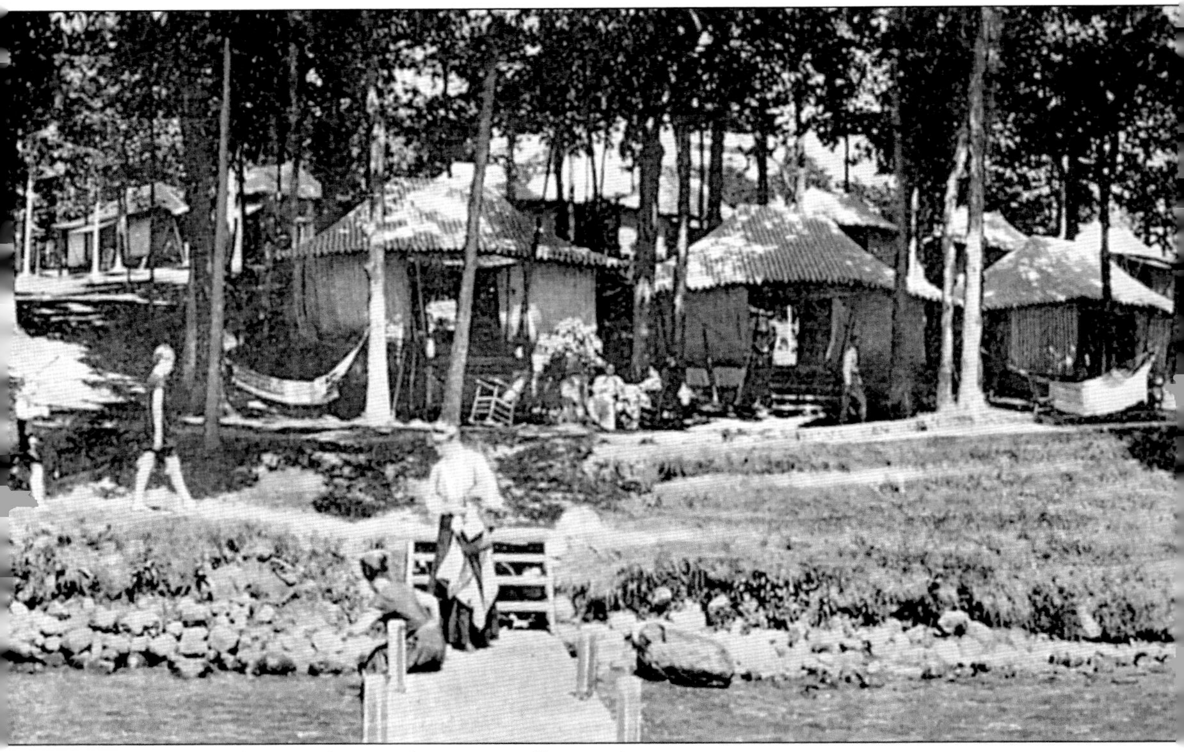

(Courtesy of the Robert Webster Sr. Collection.)

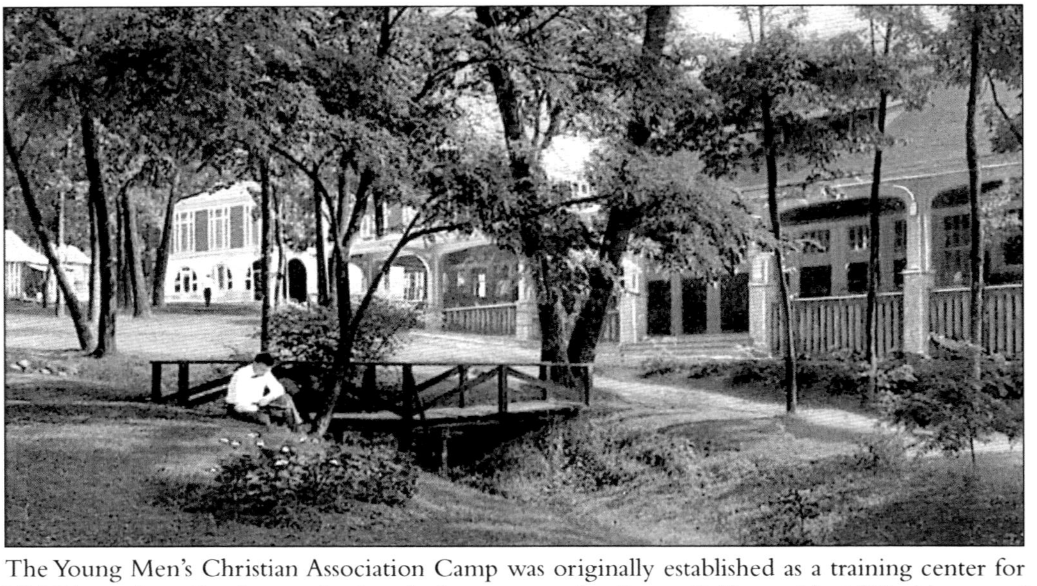

The Young Men's Christian Association Camp was originally established as a training center for YMCA workers. Previous gatherings had met at nearby Camp Collie, and in 1886, 64 acres of land were purchased for a permanent camp site. By 1926, the camp's holdings grew to 96 acres. Accommodations included 121 tents, 5 sturdy buildings, 21 resident cottages, and a dining hall that seated 900 people.

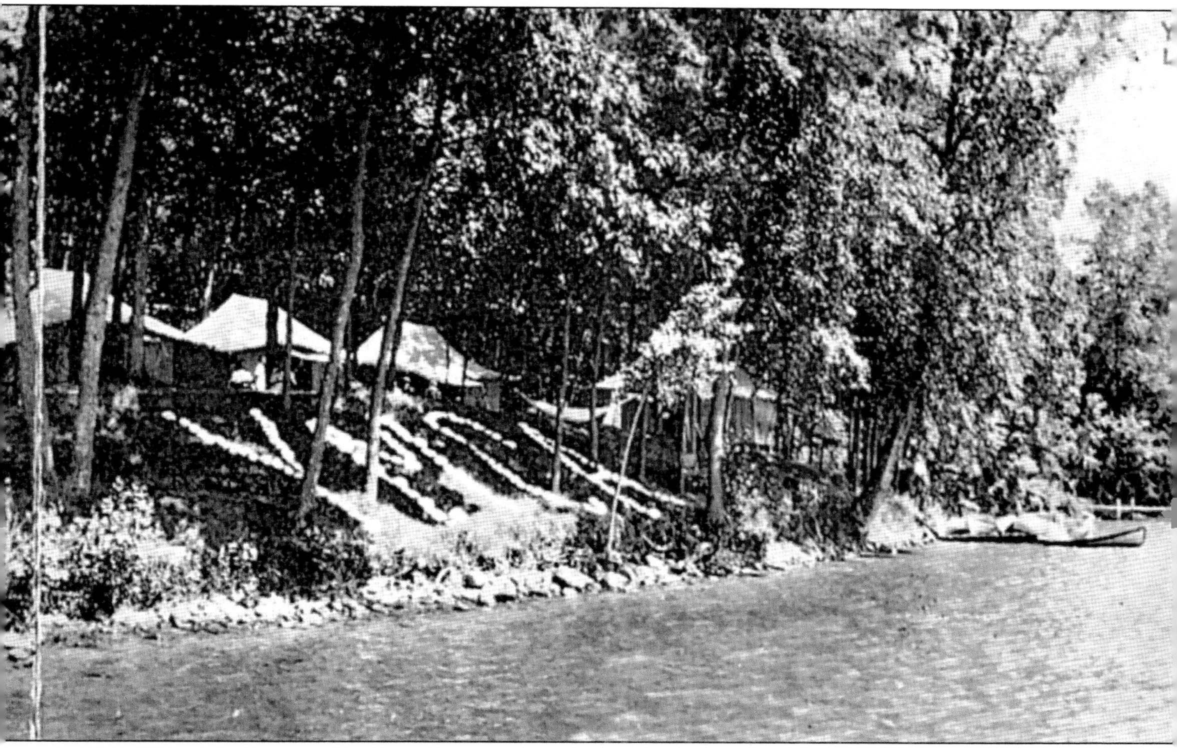

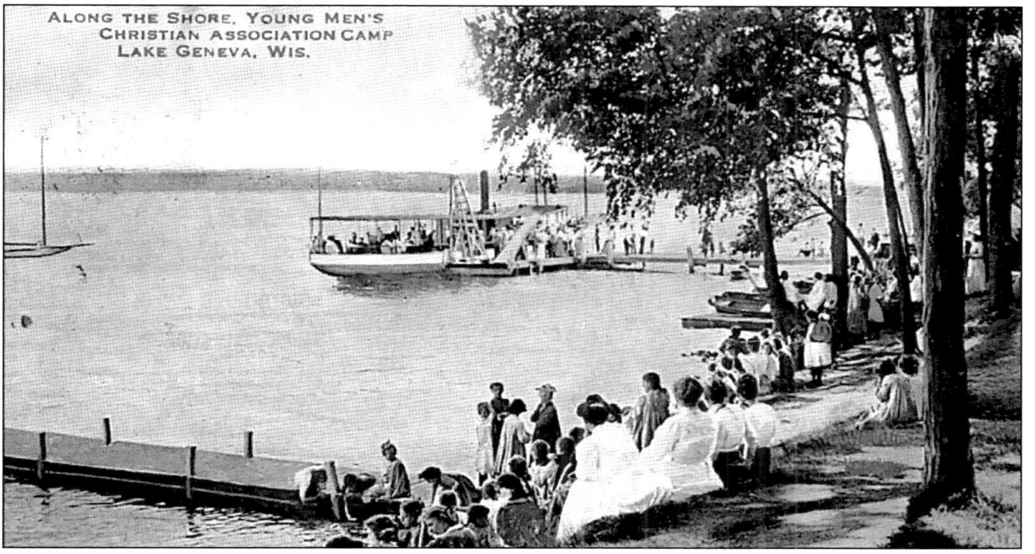

A very popular destination, the YMCA Camp served 5,260 guests in the summer of 1925. During that era it was advertised as "a place of replenishment for body and soul." Recreational needs were met by 13 tennis courts, a baseball diamond, golf course, a running track, gym, swimming piers, and a fleet of rowboats. This camp has been through many educational program changes as well as name changes: The Western Secretariat Training Institute, George Williams College–Lake Geneva Campus, and College Camp. Today, it is known as Aurora University.

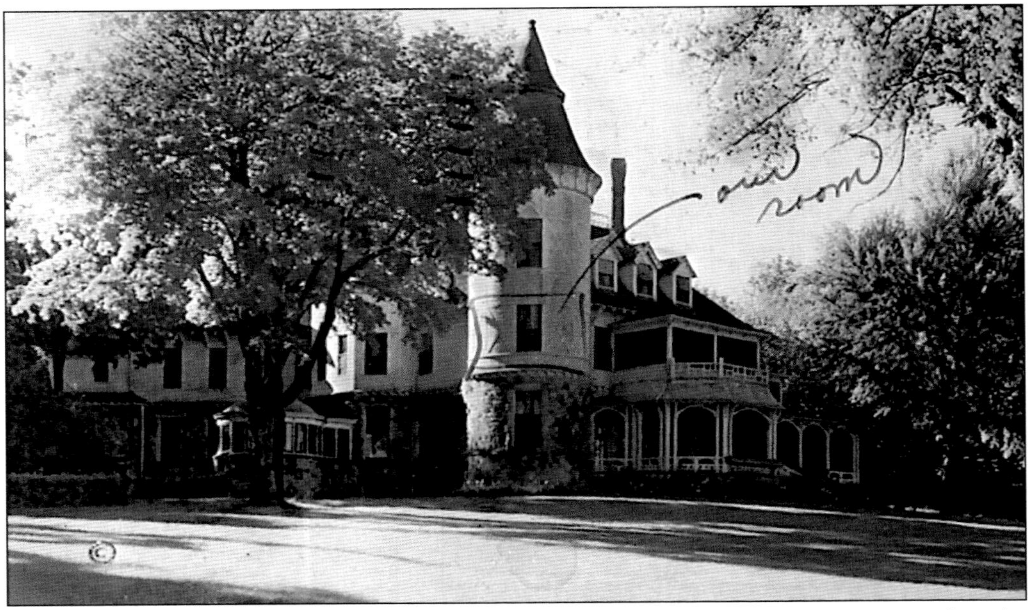

Covenant Harbor is situated on the beautiful grounds that were once known as Snug Harbor, the lakefront estate of George Sturges. Construction of the main residence started in 1881, and the home was sold to John Borden around the turn of the century. Ownership changed several times over the years and on October 4, 1947, the property was purchased by the Central Conference of the Evangelical Mission Covenant Church of America at a cost of $150,000; the first Bible camps were offered at Covenant Harbor in the summer of 1948. Cost for a week of camp was between 13 and 17 dollars. The residents occupied the original Snug Harbor buildings, but the main house was destroyed by fire in 1957. The land today is still operated as a camp and retreat center and is recognizable from the lake by the original vintage boat house.

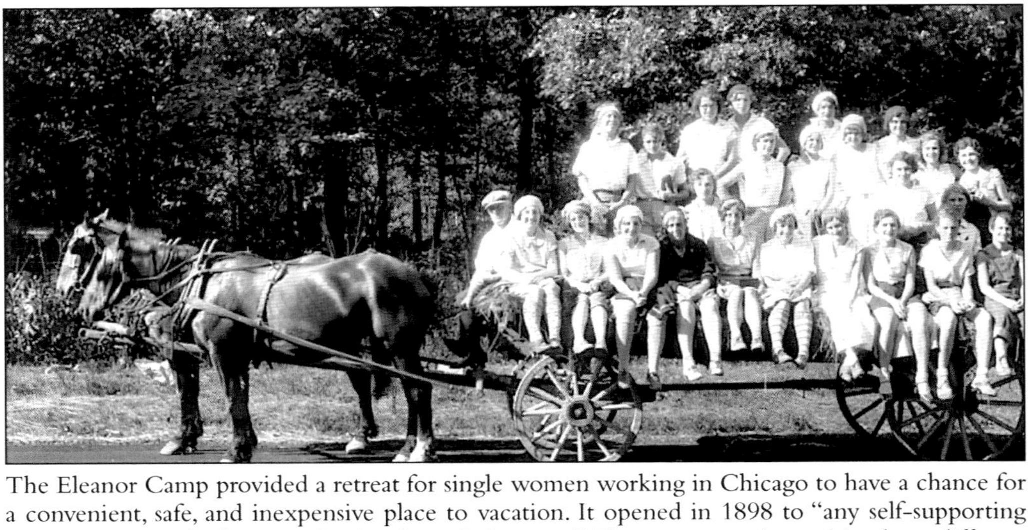

The Eleanor Camp provided a retreat for single women working in Chicago to have a chance for a convenient, safe, and inexpensive place to vacation. It opened in 1898 to "any self-supporting young woman of Chicago who is of good character." The camp was housed in three different locations, with its final home being portions of the then Rockford Camp. (Courtesy of the Brown-Gabriel Collection.)

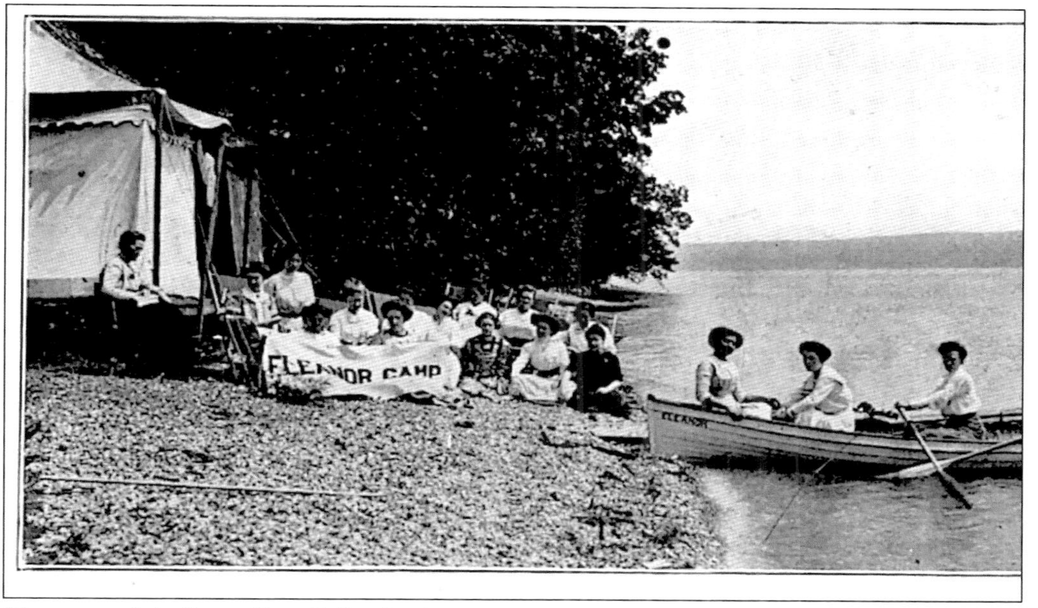

(Courtesy of the Jerry Glass Collection.)

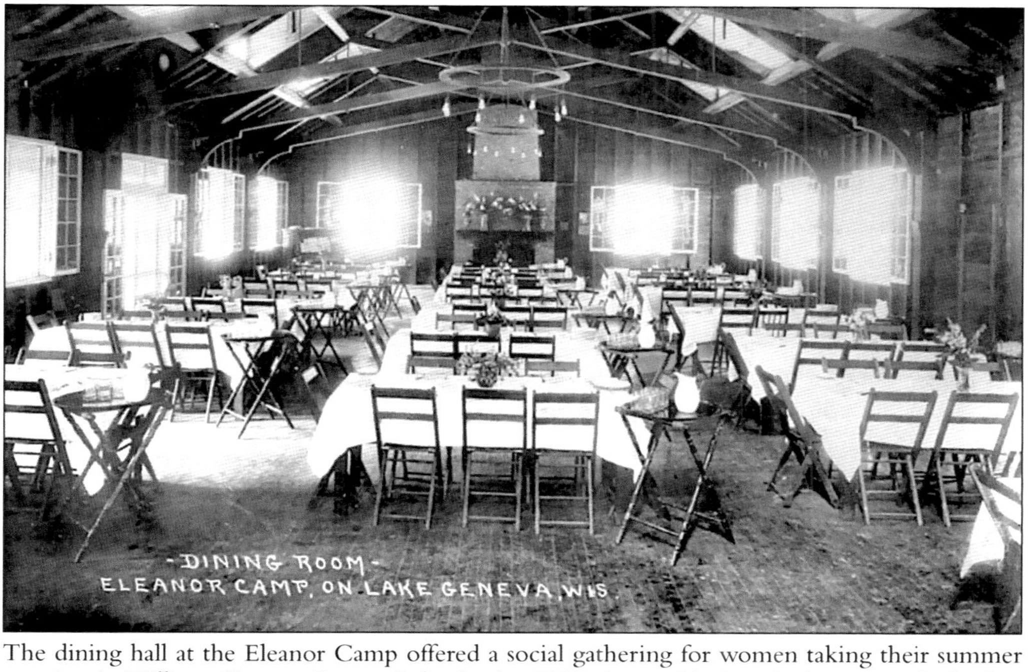

The dining hall at the Eleanor Camp offered a social gathering for women taking their summer vacation in Williams Bay on Geneva Lake. In the 1950s, it was felt that single women had other options for a vacation, and the Eleanor Camp was sold. Today, the Eleanor Camp property is Wesley Woods, a summer Methodist Camp for children and adults. The nearby Rockford Camp is Dartmouth Woods, an association of nine private homes built on the "stand-alone" cottage footprints. (Courtesy of the Jerry Glass Collection.)

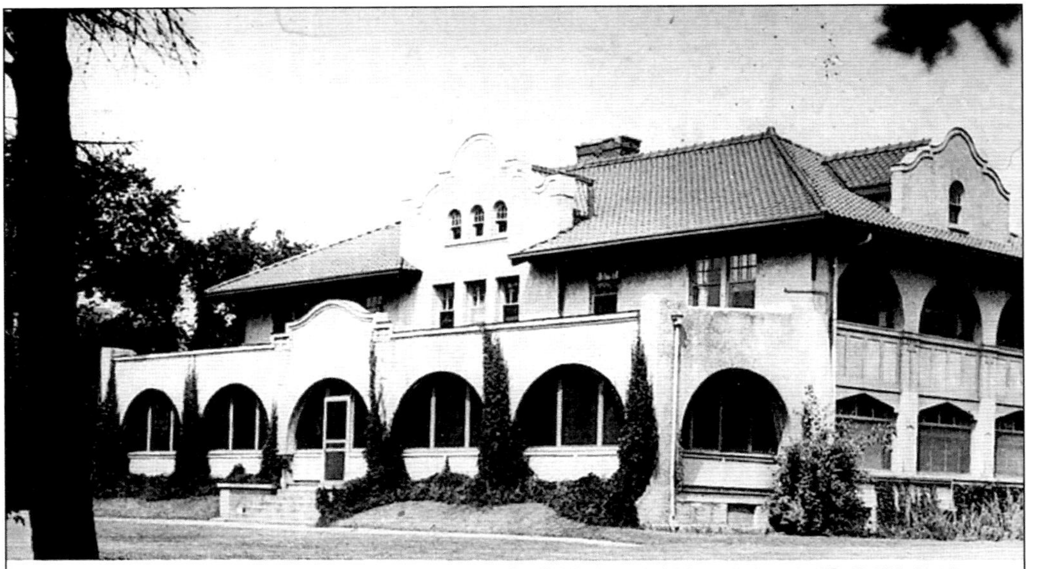

THE LODGE—CHICAGO BOYS CLUBS—CAMP KEMAH—WILLIAMS BAY, WIS.

The Crane family owned Jerseyhurst on Geneva Lake as well as this acreage in the woods surrounding Lake Como. The Lake Como property served the purpose of providing a hunting ground. It had a hunting lodge which became a sanitarium for Crane's Plumbing executives. (Today, it is the Geneva National's Hunt Club Restaurant.) The property eventually became a campsite for the children of Crane Plumbing employees, as well as a Chicago Boys Club Camp, called Camp Kemah.

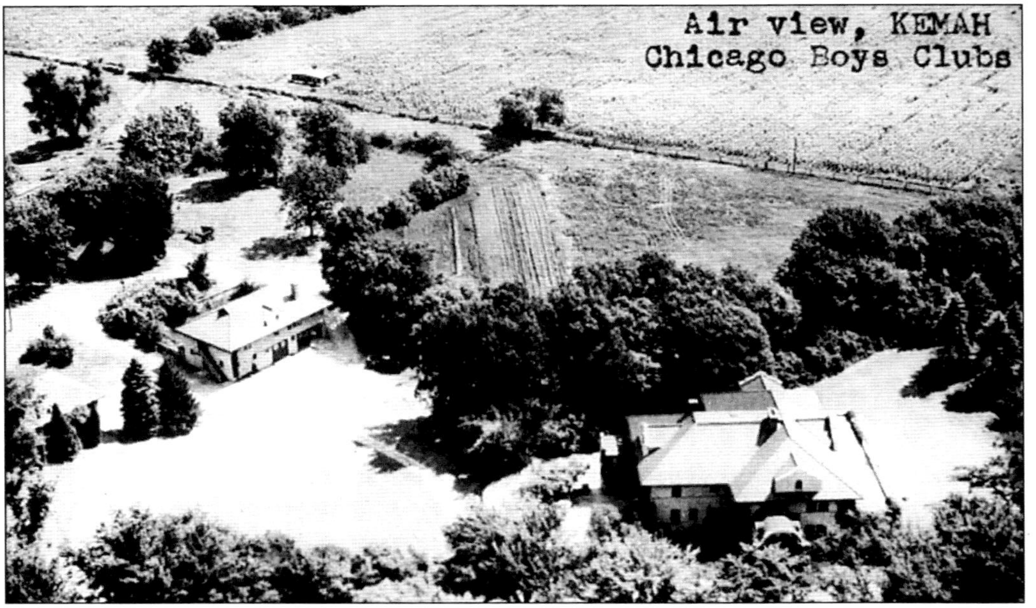

Today the property is a golfing community with 54 holes of golf; it is both a public and private club, known as Geneva National. (Courtesy of the John P. Urlakis Collection.)

Four

The Enjoyment of Lake Fun

Since the mid-1800s, Geneva Lake has been known for outdoor recreation and lake fun. Whether it is strolling the Victorian streets or along the shore path, swimming, golfing, water-skiing, taking a boat cruise, ice fishing, or snow skiing, every season can boast of fun activities for children, adults, and families. Perhaps the most vivid and popular activity of Geneva Lake is "lake fun."

Geneva Lake has a strong history of wonderful hotels, resorts, Victorian bed-and-breakfast inns, and motels, making it a "get-away" destination in all seasons. Most of the larger resorts like the Abbey, Interlaken, and Grand Geneva offer a variety of activities: swimming, horseback riding, golfing, spas, and even a water park. The Geneva Inn, on the shores of Geneva Lake, is a bed-and-breakfast inn, with water views from its dining room, as well as from the guest rooms.

Geneva Lake was such a desirable spot for get-away fun that Hugh Heffner opened a Playboy Club Hotel in the sixties. The Playboy Club offered skiing in the winter and golfing in the summer. This hotel even had a private airport. Besides welcoming visitors to Geneva Lake, the Playboy Club also drew many new residents, who moved to the lake to work at the Club. Today, the Club is known as Grand Geneva.

Many of the bed-and-breakfast inns are Victorian mansions that once were private homes. The majority of these inns are within walking distance of Lake Geneva's downtown area. However, some are outside downtown and provide a tranquil environment, away from the crowds. During the 1950s, motor inns became popular in Lake Geneva. Today, motels still welcome visitors to the lake. Some of the hotels in the lake area are timeshare. The hotels, motels, inns, and resorts provide a variety of housing options for visitors to enjoy lake fun in all seasons.

In the summer, the lake hosts a variety of boat activities. Almost every imaginable boat or water vehicle can be seen on the lake. Classic, traditional, and newer boats provide a picturesque scene not visible on many lakes. A steamboat and other wooden boats of "years past" give tours, host dinners, and provide locations for weddings and parties. Some of the grand tour boats on the lake include the *Louise*, the *Lady of the Lake*, the *Lorelei*, the *Polaris*, and the *Grand Belle of Geneva*.

Pleasure sail boating and boating lessons are popular, as are the intense sail boat regattas. The Lake Geneva Regatta Club was formed in 1872, and Geneva Lake is noted for some of the best competitive sailors in the world, including Harry C. "Buddy" Melges Jr., internationally known yachtsman, Olympic gold medalist, and winner of the 1992 America's Cup.

Swimmers, sunbathers, skiers, tubers, water trampoliners, water divers and even submariners enjoy and explore the lake. Water slides are popular along the lakeshore. Hot air balloonists, water gliders, and small-craft airplane pilots get a spectacular "above the water" view of lake activities.

Fisherman, regardless of the season, can always be found on Geneva Lake. In the summer, spring, and fall, fishermen head out in row boats or fish from piers. Their silhouettes can be seen against the sunrise and sunset. In the winter, ice boat houses appear on the lake, providing protection to fisherman as they ice fish, sometimes cooking and picnicking on the lake in the bitter cold.

Golfing is a popular pastime for both the serious and casual golfer. The lake has several country clubs including Lake Geneva, Big Foot, and Geneva National, as well as championship public courses and miniature golf. The courses have carefully manicured greens, lush fairways, and beautifully tended trees. Some have wooded hillsides and views of lakes. In the winter, golf courses host skeet and trap shooting, as do private farms like Willow Bend. Hunting and gaming are also popular sports in the lake area.

Residents and visitors alike enjoy horseback rides, horseshoes, and hay rides, and in the winter, sleigh rides. Many of the farms have petting zoos and provide an opportunity for children and adults to learn about farming and farm animals.

Road biking, trail biking, cross country skiing, snow skiing, snow shoeing, hiking, and tennis are other activities found in the lake area. A favorite tradition is croquet, played in all-white attire. In addition to athletic activities, the lake area provides greyhound dog racing, outdoor concerts, operas, plays, creative art lessons, quilting guilds, antique car and boat exhibits, and a county fair.

The Geneva Lake area also provides antique and boutique shopping in Victorian buildings, and a number of day spas. One can always visit historical sites, such as Yerkes Observatory, Chief Big Foot's landmarks, or Andy Gump's Statue (1947) located in Flat Iron Park. Lastly, there is always the option to quietly enjoy the beauty of the lake by sitting back, watching the water, soaking up the sun and taking time to reflect, write, read, and listen to the birds.

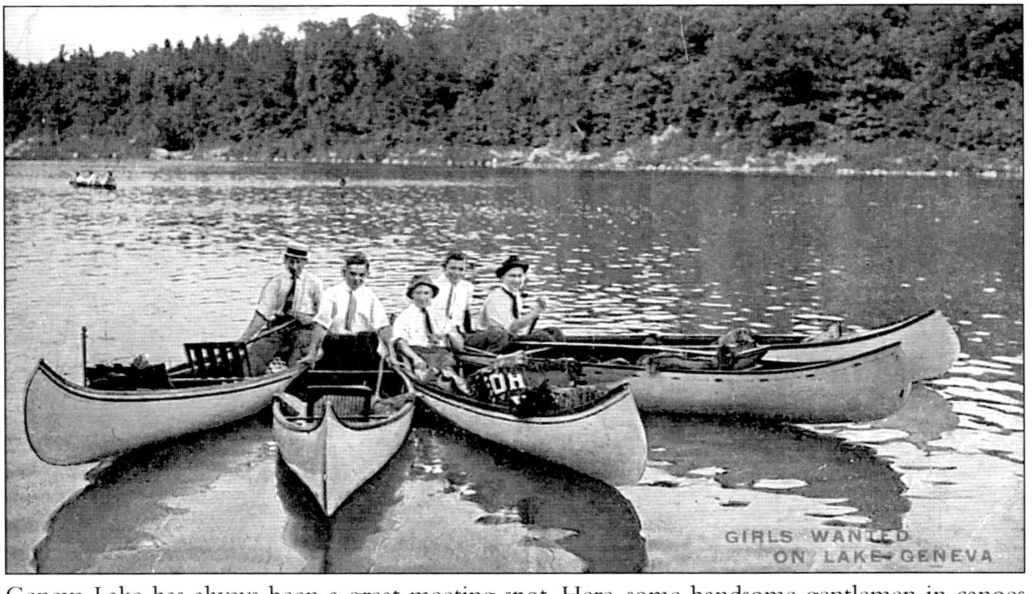

Geneva Lake has always been a great meeting spot. Here, some handsome gentlemen in canoes are all decked out hoping to find some pretty girls. Chuck's in Fontana, a local "hangout," is one of the locations where many couples were introduced to each other and later became bride and groom. There is even an annual reunion of married couples that met at Chuck's. (Courtesy of the Robert Webster Sr. Collection.)

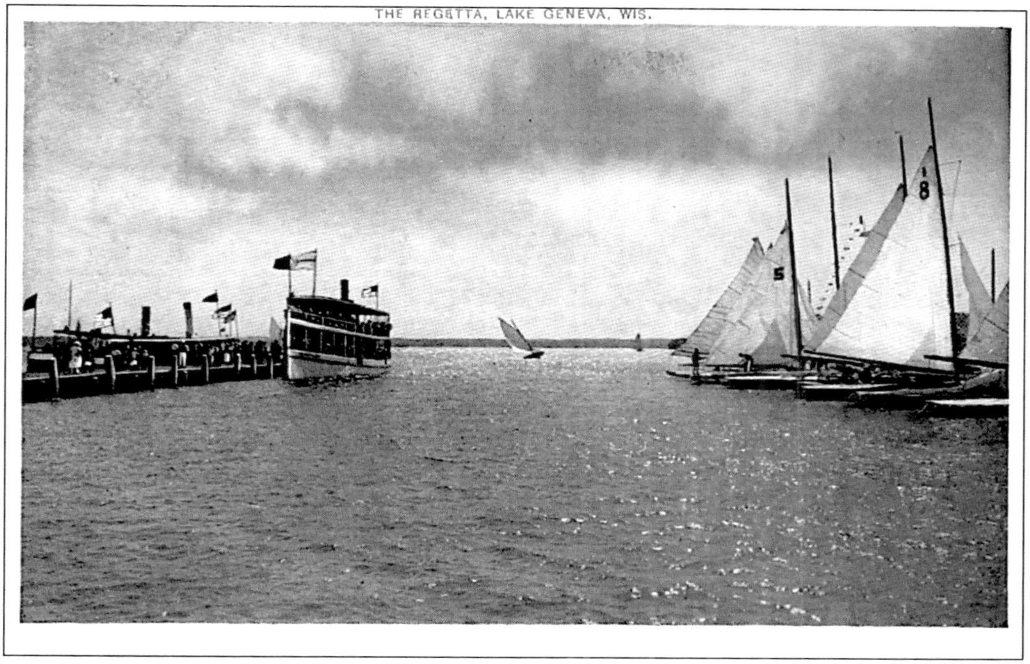

The Lake Geneva Yacht Club has been host to many regattas over the years. The yacht club facilities and sparkling clear waters of Geneva Lake have provided idyllic conditions to lure a wide variety of boat classes to compete from all over the United States.

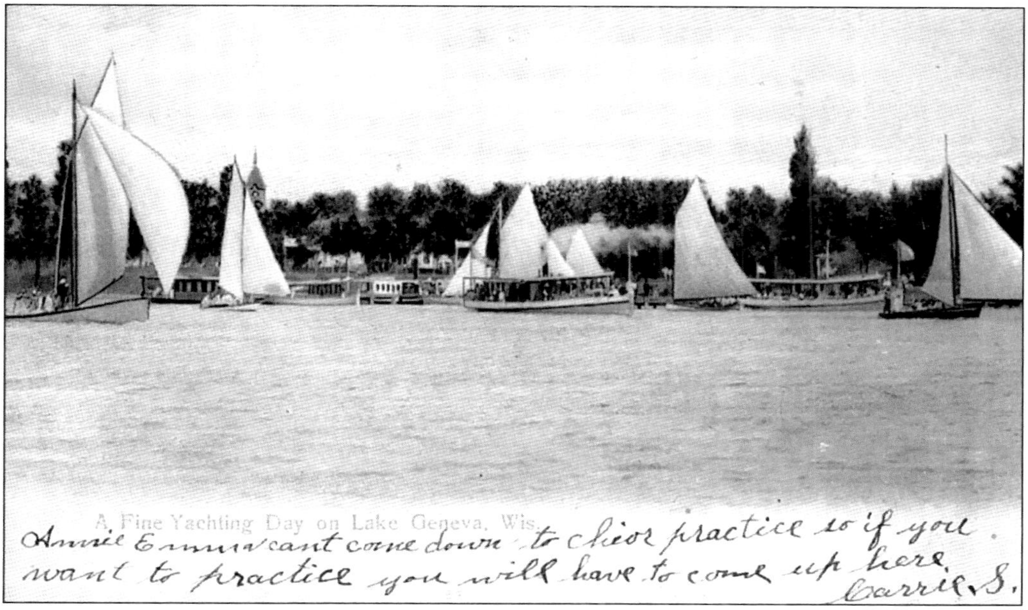

The first recorded sailboat race of the Lake Geneva Yacht Club was in 1874. The earliest boats that raced were called "sandbaggers," so named because the crew had to pile sandbags for ballast along the windward rail to counterbalance the huge area of sail canvas. (Courtesy of the Robert Webster Sr. Collection.)

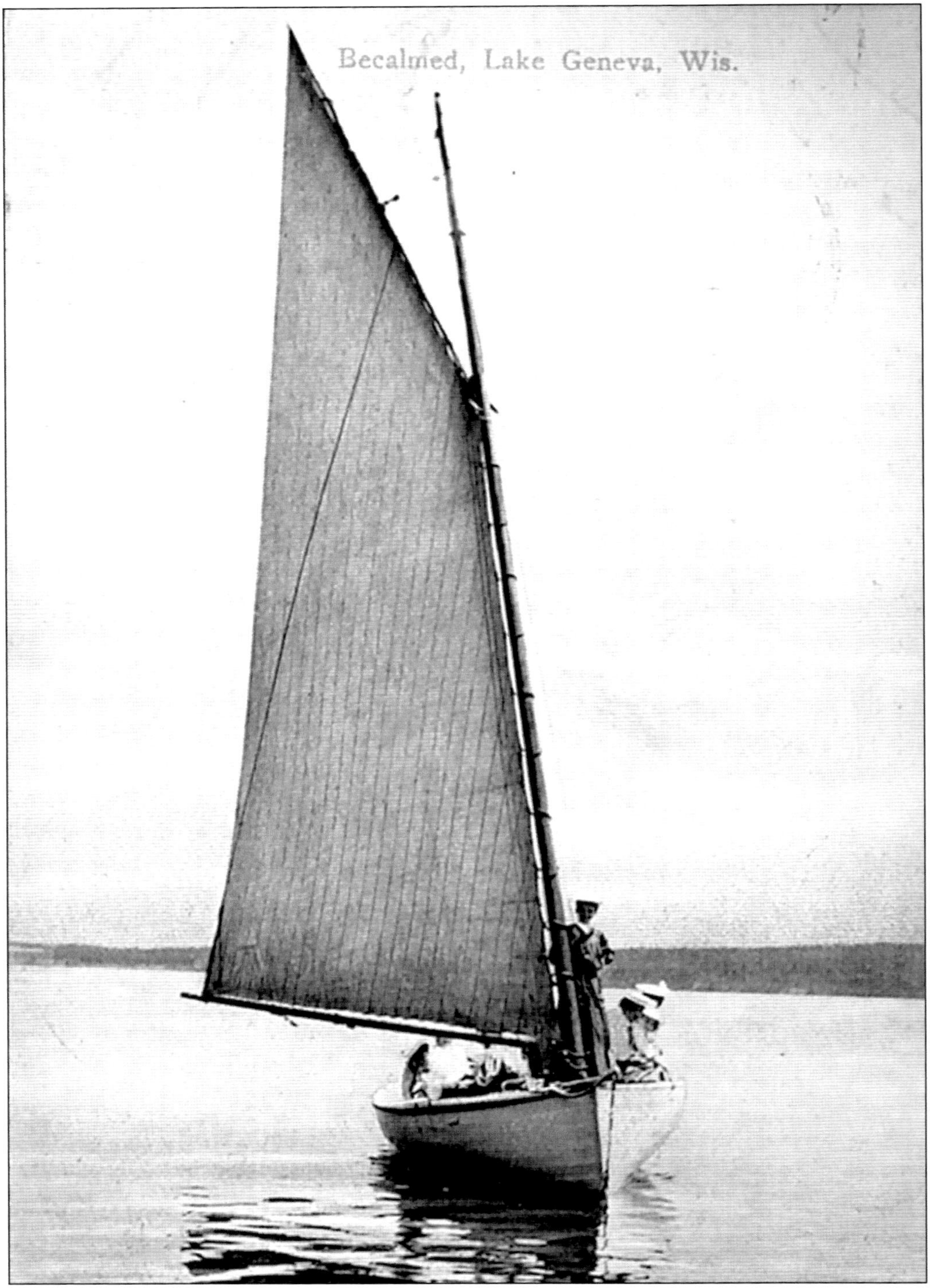

Sailboat racing is all about wind and speed. This crew unfortunately has neither! (Courtesy of the Robert Webster Sr. Collection.)

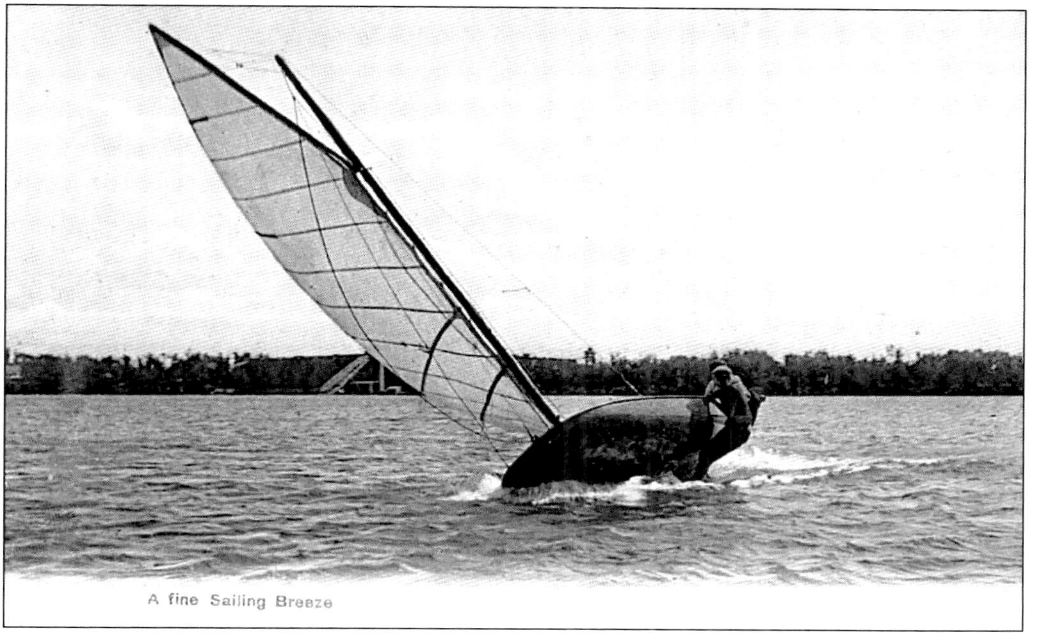

The "sandbaggers" started to phase out during the early 1900s in favor of several classes which offered a longer, narrower style boat. The forerunner of the modern scow, they became very popular and were less strenuous to sail. (Courtesy of the Robert Webster Sr. Collection.)

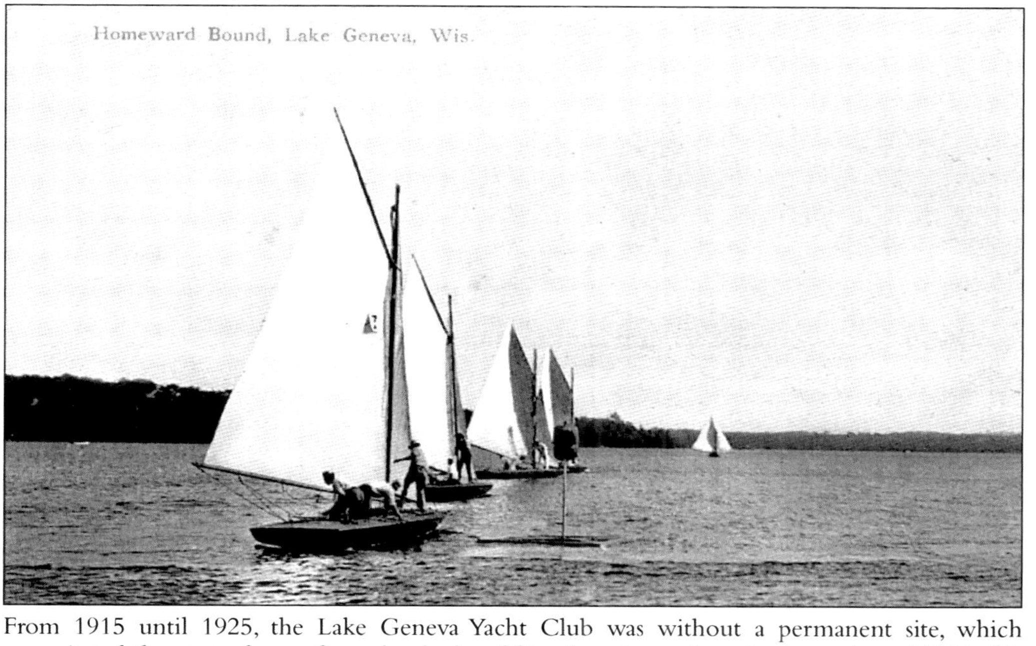

From 1915 until 1925, the Lake Geneva Yacht Club was without a permanent site, which necessitated the start of races from the docks of friends and members. In the spring of 1926, this situation was rectified when friends and officers of the LGYC identified a property on the south shore for their new headquarters. They remodeled the residence into a clubhouse and installed the piers and slips.

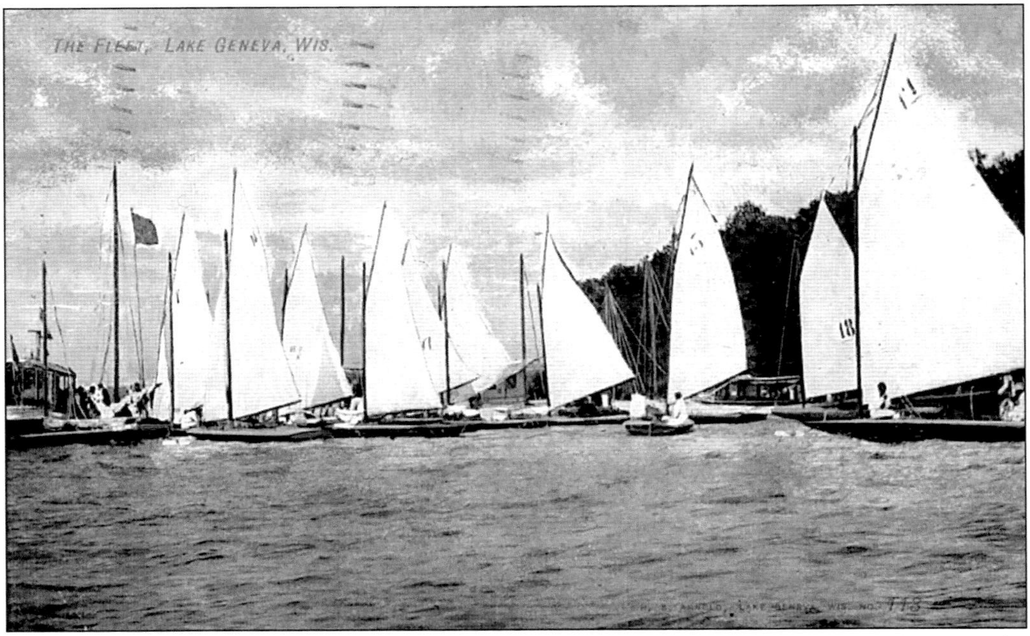

Legendary sailor and entrepreneur Buddy Melges worked with his father, Harry, to become the world's largest builder of inland lake scows. Originally called Mel-Ban Boat Works, the company was created in 1945 by Harry Sr. and his partner, Ephraim Banning, in nearby Zenda, Wisconsin. Evolving into Melges Boat Works, the corporation produced classic "A Boats" and scows, noted for winning many races; they can be viewed today in the morning or early evening regattas.

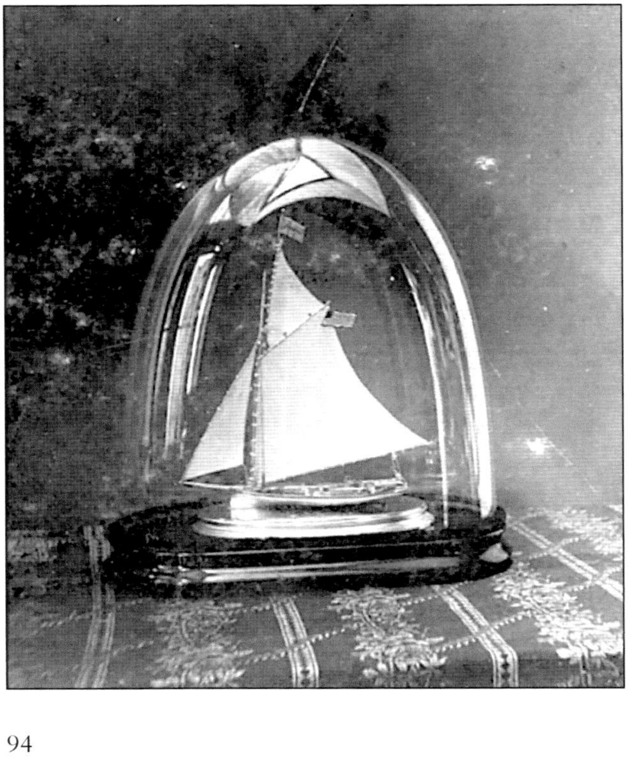

Since 1874, sailors have competed every year for this prestigious trophy, the Sheridan Prize. The award was named for General Phillip Sheridan (who was very fond of sailing and a frequent visitor to Geneva Lake), and local yacht enthusiasts held an annual regatta in his honor. The first race, won by the Nettie, was held with seven yachts on August 31, 1874. The Nettie, 24.5 feet long and owned by Julian Rumsey, was a much-admired vessel; as a special tribute to the boat and the skilled skipper, the Sheridan Regatta trophy was made as a miniature replica of the trim little yacht. This treasured trophy is still awarded today. (Courtesy of the Brown-Gabriel Collection.)

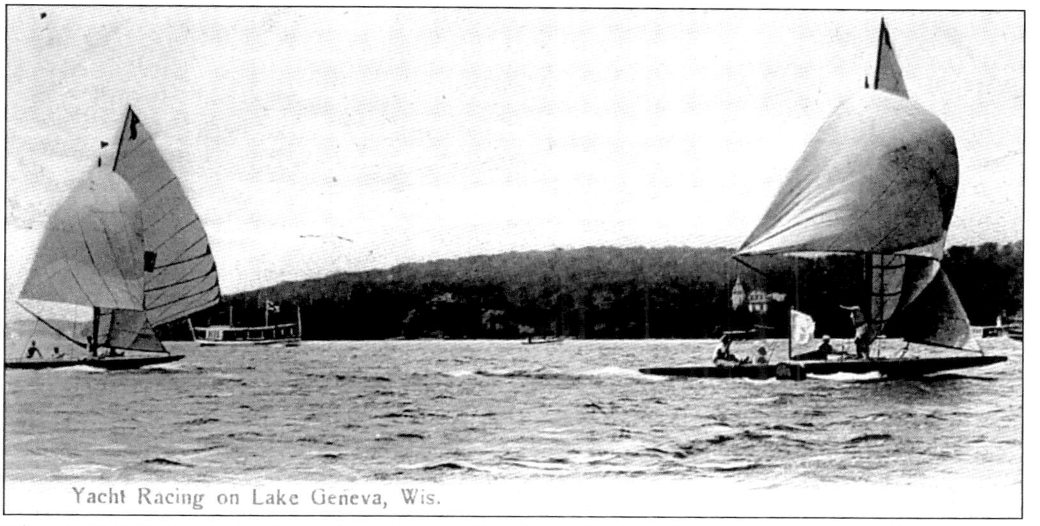

The LGYC Sailing School was founded in 1938. Organized by Herb Taylor, a yacht club member, it maintained the goal of instructing young people around the lake to sail for pleasure or for competition. Reorganized in 1953 as the Geneva Lake Sailing School, a nonprofit educational corporation, it continues to share the facility with the LGYC. Well-known and respected, the school has turned out some of the top sailors from the area, dominating national and international sailing events.

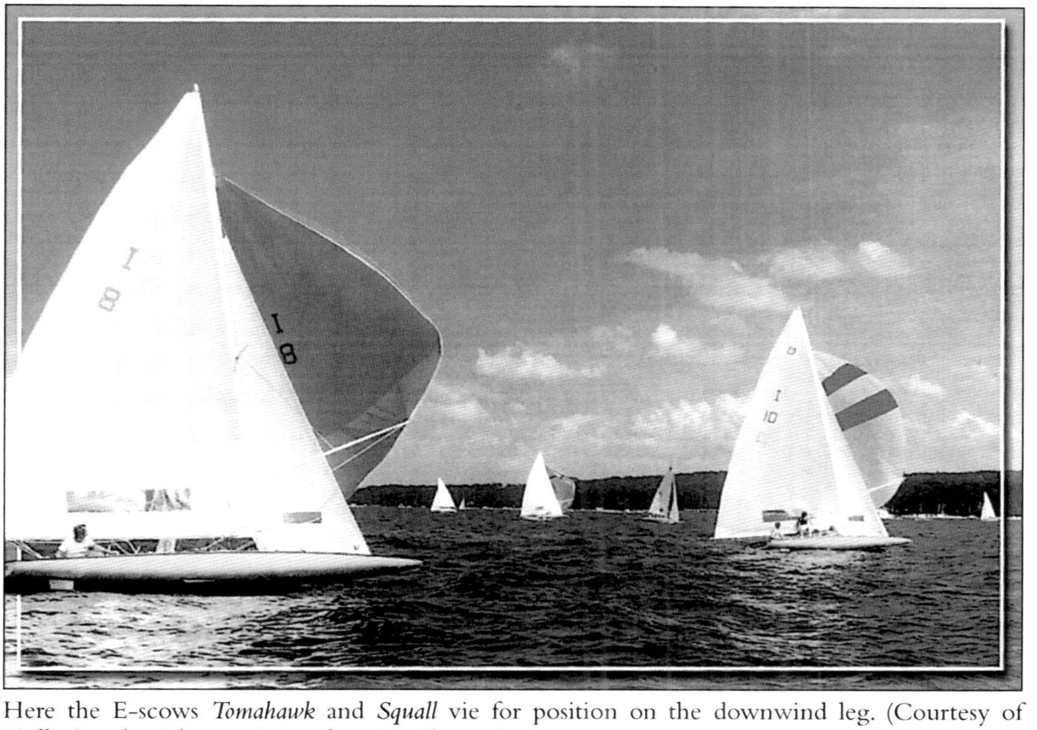

Here the E-scows *Tomahawk* and *Squall* vie for position on the downwind leg. (Courtesy of Holly Starck with permission from Virgil Wuttke.)

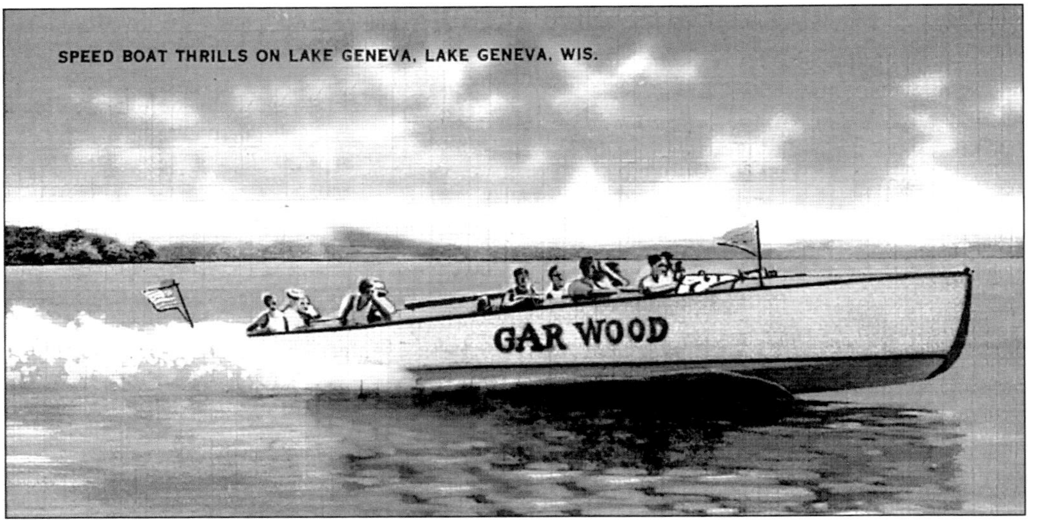

Inboard motorboats became fashionable in the 1940s. The Garwood model was particularly popular as it was known for its speed. Motor boats in all sizes, shapes, and colors are an active part of the lake, along with classic Streblows, custom wooden boats initially made in the early 1950s at the lake by Larry Streblow. (Courtesy of the Jerry Glass Collection.)

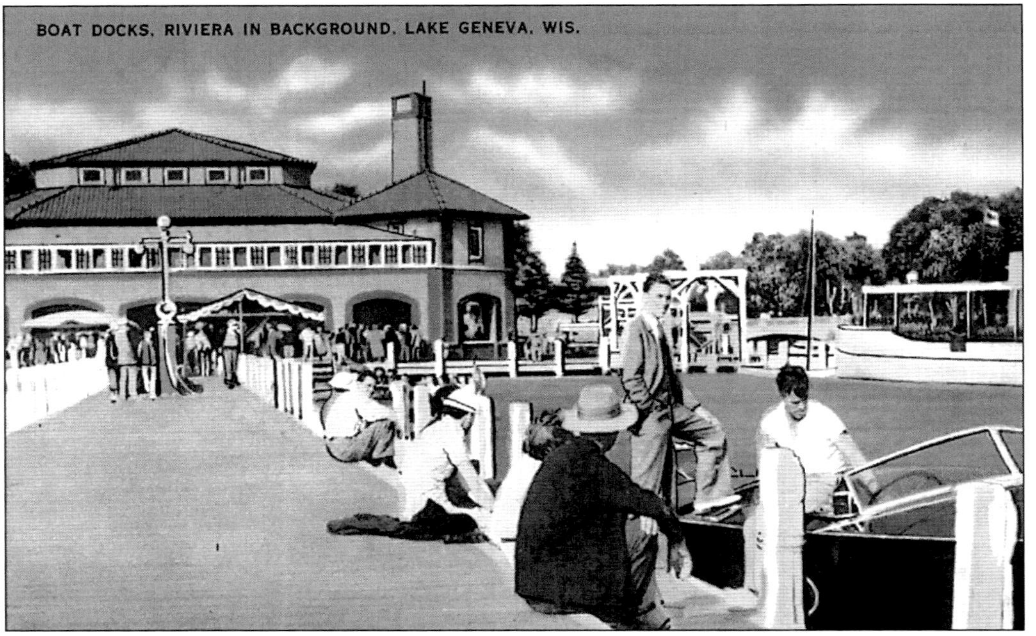

The majority of Geneva Lake boats have names that are fun and significant to the lake and certainly to the owners: *Elsie, Full Throttle, Alouette, Fireball, Lu-Ka-Li-Le, Imp, Stardust, Allegheny, Matriark, Benjamin R. Bates, Helen A., El Do VIII, Bopper, Elixir, Normandie, Doreen, Seven C's, Slingshot, Succotash, Alacrity, dot.com, Miss Carolyn, Maggie B., LaTourette, Mondo, Ada E., Ol' Duffer, Ajax, Nokomis, Cream of the Kropp*, and *Avallon*. On a sunny mid-summer day, these boats along with kayaks, canoes, row boats, pantones, and jet skis can be seen all at one time on Geneva Lake.

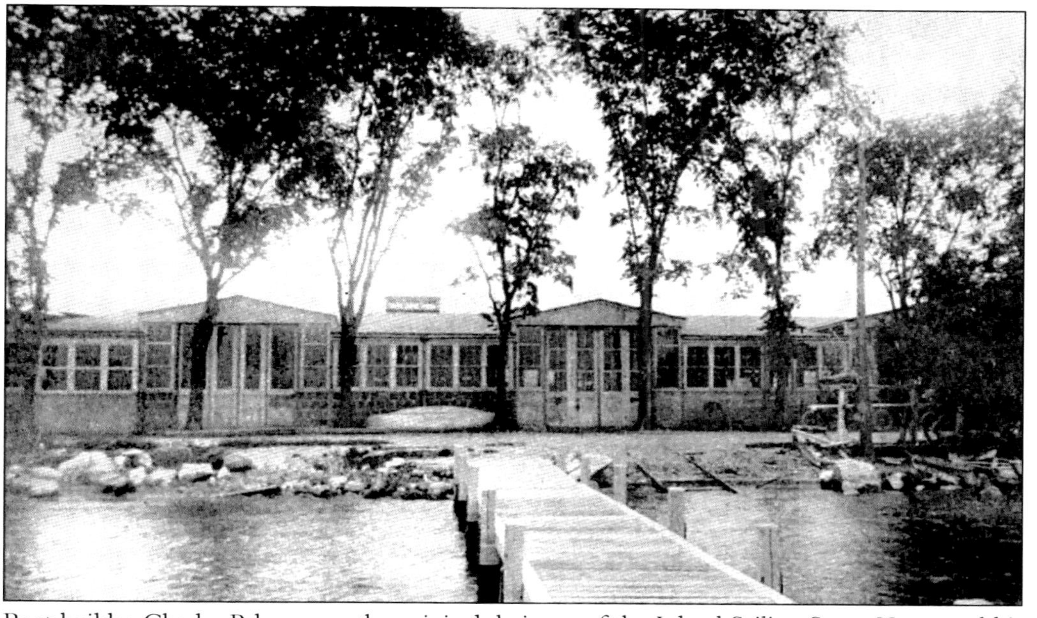

Boat builder Charles Palmer was the original designer of the Inland Sailing Scow. He started his Palmer Boat Works in 1905 just east of St. Benedict's Church, and later moved it to the building shown on this postcard on the Fontana lakeshore just north of what is now the Fontana public beach. It was destroyed by fire in 1934.

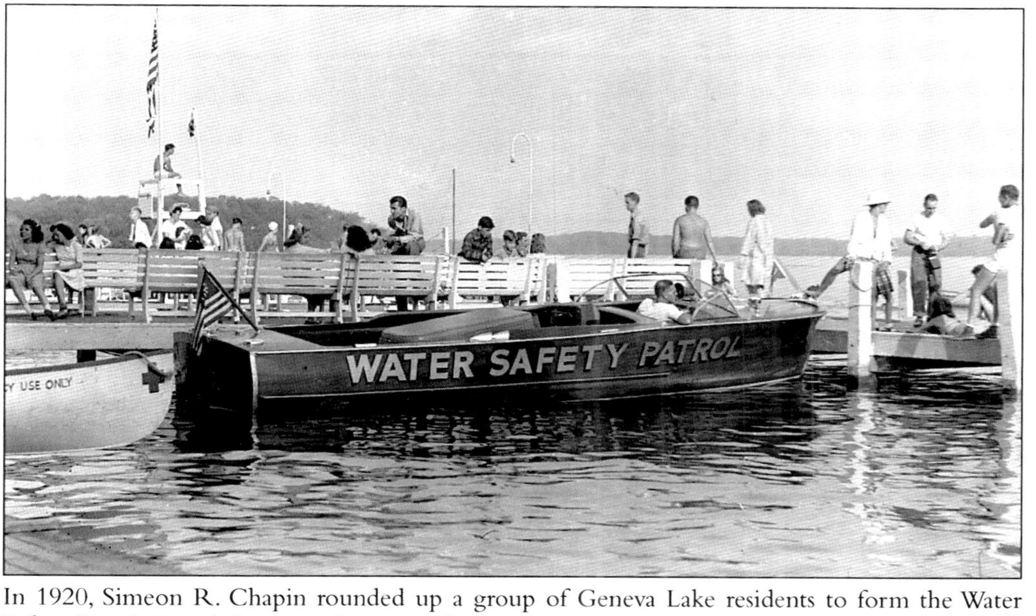

In 1920, Simeon R. Chapin rounded up a group of Geneva Lake residents to form the Water Safety Patrol. Its mission was the same then as it is now: to teach people how to swim and to keep them safe on the lake. Today, it is funded mostly through private donations. From its modest beginnings of manning the beaches with a few life guards in 1925, it has grown to encompass 1 full-time director, more than 80 dedicated guards and swimming instructors, and 5 state-of-the-art equipped patrol boats. (Courtesy of the Geneva Lake Water Safety Patrol.)

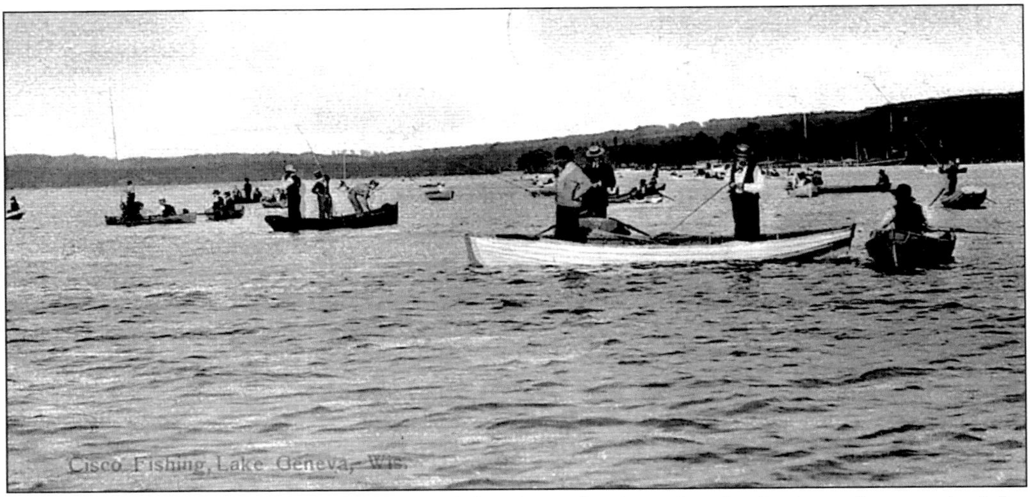

"The Ciscoes are running!" was the signal for the gathering of enthusiastic anglers on the lake. Each fisherman operated two lines, one in either hand. With a very small, shiny bead at the end for bait, the fishermen would alternately move their hands up and down about three to five inches in order to snag the fascinated fish on the hook. They could average 25 dozen ciscoes in a day (no limit!) and were paid $1 per dozen. While this unusual species is designated as a type of whitefish, its gleaming silver body looks to the amateur more like a smelt. Ciscoes average about ten inches in length and about 1/3 of a pound. Usually only appearing in cooler weather, they would feed for a short span on a lake fly that hovered above the water. Fishermen took advantage of this limited time frame and fished abundantly. The fish could also be caught through the ice in the winter.

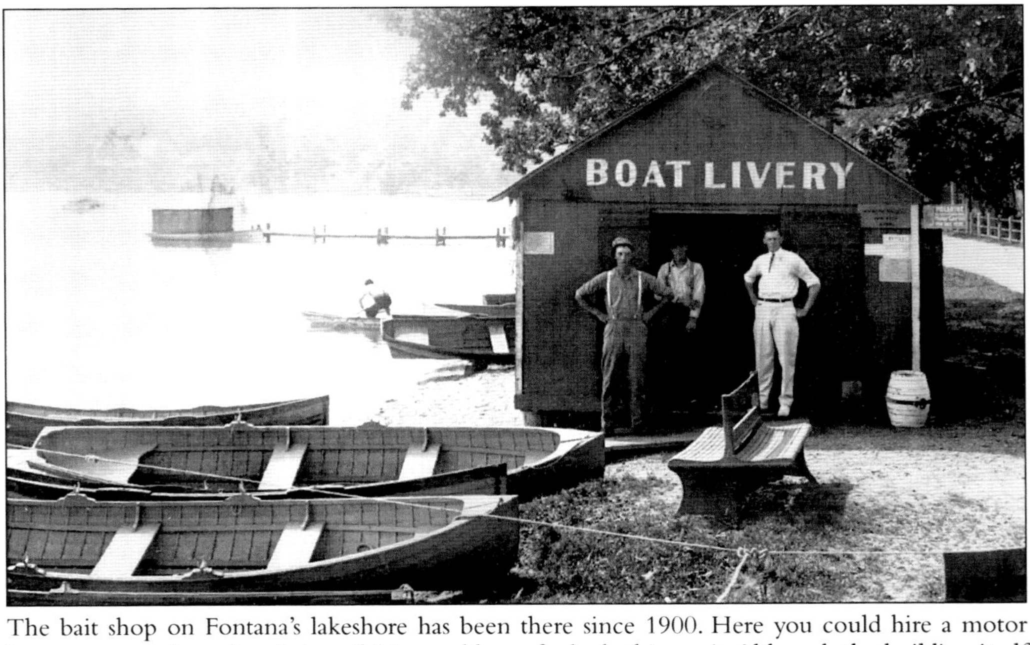

The bait shop on Fontana's lakeshore has been there since 1900. Here you could hire a motor boat, rent a rowboat, buy bait or fishing tackle, or find a bathing suit. Although the building itself has been rotated 90 degrees, it is still there today. (Courtesy of the Brown-Gabriel Collection.)

The one that got away! (Courtesy of the Brown-Gabriel Collection.)

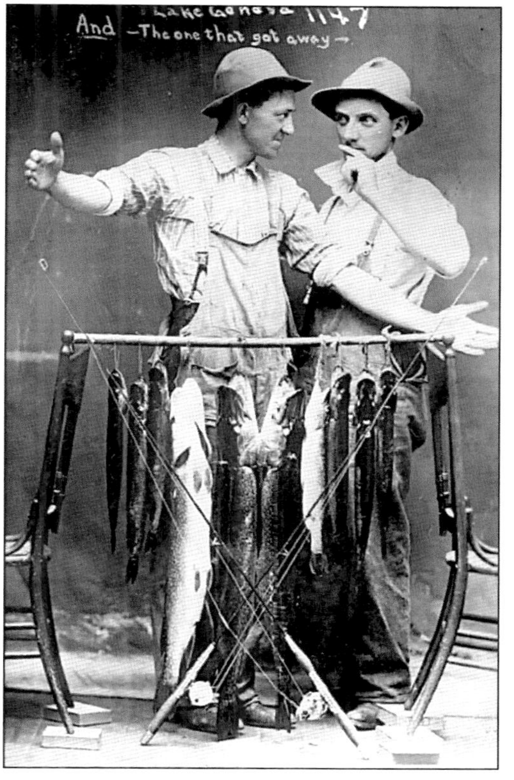

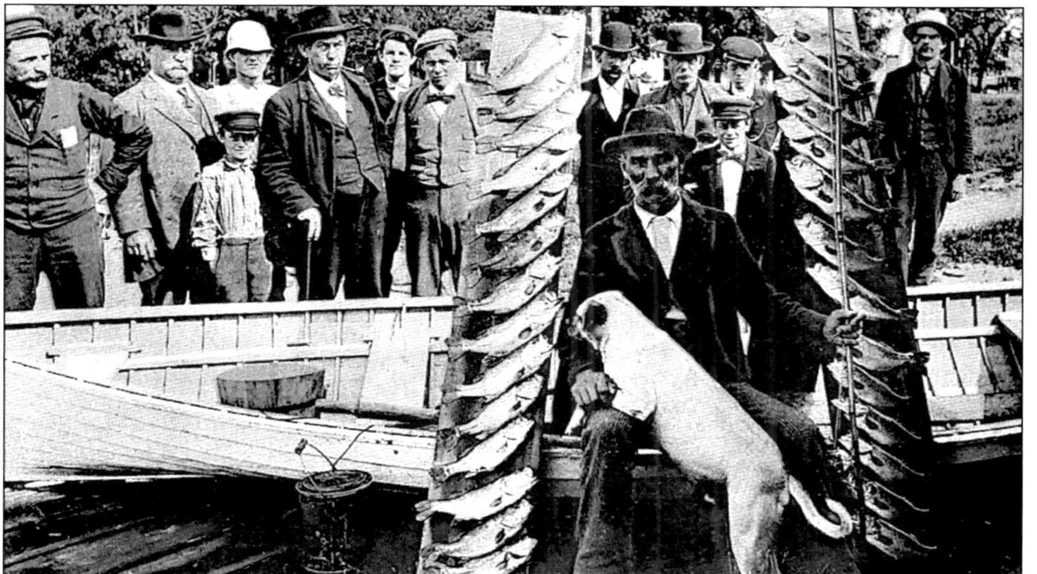

Postmarked 1917, this card comments: "Hello Roy, I haven't heard from you yet. You may think this picture is a fishy fish story, but don't believe it because I heard that one fellow caught about 92 dozen fish in one day. C.F."

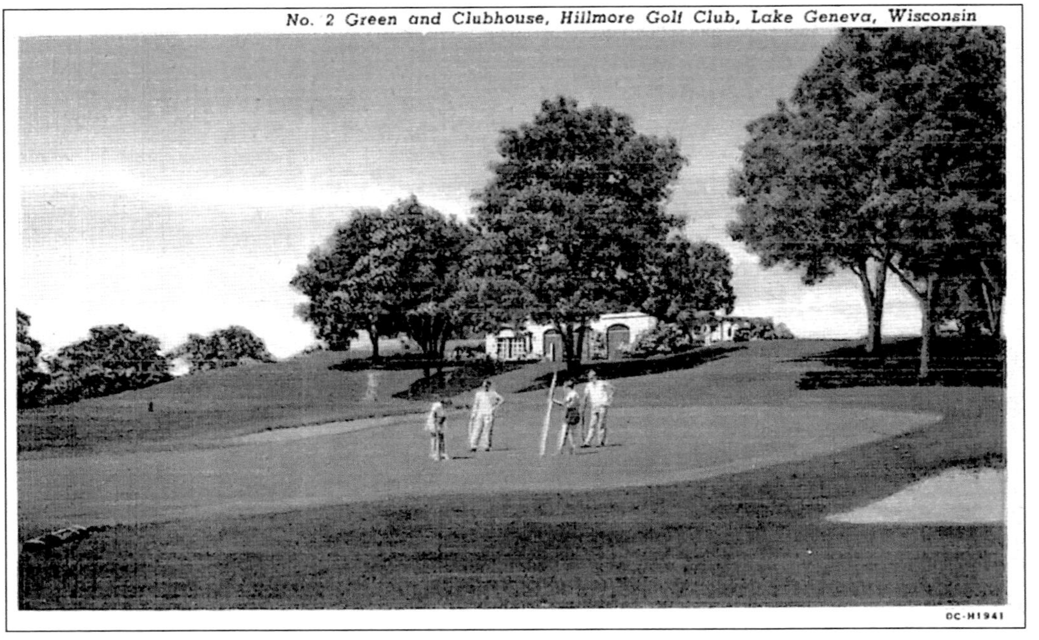

Hillmoor Golf Club began with nine holes in 1923. The following year the second nine holes were added, along with a small clubhouse and soda fountain.

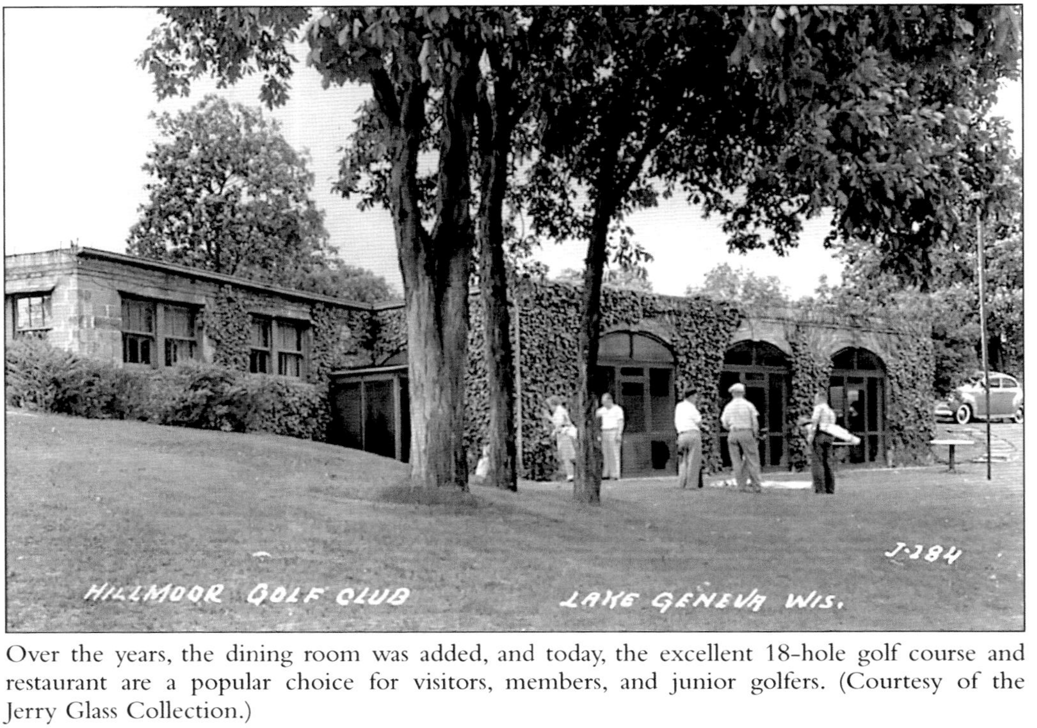

Over the years, the dining room was added, and today, the excellent 18-hole golf course and restaurant are a popular choice for visitors, members, and junior golfers. (Courtesy of the Jerry Glass Collection.)

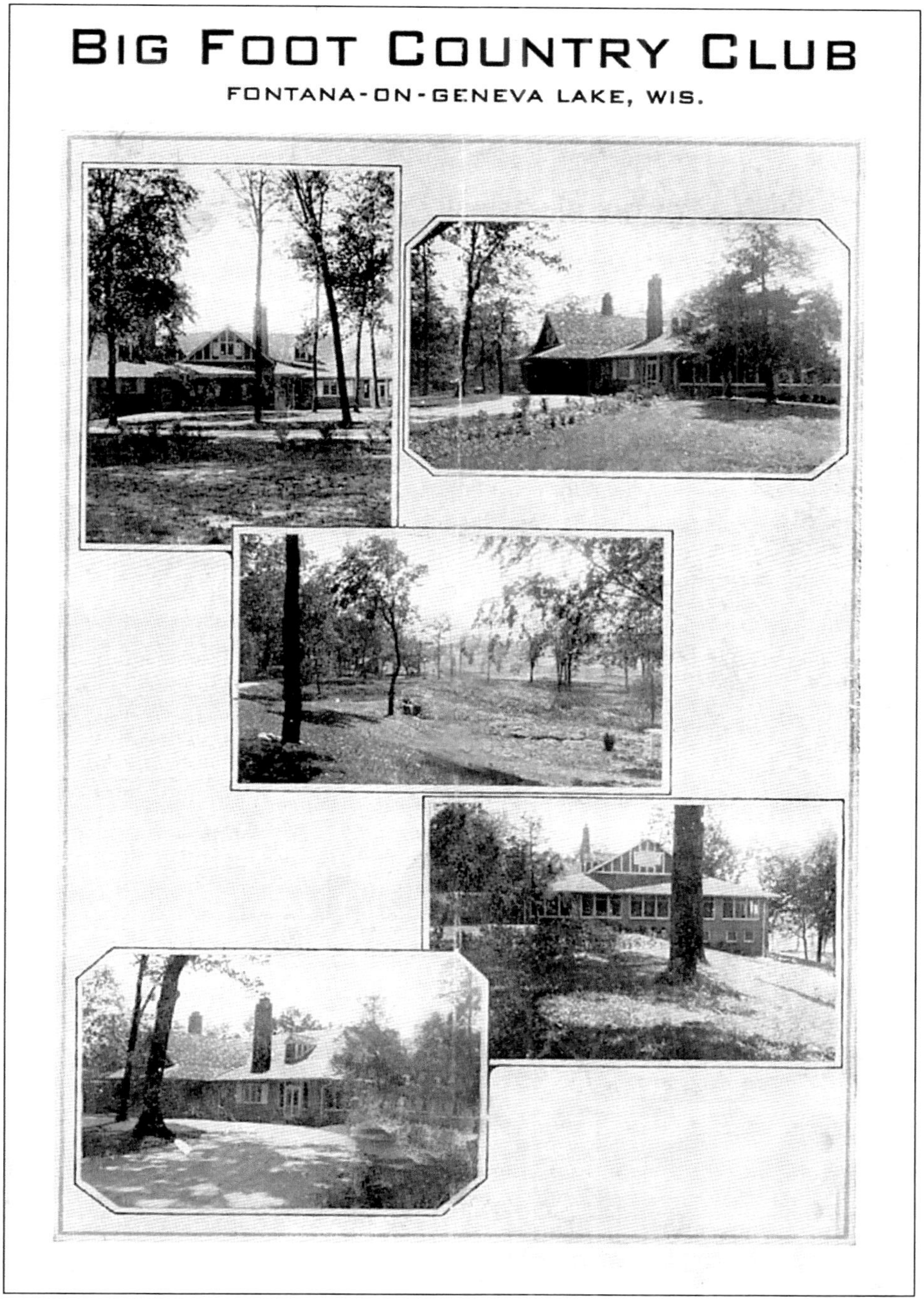

In 1923, the Geneva Lake Improvement Association was formed; this group is acknowledged to have been the founding body of the Big Foot Country Club. The group bought 700 acres from the Leiter estate, and the clubhouse was built at the site of the old farmhouse in 1926. Located in Fontana, the rolling hills, beautiful woods, and fast running brooks make the golf course one of the prettiest and most challenging in the area. The Potawatomi Indians believed that the seven pools located around the clubhouse were sacred. (Courtesy of the John P. Urlakis Collection.)

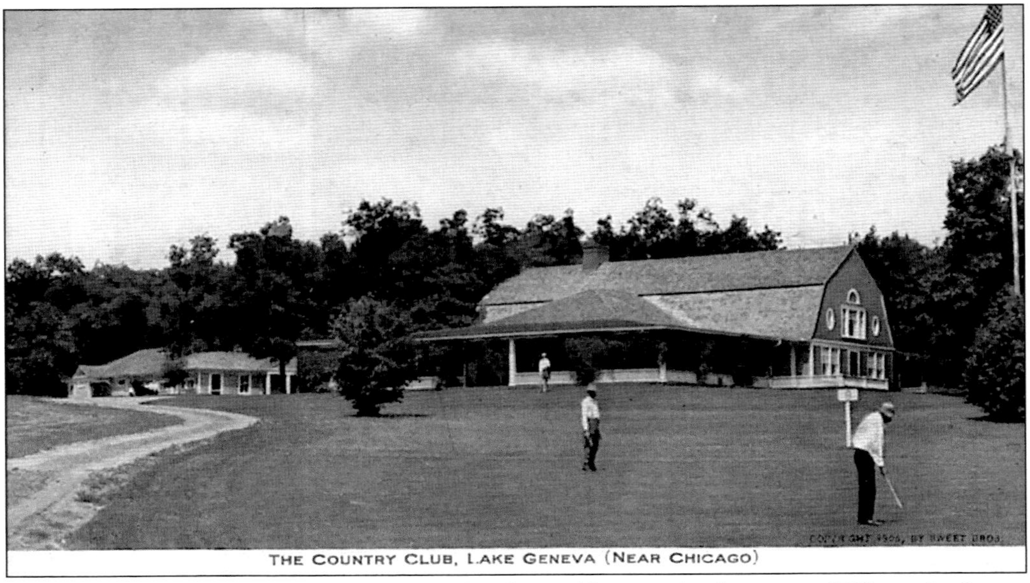

Lake Geneva County Club (LGCC) was the first golf course in the state of Wisconsin. It was organized in 1895, incorporated in January 1896, and opened its clubhouse and golf course in May 1896. The original clubhouse was consumed by fire; the present-day building was constructed in 1916 and designed by Robert B. Spencer Jr. A six-hole course was laid out so that it could be expanded to nine holes the next year, and to eighteen holes soon thereafter. (Courtesy of Bob Kelly.)

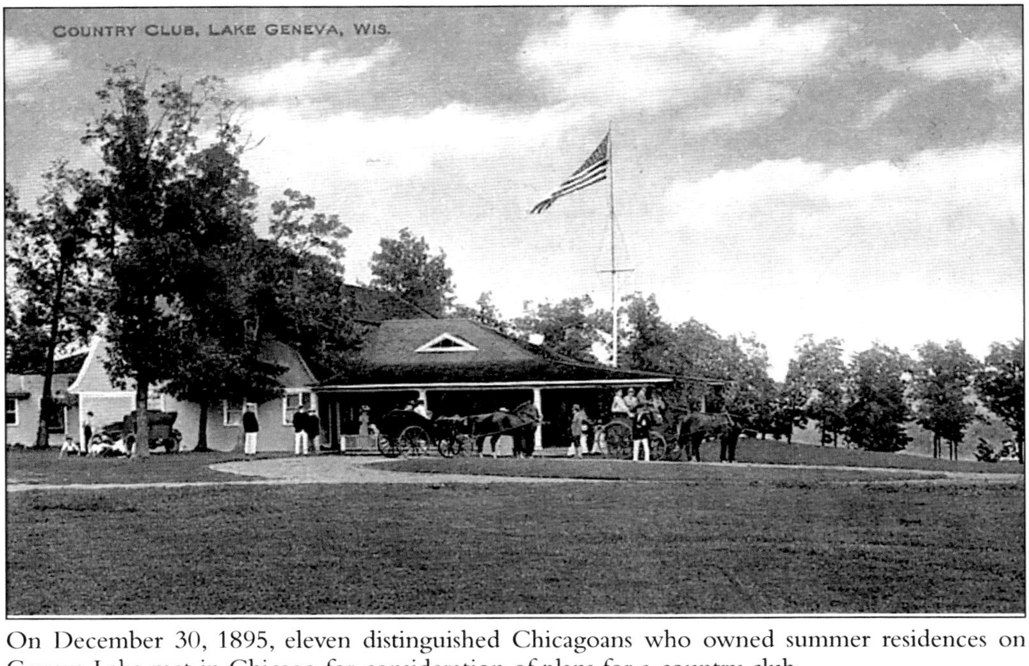

On December 30, 1895, eleven distinguished Chicagoans who owned summer residences on Geneva Lake met in Chicago for consideration of plans for a country club.

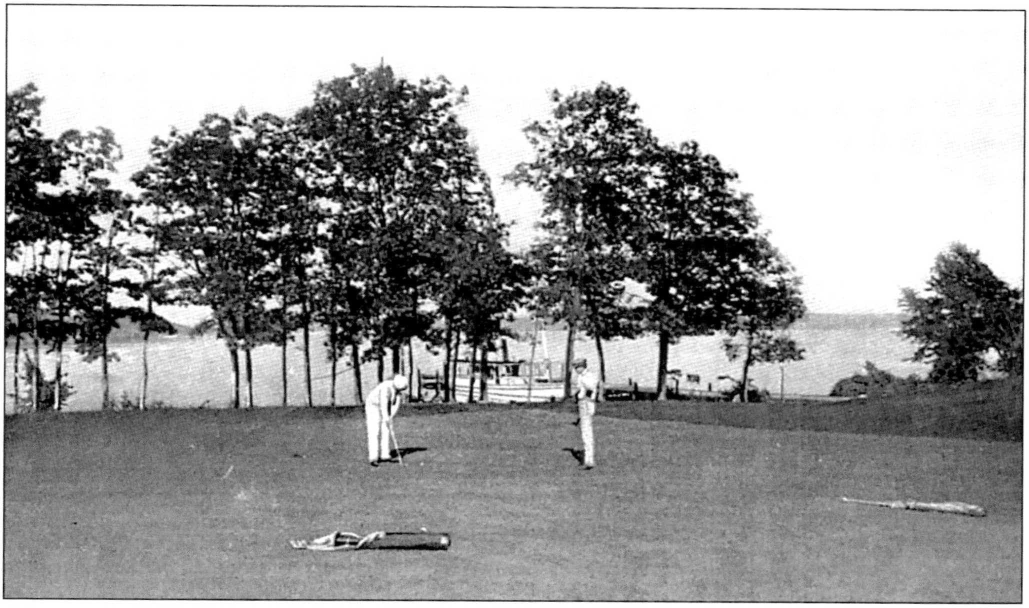

Lake Geneva Country Club hosts golf, tennis, swimming, and a junior program. It is also the site for the paddle tennis court initiated by John Lehman and is registered as a yacht club. Members gather to socialize at its well known "Friday Night Fish Fry." (Courtesy of the Jerry Glass Collection.)

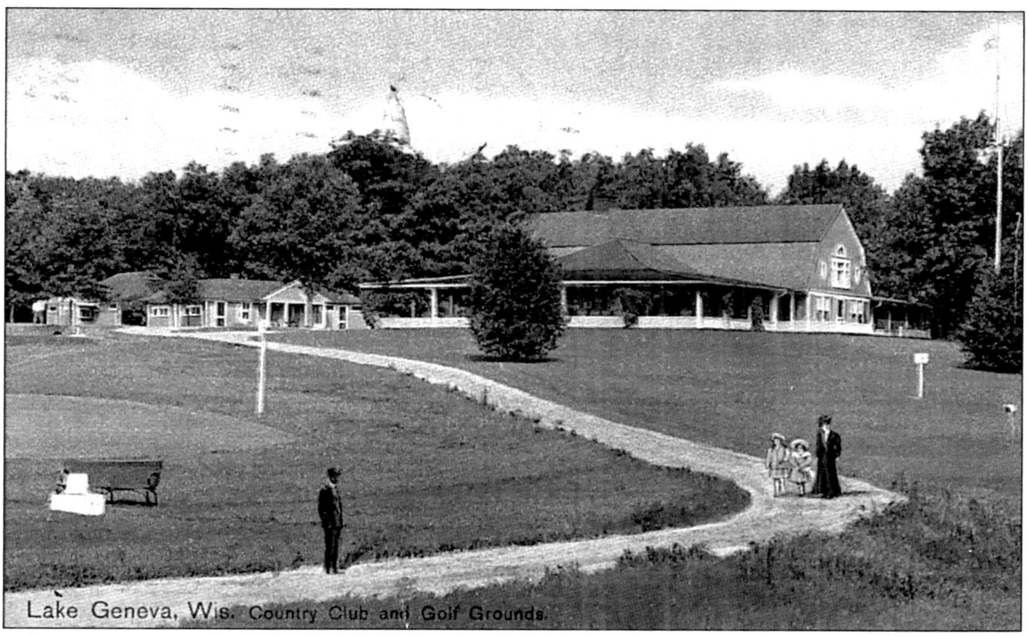

Lake Geneva Country Club is accessible by both land and water. The road, formerly a path to the country club, was created prior to the invention of the automobile. Members in years past arrived at the club via this path (today's road) by walking, on horseback, or in horse-drawn buggies. Boat transportation to and from the club was an option then, as it is now.

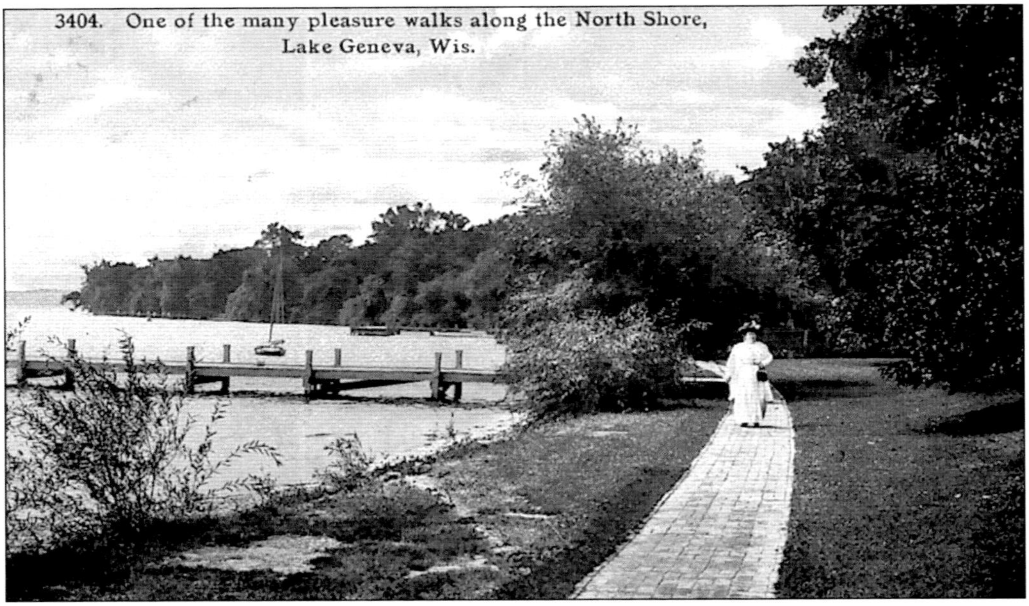

The Geneva Lake shore path is quite unique. The 21-mile footpath around the lake is said to be an old Indian trail. While it is technically open to the public (with the understanding that walkers stay on the path), this right has been challenged over the years. There was actually a lengthy litigation, which ended in 1975 when the court determined that "the public has the right of free and unobstructed use of the lake front path." Some elect to walk the entire trail in one day, while others break it up into sections and take days to traverse the shore. Each home owner or association is responsible for maintaining their portion of the path so that visitors can enjoy viewing the mansions, camps, and cottages.

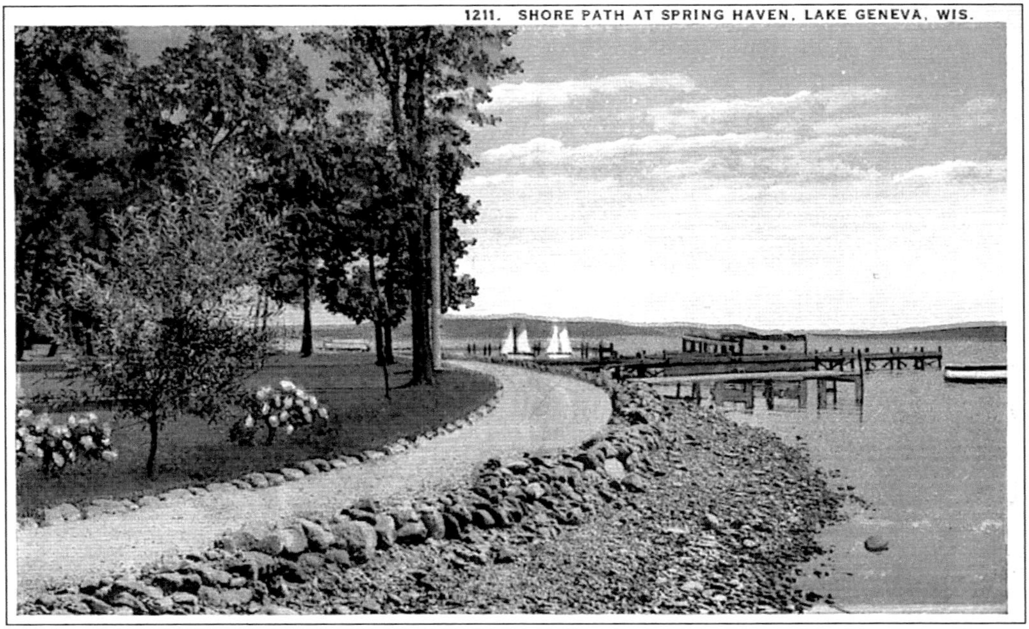

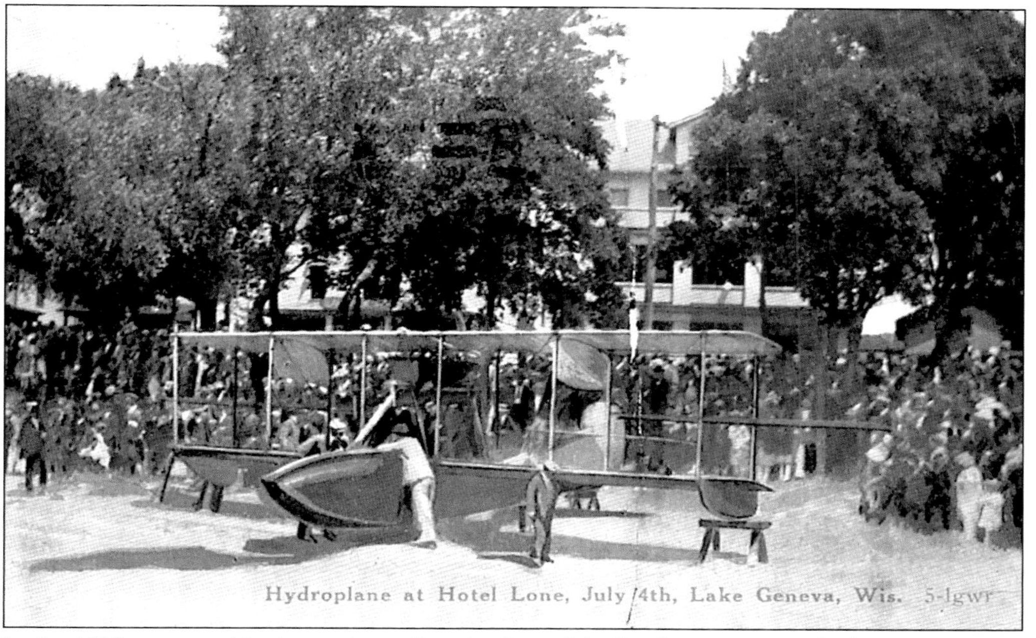

In the 1920s, you could take a spin on Ray Applegate's hydroplane—reportedly for $5. (Courtesy of the Jerry Glass Collection.)

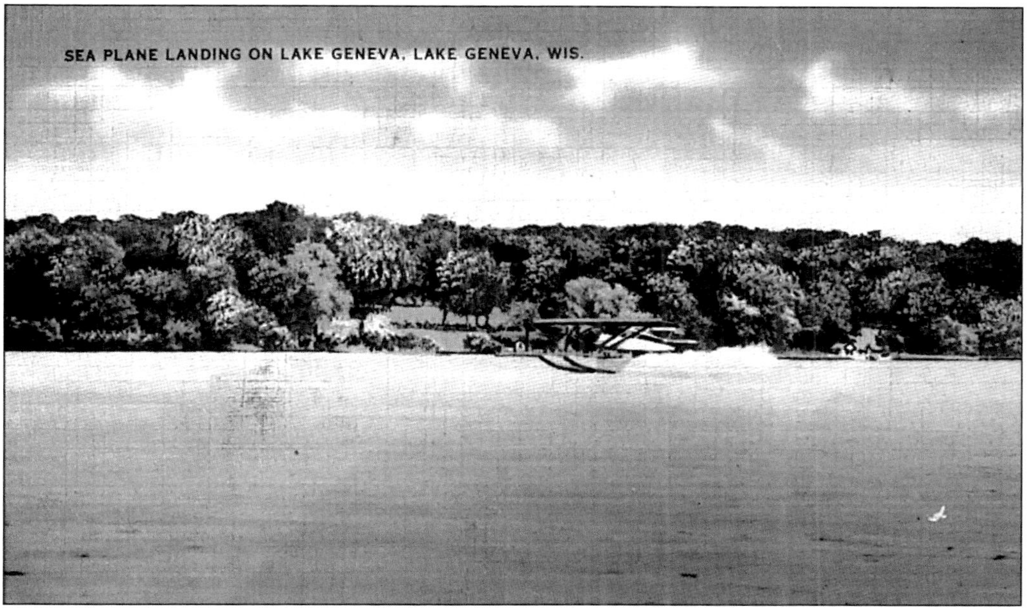

Hydroplanes can still be seen landing on Geneva Lake today. (Courtesy of the Robert Webster Sr. Collection.)

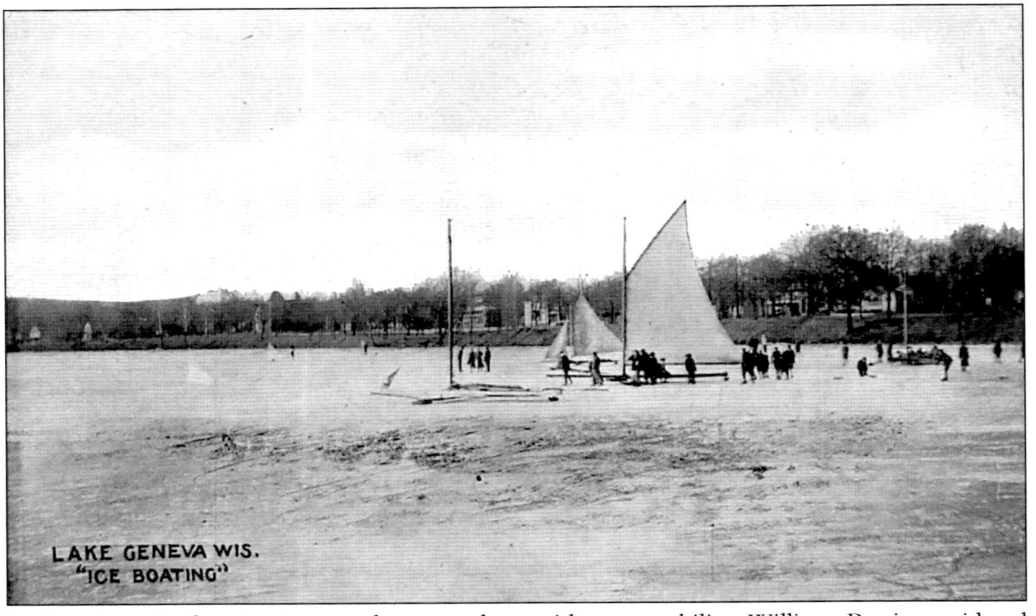

In the winter, ice boating is a popular sport, along with snowmobiling. Williams Bay is considered to be the Ice Boat Center of the World. Owners of colorful ice boats, Mother Nature dependent, gather for racing and socializing on the lake from December thru March. (Courtesy of the Robert Webster Sr. Collection.)

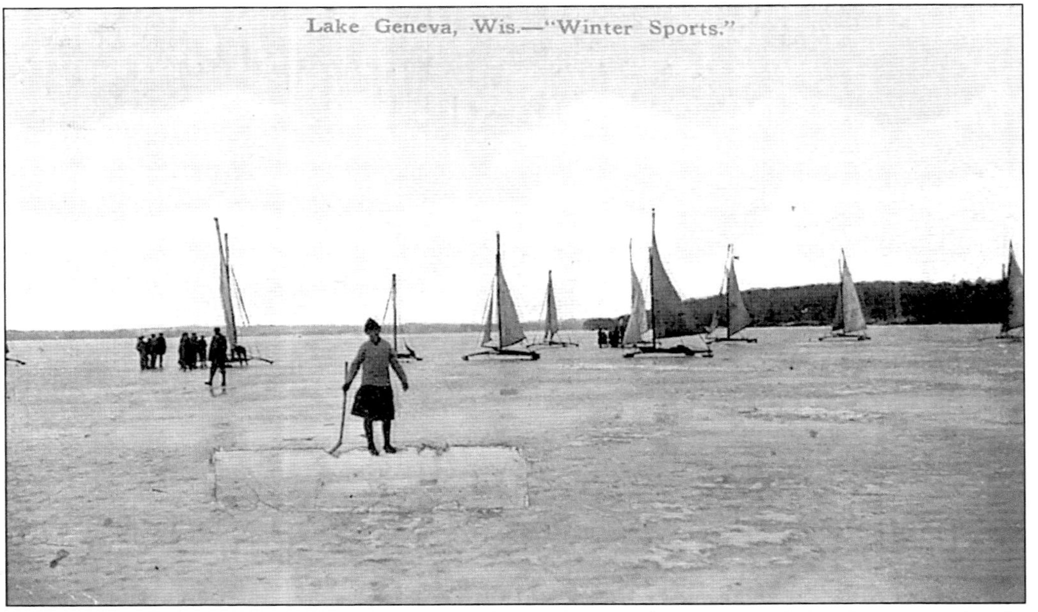

Walter Jewell, a skilled boat builder, established a boatyard just east of Conference Point in Williams Bay, later moving it the west shore of the Bay. After several years, it was taken over by Walter Beauvais, who was the designer of the famous Beau Skeeter Ice Boat. The current headquarters of the Gage Marine Corporation is thought to be on that site.

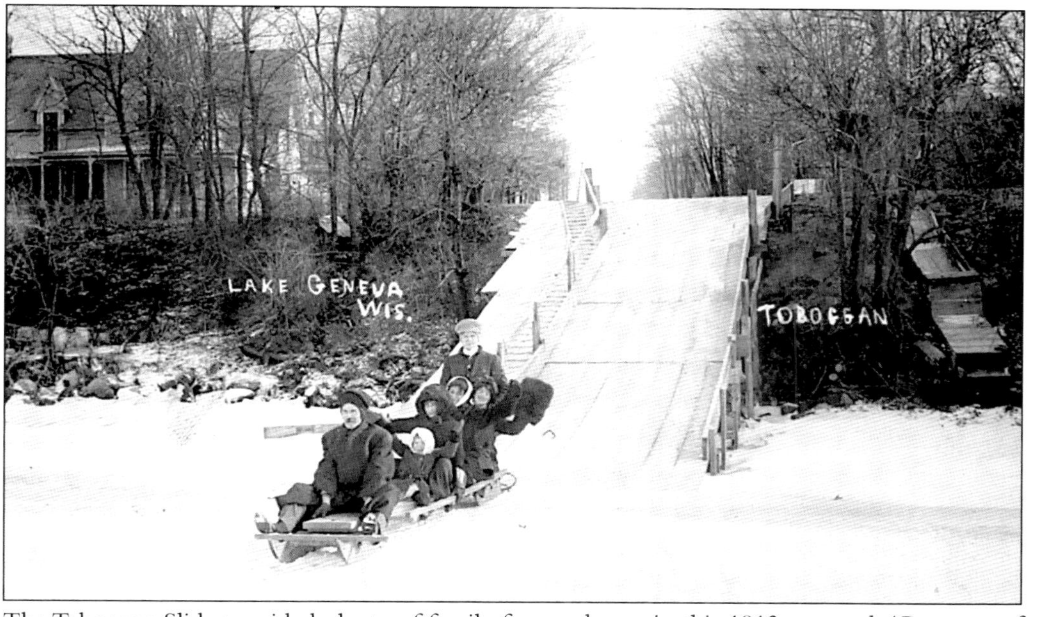

The Toboggan Slide provided plenty of family fun, as shown in this 1913 postcard. (Courtesy of the Brown-Gabriel Collection.)

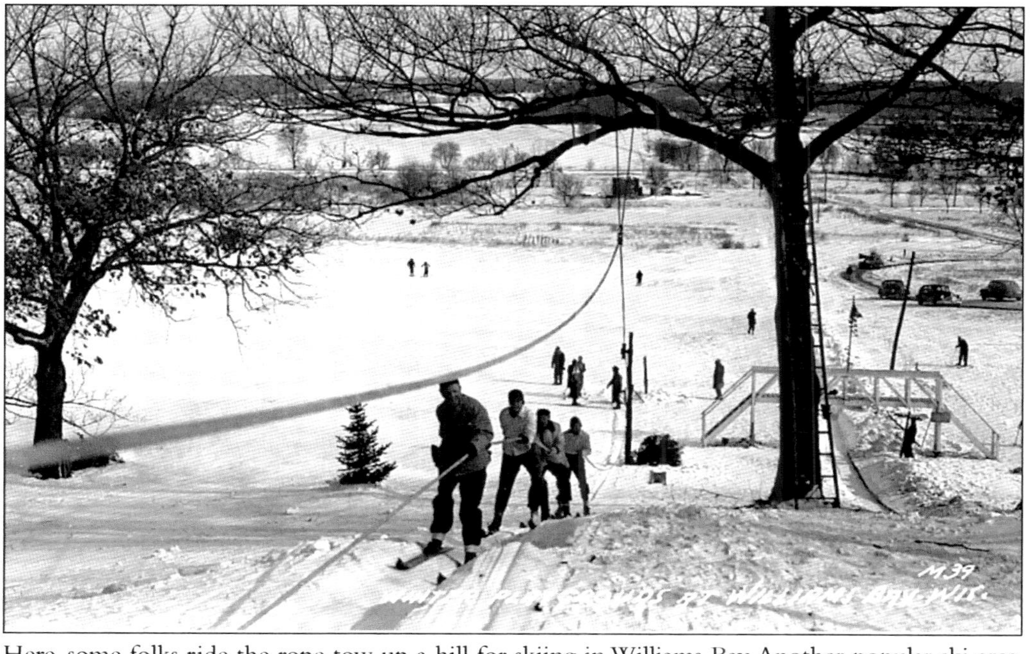

Here, some folks ride the rope tow up a hill for skiing in Williams Bay. Another popular ski area, Majestic Ski Hill, was located on the south side of the lake between the towns of Fontana and Lake Geneva. (Courtesy of the Brown-Gabriel Collection.)

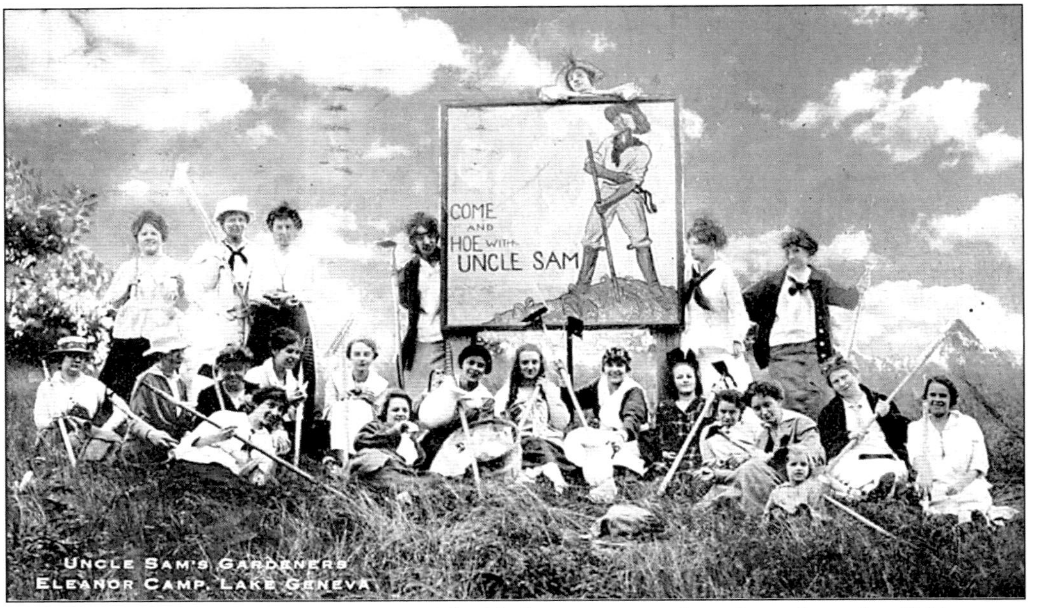

Gardening enhances the lake beauty and highlights summer colors. As early as the 1900s, some of the lake estates would compete in growing the best vegetables and flowers. Here, some participants of Eleanor Camp make their contribution to aid in the war effort. (Courtesy of the Brown-Gabriel Collection.)

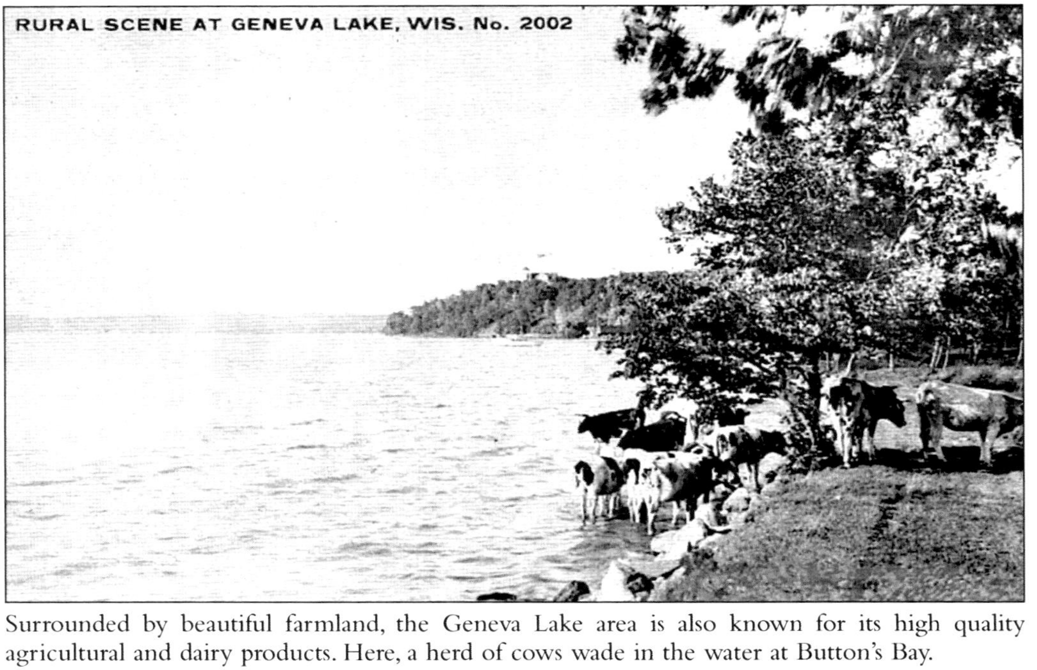

Surrounded by beautiful farmland, the Geneva Lake area is also known for its high quality agricultural and dairy products. Here, a herd of cows wade in the water at Button's Bay.

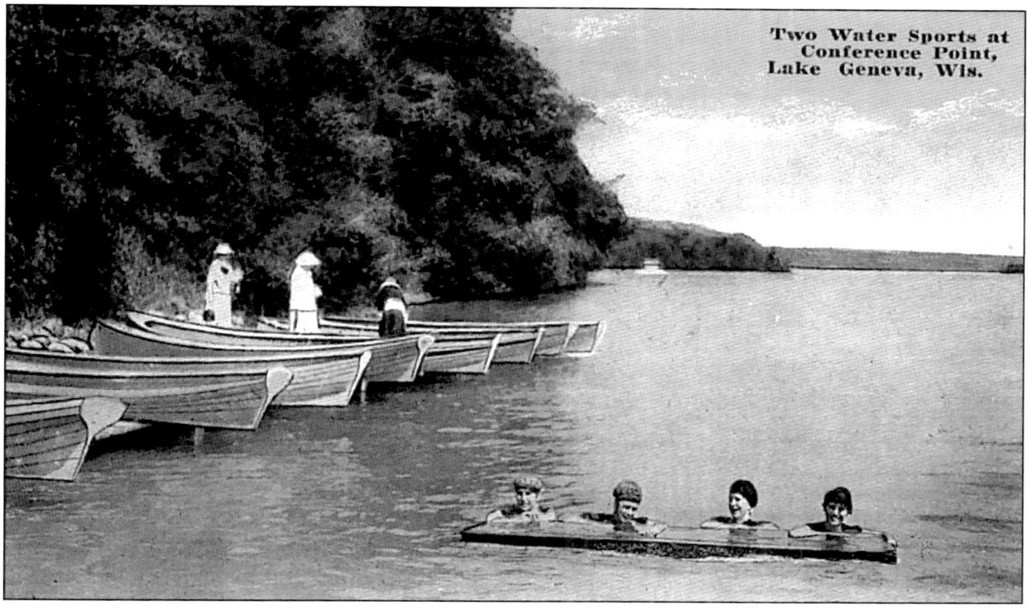

A variety of water sports have always been popular on the lake.

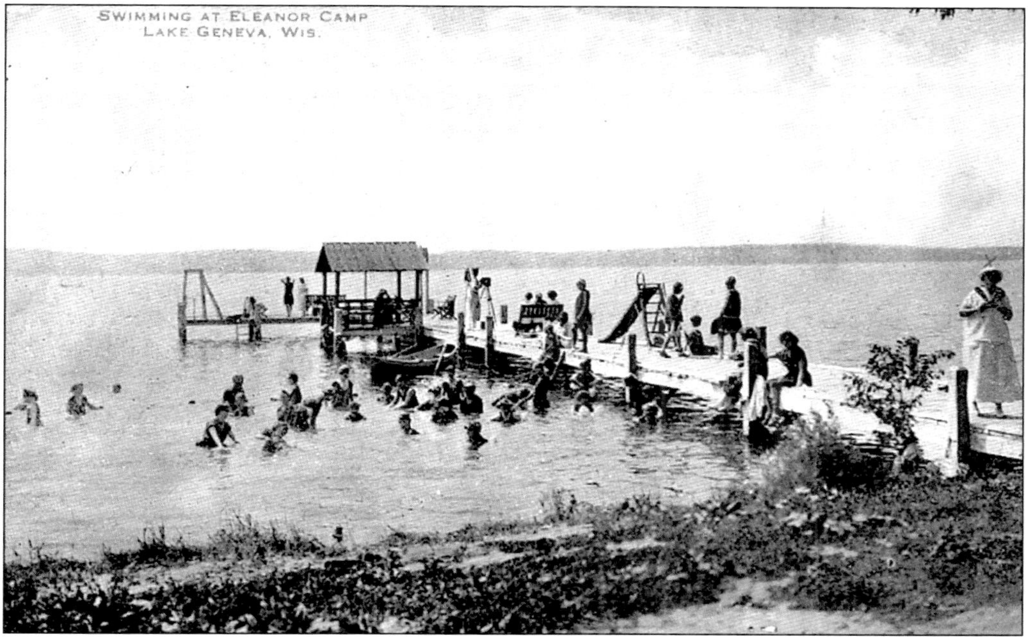

The first Eleanor Camp provided summer vacations for forty-six women, spread over the summer. The camp was moved from their Black Point location to Conference Point, allowing more women to enjoy summer camp together at one time. That year, 127 women attended camp, sometimes 30 at a time. Swimming at Eleanor was always part of the fun at summer camp. (Courtesy of the Jerry Glass Collection.)

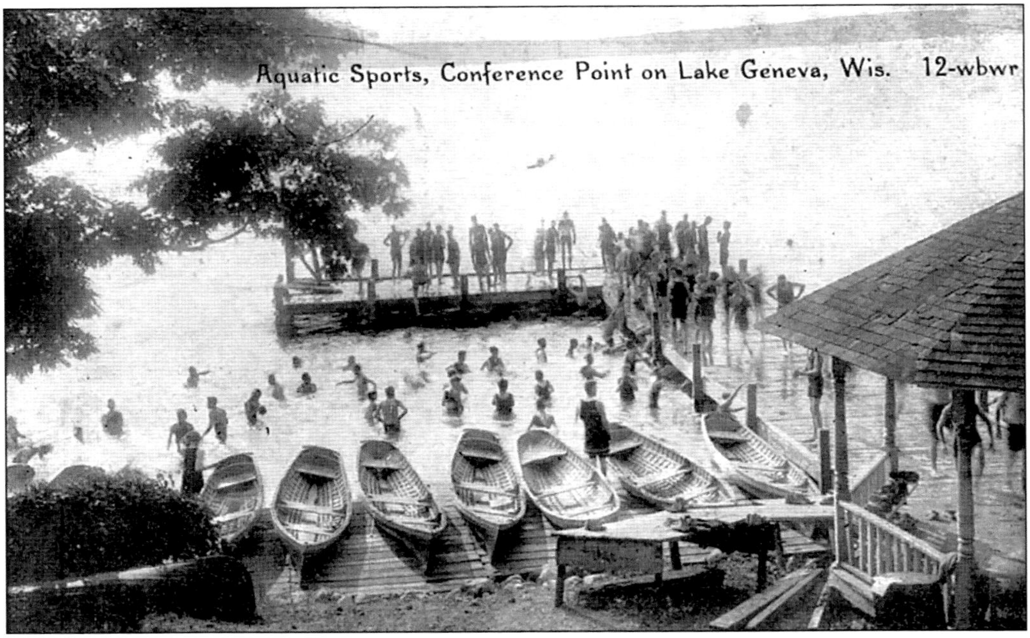

Aquatic sports have always been part of Geneva Lake recreation. Today, the tradition continues as athletes are challenged by the hilly terrain and the cool waters of the lake in the annual Lake Geneva Triathlon. (Courtesy of the John P. Urlakis Collection.)

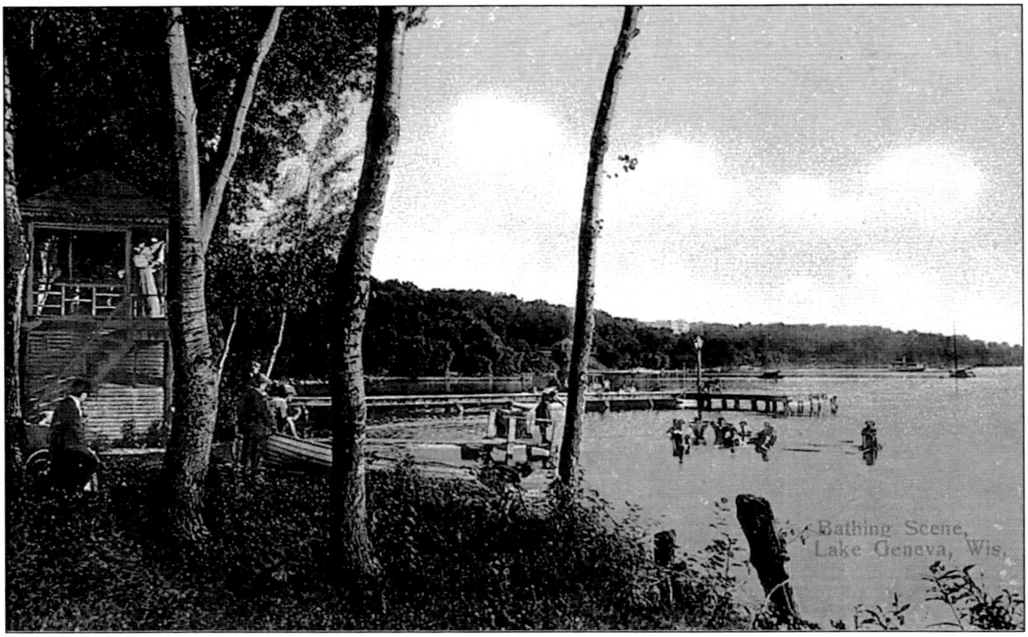

Postcards were the emails of yesteryear. For about five cents, a postcard could be purchased and then mailed for a penny. Friends and family wrote back home from their summer homes and camps. The messages were short. Many times, the writing was on the front of the postcard. Postcards were also sent as a way of communicating to friends and family in the same town or down the street.

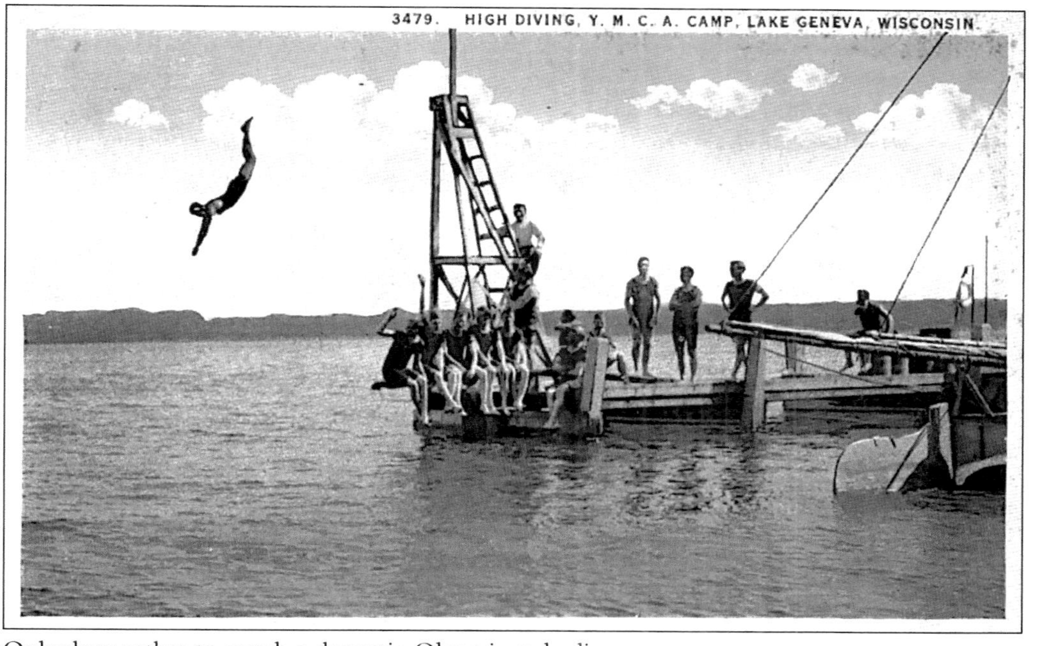

Onlookers gather to watch a dramatic Olympic style dive.

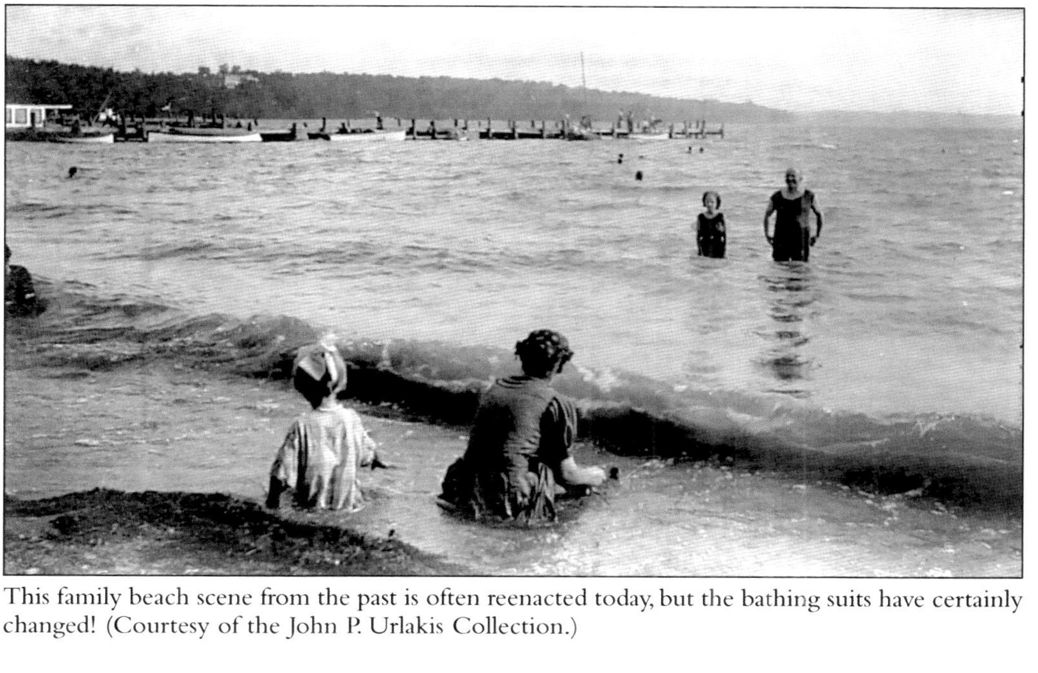

This family beach scene from the past is often reenacted today, but the bathing suits have certainly changed! (Courtesy of the John P. Urlakis Collection.)

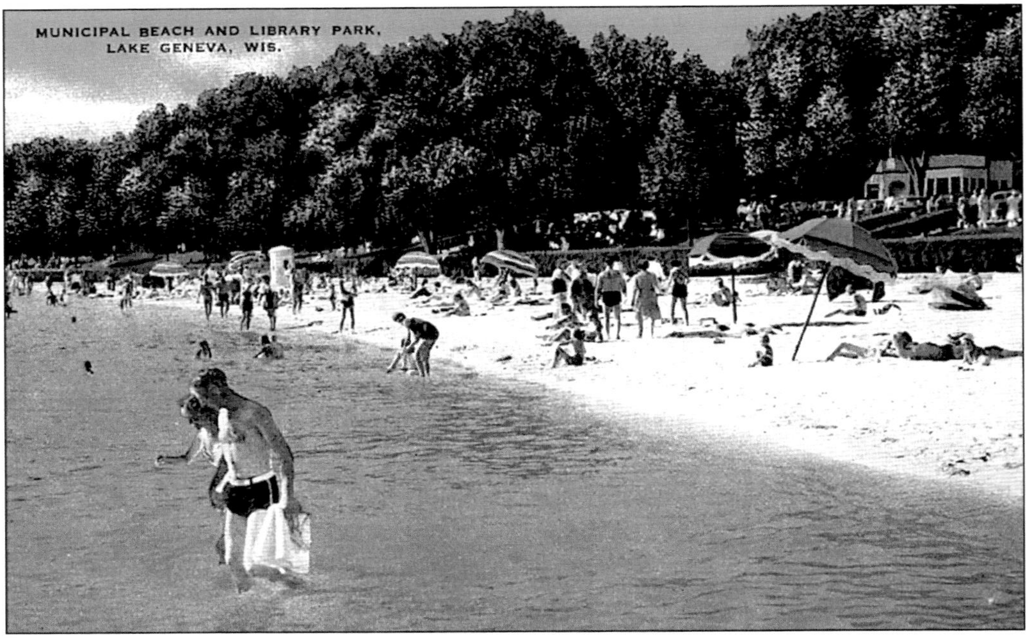

Sunbathers and swimmers with boats in the background are still a common sight on Library Park Beach. . .

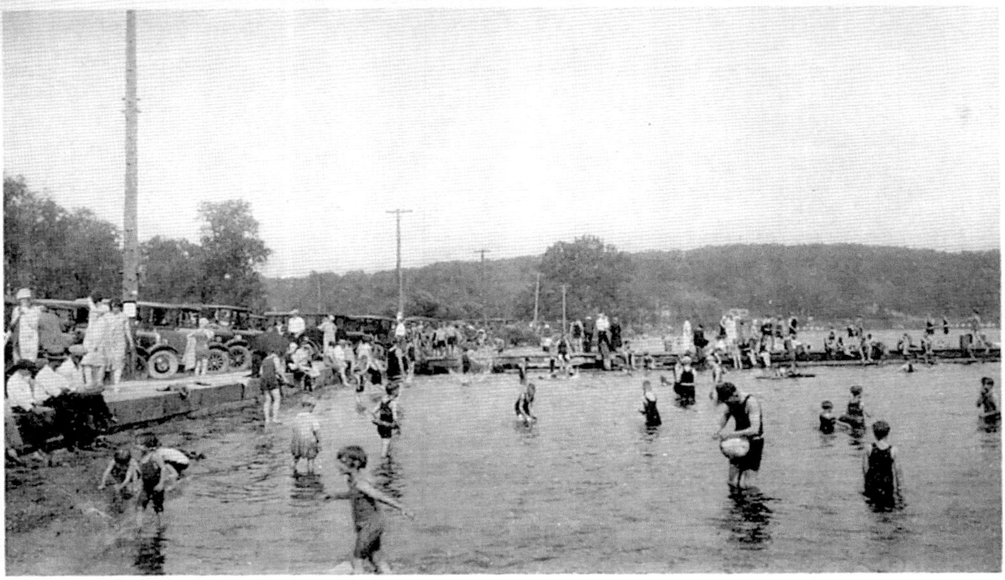

BATHING BEACH, WILLIAMS BAY, WISCONSIN

. . . as well as on Williams Bay Beach.

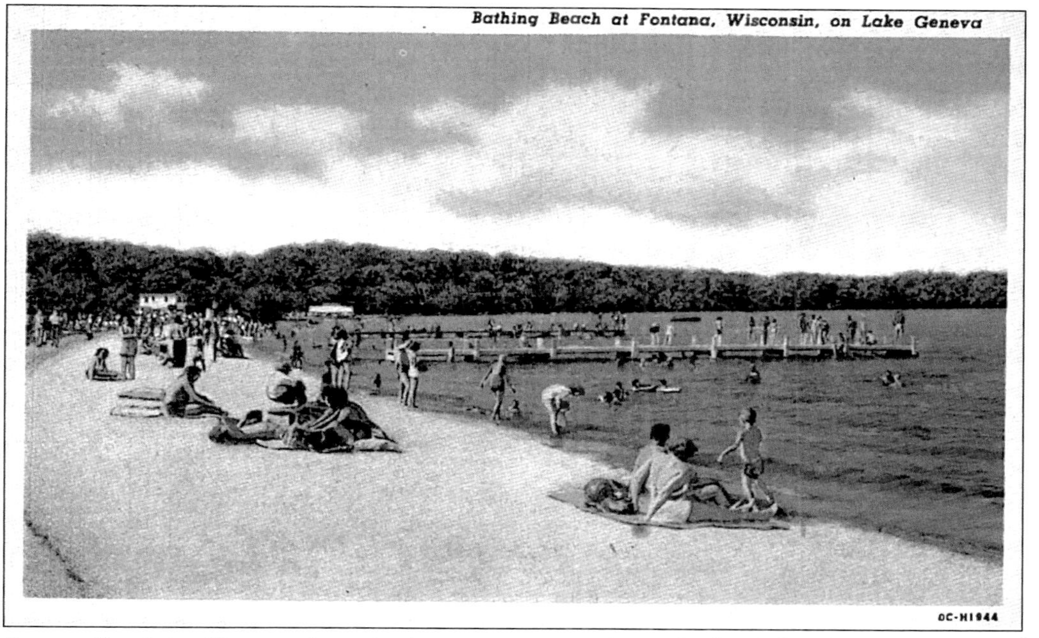

Fontana Beach is still a popular gathering spot to sun, swim, and relax. It has the convenience of close-by restaurants, parks, boat rentals, and piers.

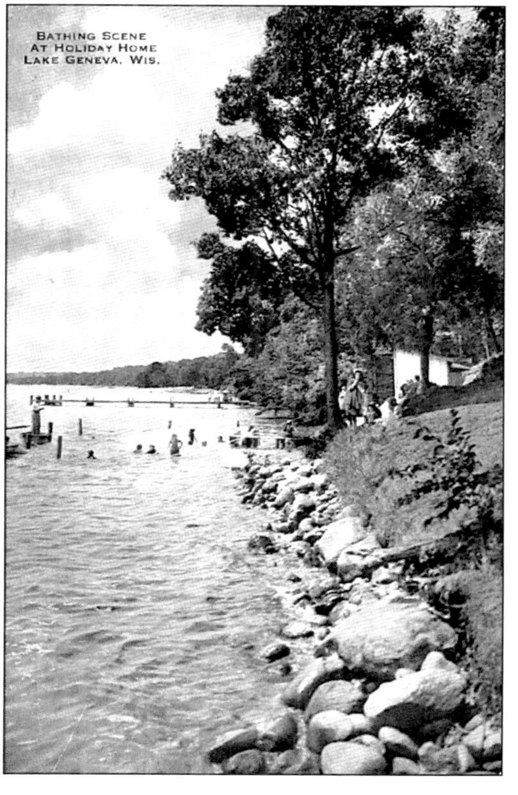

Geneva Lake's crystal clear water welcomes swimmers for a refreshing early morning dip or a relaxing evening exercise.

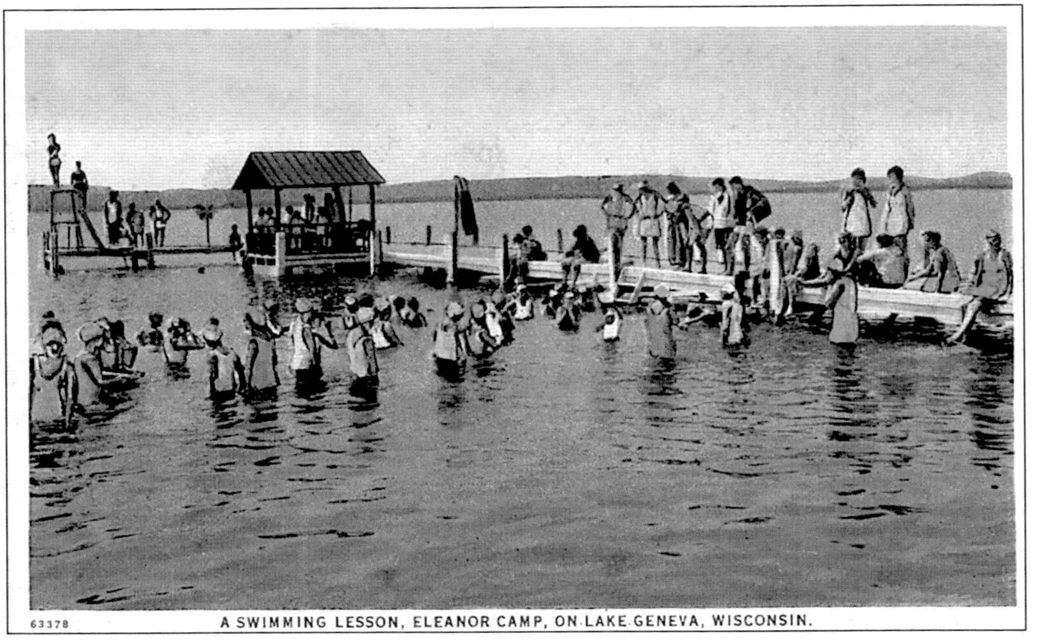

Swimming lessons and water safety are part of the lake's culture, with instruction offered for nearly a century by the camps and the Water Safety Patrol.

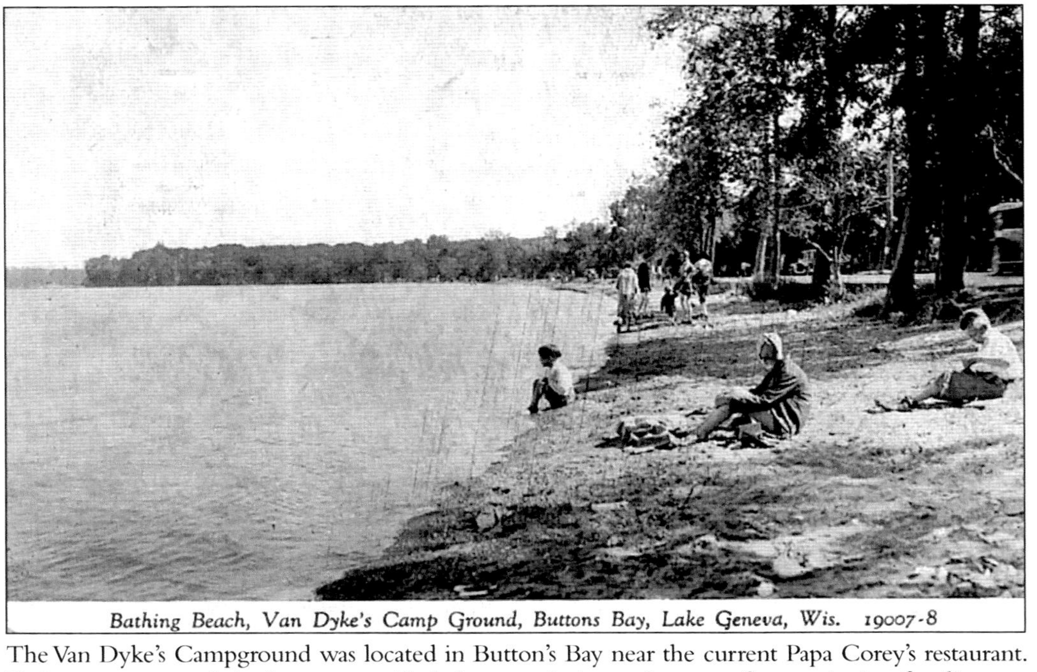

The Van Dyke's Campground was located in Button's Bay near the current Papa Corey's restaurant. Various campgrounds in the area provided close proximity to the water for vacationing families.

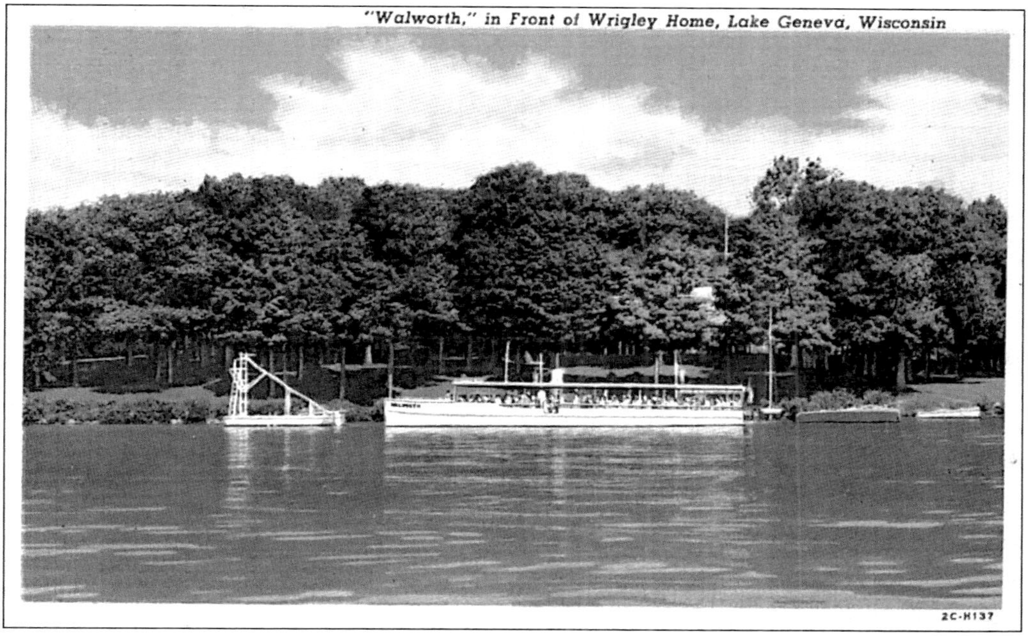

For almost 50 years, the steamship *Walworth* faithfully carried the mail and passengers around the lake. Launched in 1916, she was designed to be the flagship of Mr. Tilford Stuyvesant's excursion fleet. More functional than graceful, her smooth, straight lines allowed her to cut easily through the water. The *Walworth* was scrapped in 1965.

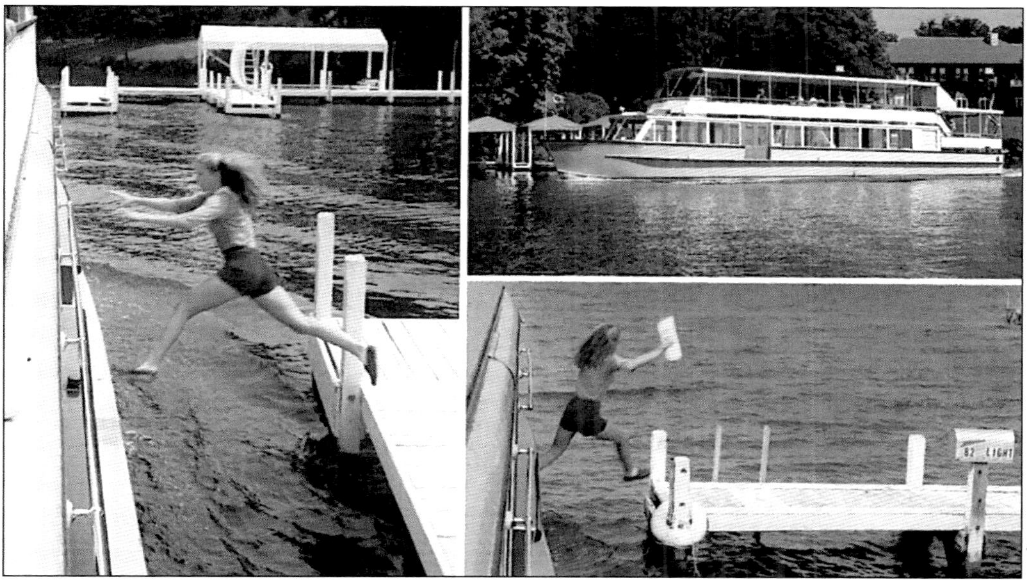

In 1967, the *Walworth II* was launched, replacing the earlier well known mail boat. This popular excursion boat delivers mail and newspapers to piers during the summer months, while simultaneously providing tours of the lake. Excitement builds for the passengers as the mail-person jumps from the boat, delivers the mail, and leaps back—usually while the boat is still speeding along! (Courtesy of Virgil Wuttke.)

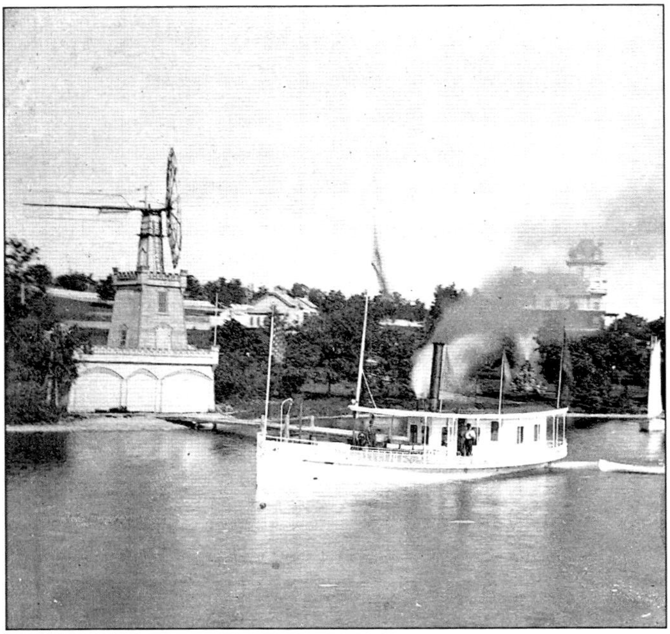

The *Arrow*, built for George Sturges of Snug Harbor, was a large and impressive craft. It was actively used by the Sturges family until August of 1891, when an untimely fire in the engine room led to her sale to Arthur Kaye, proprietor of Kaye's Park. The huge windmill in the background was on the grounds of the Leiter estate. (Courtesy of the Brown-Gabriel Collection.)

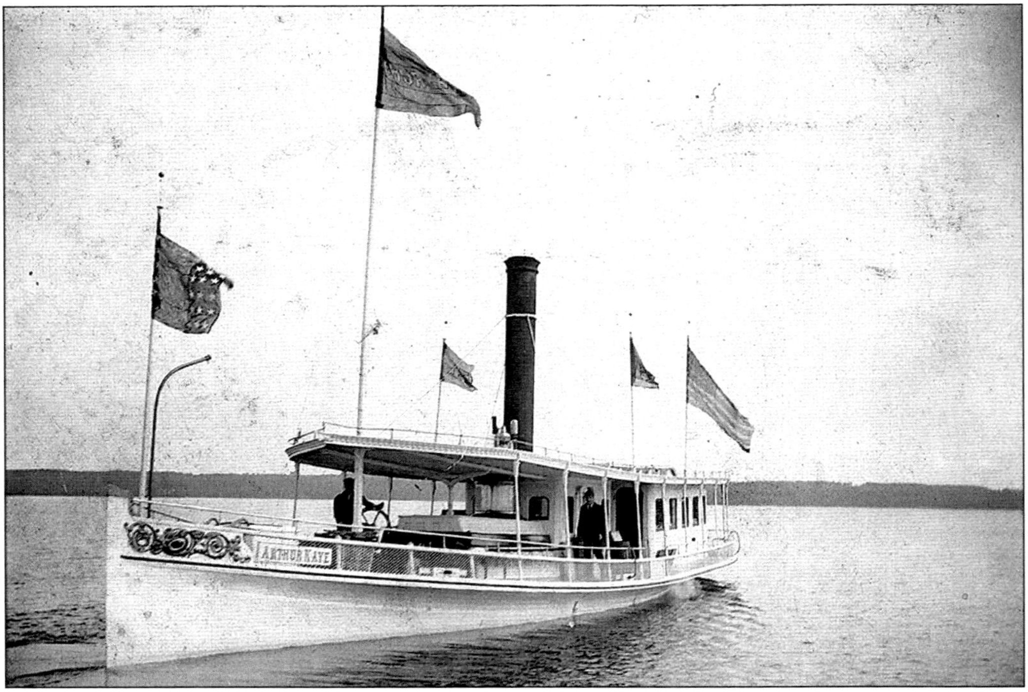

Mr. Kaye rebuilt and restored the partially burned *Arrow* and renamed her—you guessed it—the *Arthur Kaye*. Guests of the resort were entertained on the excursion steamer by the colorful character Captain William Wood until 1898, when the vessel ignited a second time, burning to the water line and sinking. The engine and machinery were later rescued and used in another yacht. (Courtesy of the Brown-Gabriel Collection.)

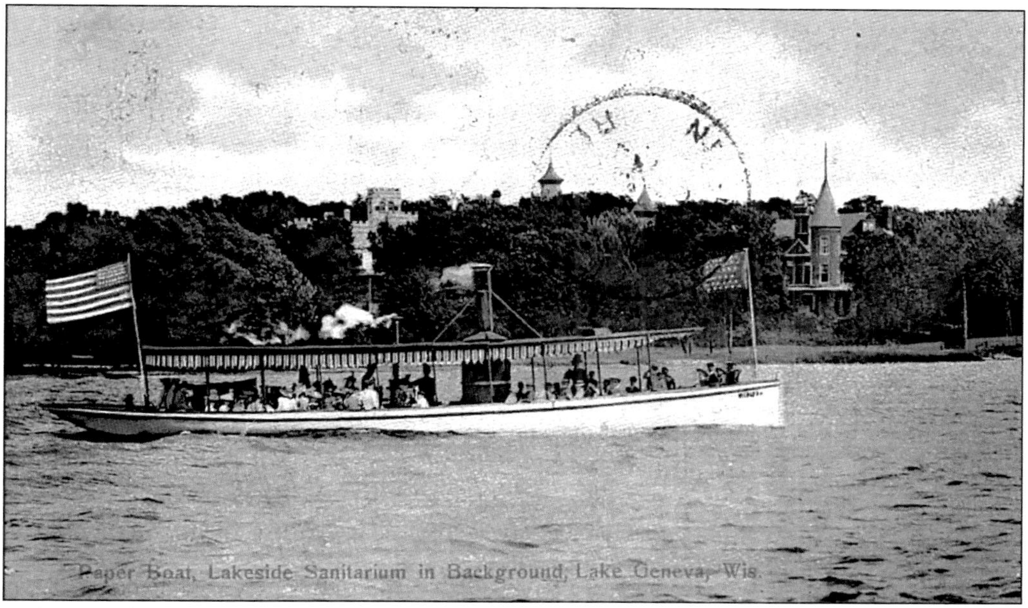

Walter Jewell, a skilled craftsman and boat builder from Williams Bay, created the *Ripple* in 1880. Smaller and more delicate, it was a trim vessel with graceful lines. The following year the owners of Lone's Boat Livery purchased the steamer, and the *Ripple* became known as the "Paper Boat," delivering newspapers to lakeshore residents until 1911.

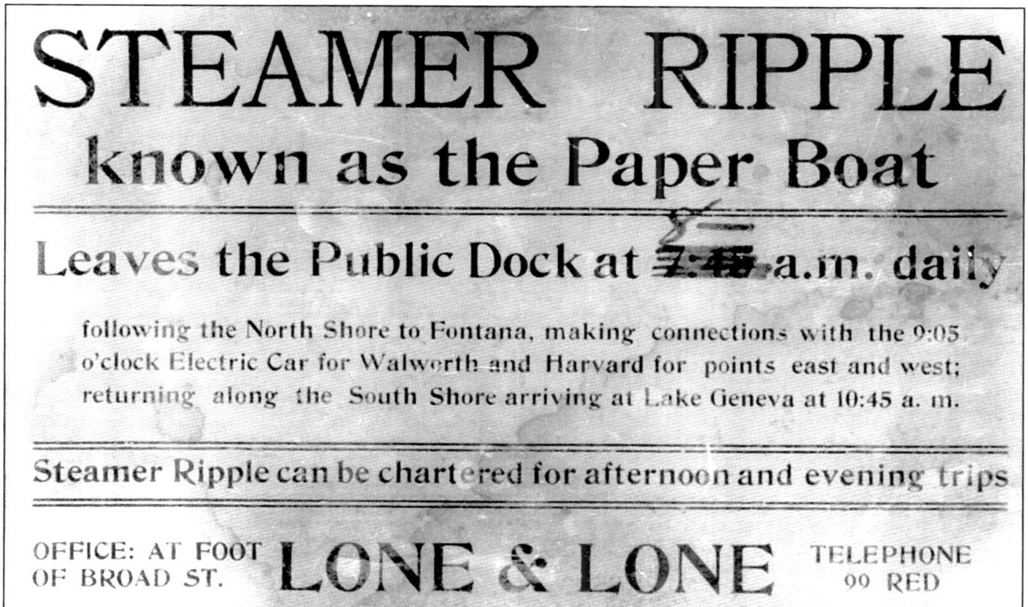

(Courtesy of the Brown-Gabriel Collection.)

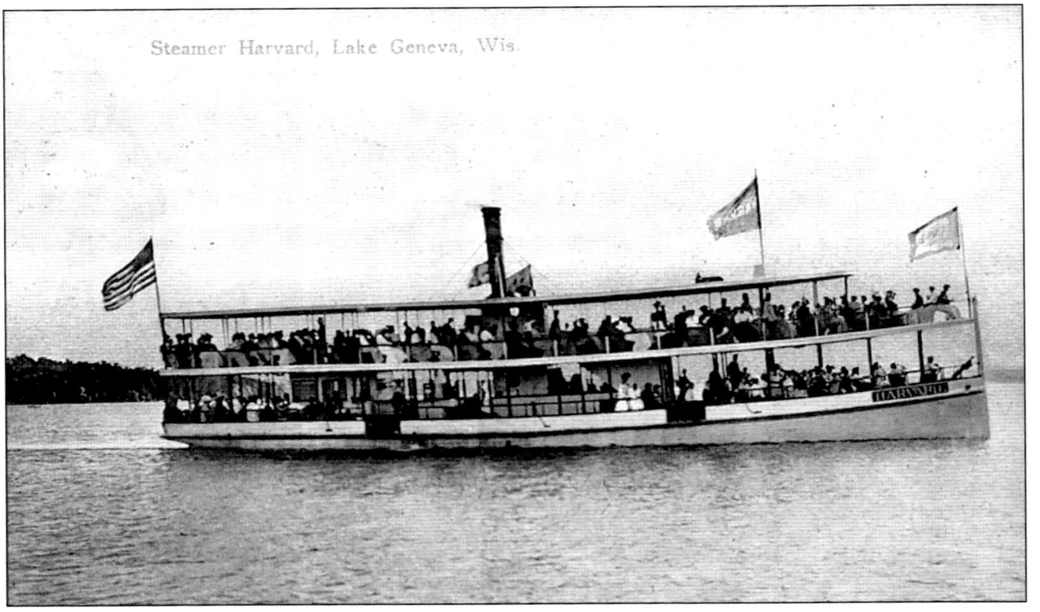

The hull of the steamship *Harvard* was launched in the spring of 1892, while its upper deck was constructed once it was in the water. After many years of service, renovation was not feasible due to the Depression and the decrease in tourism. It was retired in 1931, and the hull sunk just outside of Williams Bay. The *Harvard* gave two-hour tours of the lake, often while a piano and brass band played for the passengers. On Saturday nights, couples would dance on the romantic moonlight cruises around the lake.

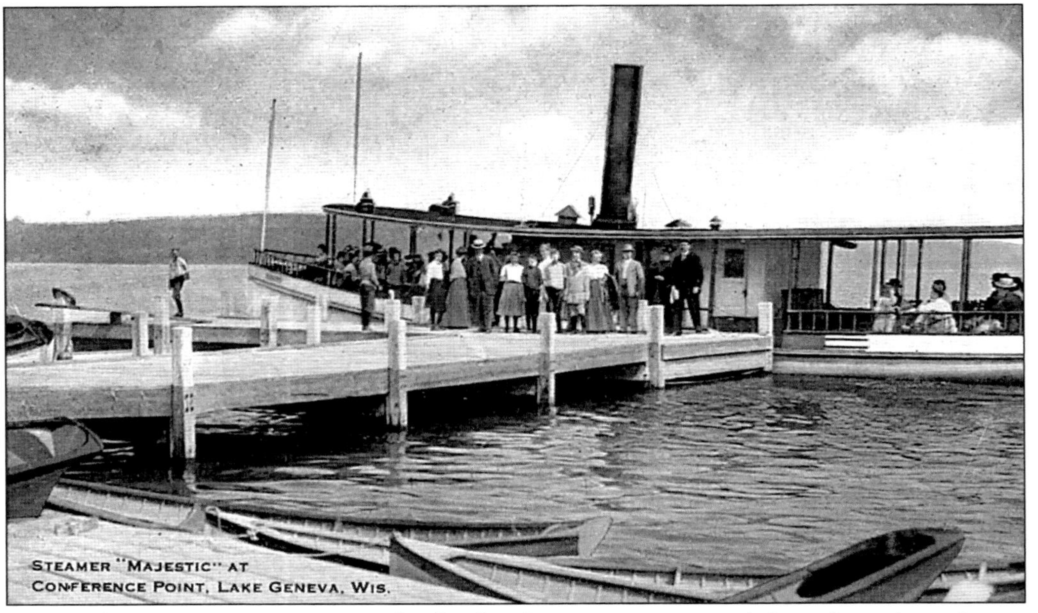

The regal steamer *Majestic* was popular for ferrying passengers to and from the train station, as well as giving tours of the lake. Built in 1891 for Wesley Johnson's Lake Geneva Steamer Line, she was 68 feet long and provided faithful commercial service until 1920.

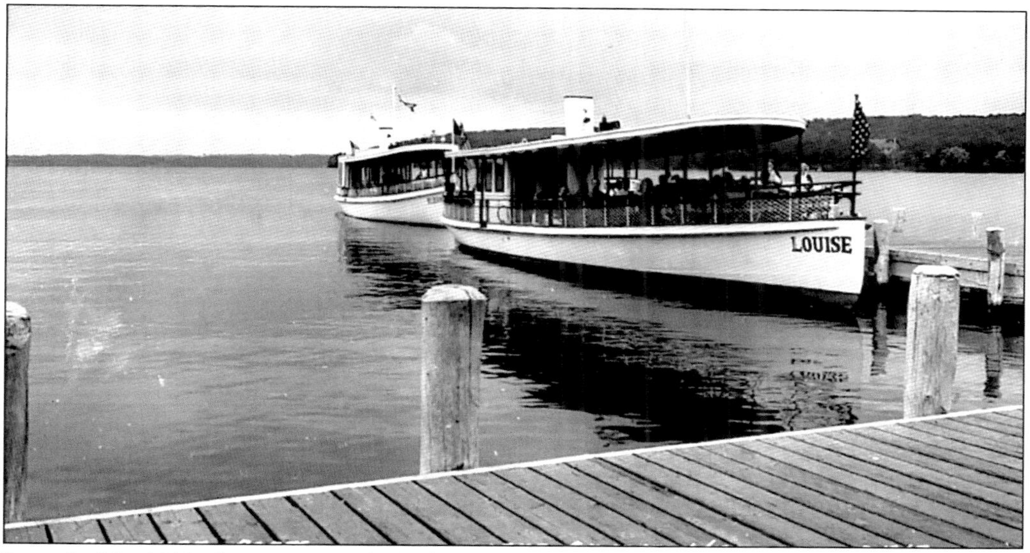

Launched in 1902, the *Louise* was built for John J. Mitchell of Ceylon Court. The 75-foot yacht, which was maintained by a captain and a steward, was the scene of many gracious gatherings. Completely restored by Russell and William Gage, it is one of only a few steam vessels in the country currently in operation.

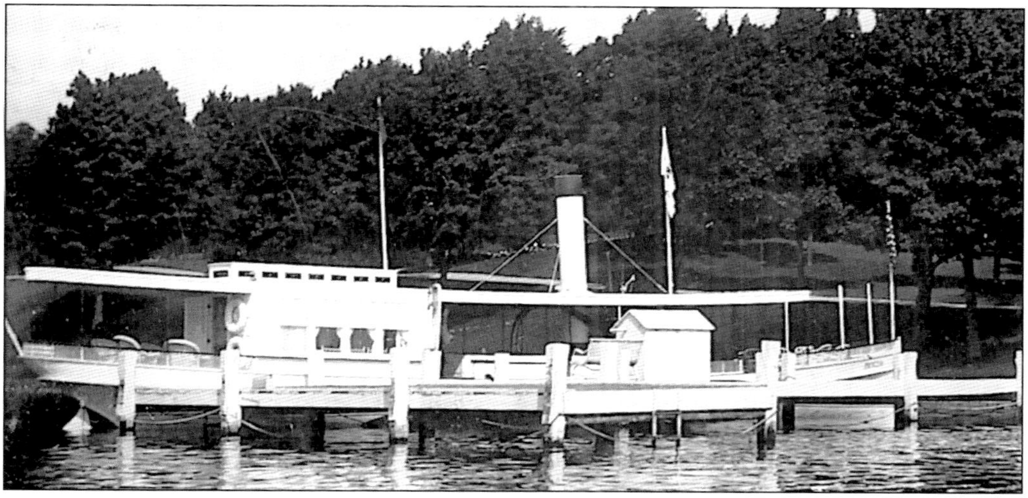

The *Princess* was built in Detroit around 1898 and delivered to Mr. O.W. Potter of Lake Geneva. In 1916, the yacht was purchased by Frederick Countess, a senior partner with S.B. Chapin, a stock brokerage firm in Chicago. At that time, Mr. Countess owned the James Moore estate. He renamed the boat *Eleanor* (after his wife) and enjoyed it for many years. In 1926, the yacht was sold with the Moore-Countess estate to a group of investors who wanted to turn the property into an exclusive country club offering golf, horseback riding, tennis, and cruises aboard the *Eleanor*. The venture failed due to zoning restrictions. An auction was held in 1930 to liquidate the clubs assets, and the *Eleanor* was sold to the excursion company. A gasoline engine was installed, and the *Eleanor* was used for commercial service until 1942, when hull deterioration necessitated dismantling the boat for scrap to aid the war effort. (Courtesy of the Brown-Gabriel Collection.)

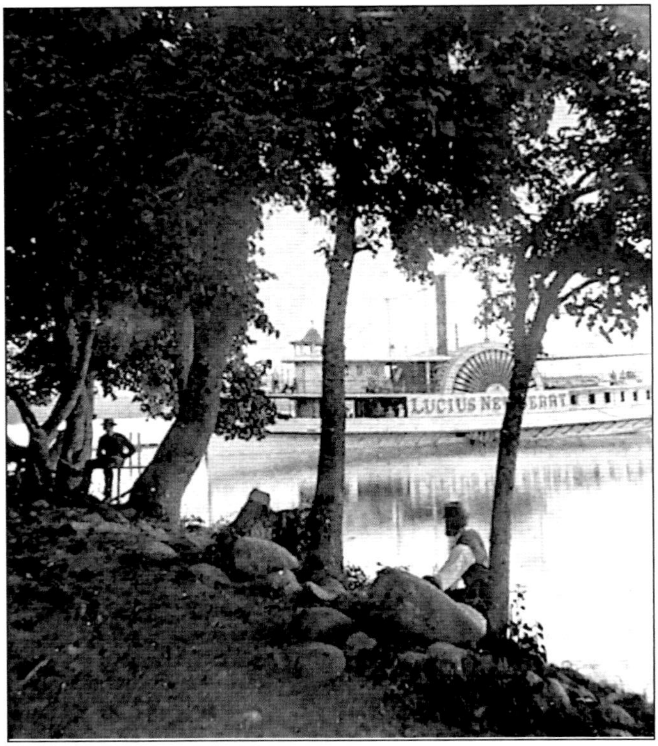

Considered by many to be the finest commercial steamer of the era, the *Lucius Newberry* was the largest vessel to float on Geneva Lake. Launched in 1875, the boat featured a main cabin with Brussels carpeting, etched mirrors, custom-made furniture, a kerosene chandelier, and an ornately carved bar. After several owners, it was renamed *The City of Lake Geneva* in 1890. Tragically, in December of that year, she caught fire while tied to the public dock in Lake Geneva. Her lines were cut to prevent nearby boats from catching fire also, and the flaming hull drifted in a gentle breeze for about 30 minutes until it sank on the lake in front of the Allerton home. The remains were discovered by divers in 1981. (Courtesy of the Brown-Gabriel Collection.)

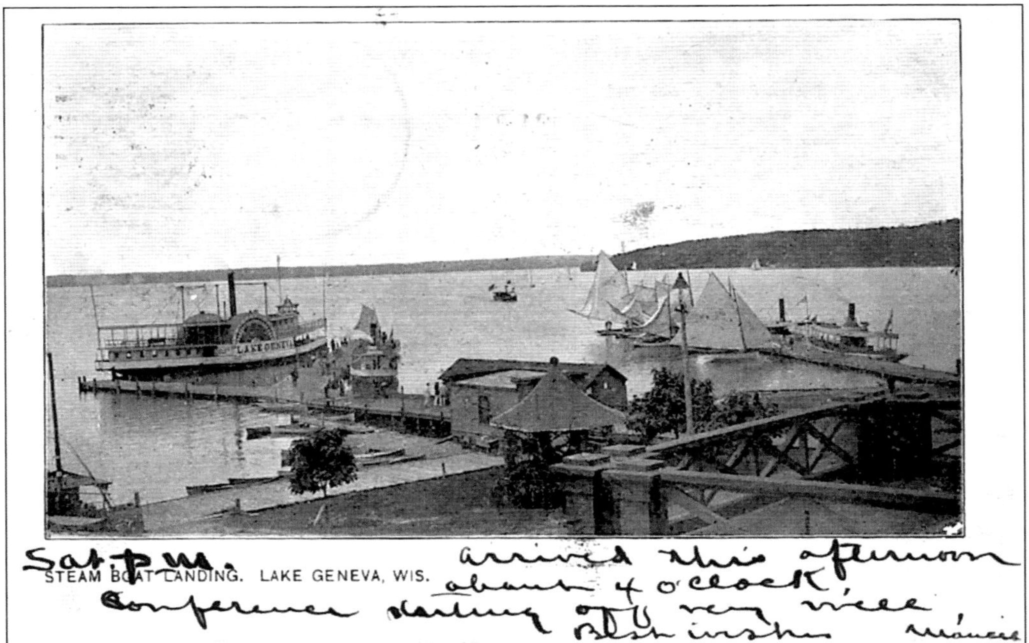

Here, you can see the different types of watercraft at this steamboat landing in the City of Lake Geneva. The *Lucius Newberry,* renamed *The City of Lake Geneva*, is the large steamer at the dock.

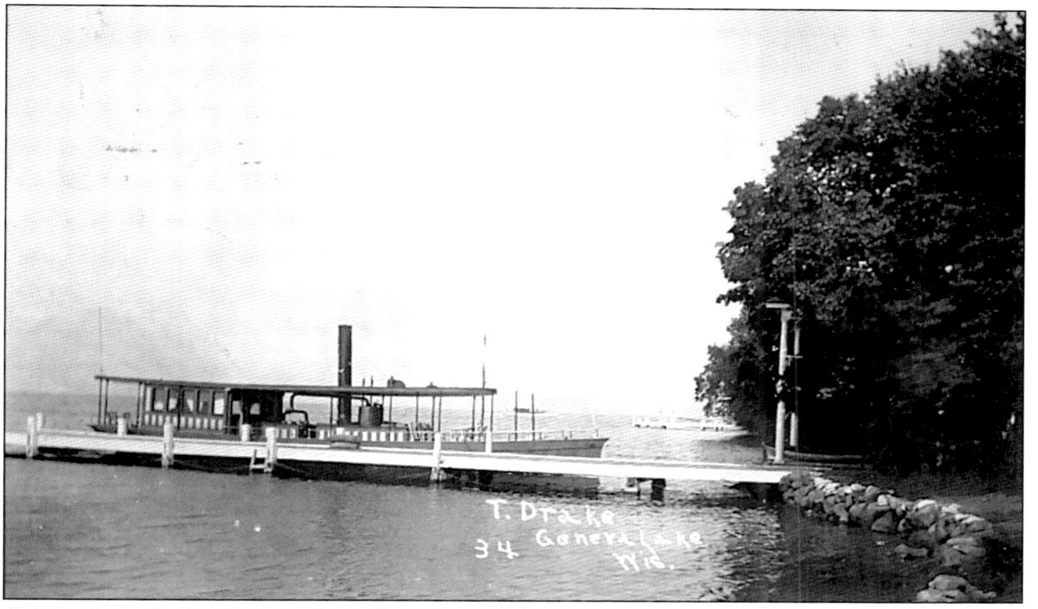

Originally built for George C. Walker, the *Ethel Mary* was purchased in 1902 by Tracy Drake, owner of the Drake Hotel in Chicago. Painted bright green with black smokestacks and white trim, she earned the nickname "Green Rabbit." Mr. Drake renamed her *Aloha,* to correspond with the name of Drake's estate, Aloha Lodge. She could be seen gliding along the waters of Geneva Lake for the next 30 years. (Courtesy of the Brown-Gabriel Collection.)

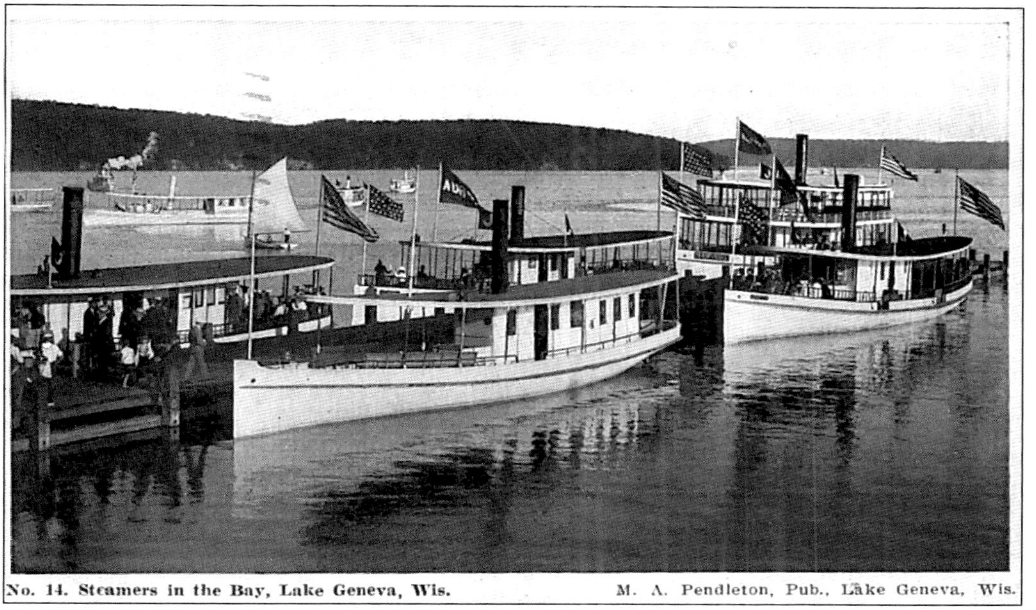

No. 14. Steamers in the Bay, Lake Geneva, Wis. M. A. Pendleton, Pub., Lake Geneva, Wis.

Even though the road was built around Geneva Lake in the early 1900s, boat travel was the main mode of transportation to the lakefront estates.

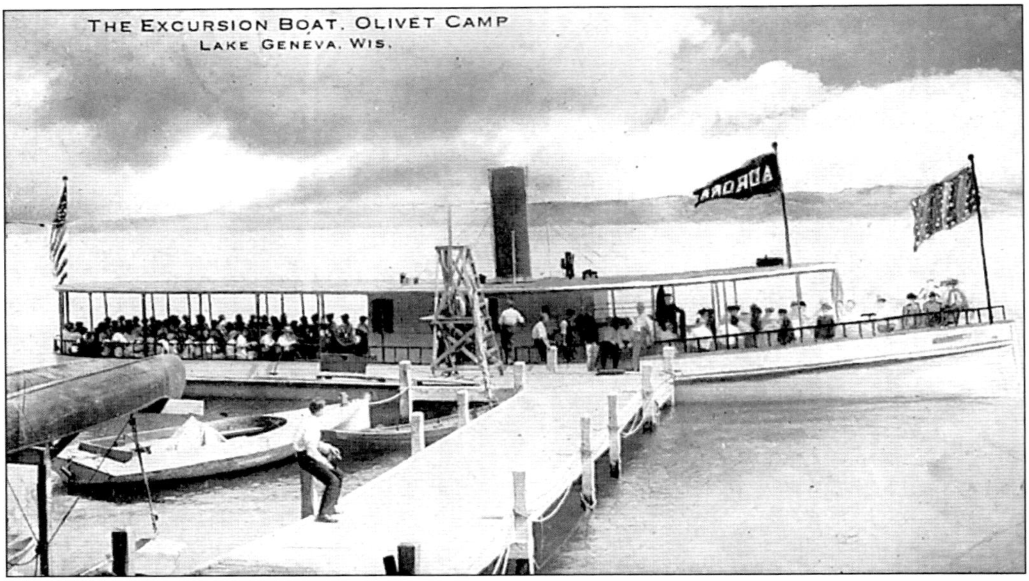

Three boats were built in the late 1890s that would be the mainstay of the excursion fleet for the next 30 years. They were the *Geneva,* the *Bavaria*, and the *Aurora*, and were similar in size and design. These boats were frequently used to deliver passengers from the train station in Williams Bay to their lake house destination. (Courtesy of the Brown-Gabriel Collection.)

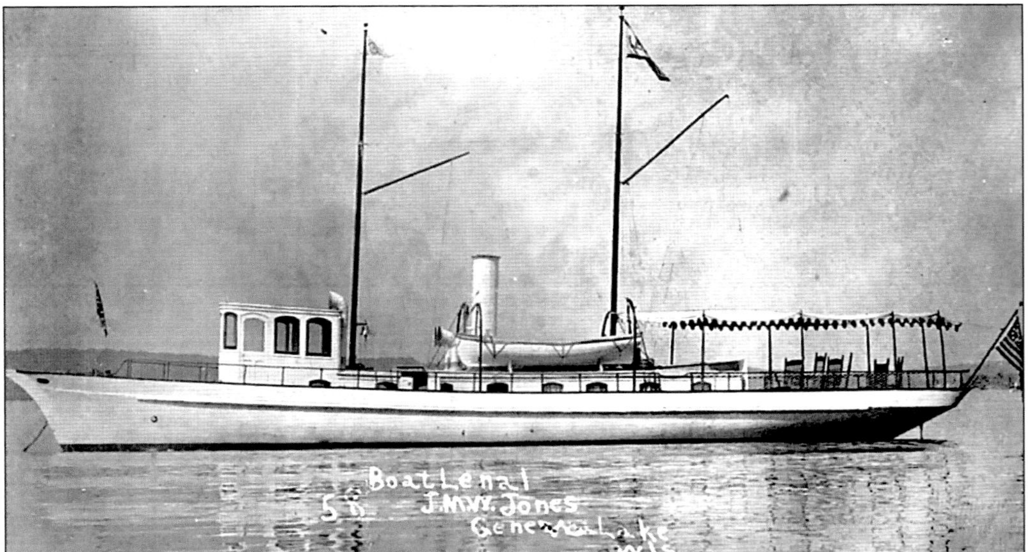

Inspired by the excitement of the World's Colombian Exposition, several Geneva Lake residents bought buildings and artifacts at the close of the fair in 1894 and shipped their purchases home. Such was the case with the *Lenal*, used for passenger service between the Chicago and North-Western Railroad in Chicago's Grant Park to the World's Fair in Jackson Park. Brought to Geneva Lake by Mason B. Starring, the vessel had a strong engine and was in frequent use on the lake. It was the only steamer on Geneva Lake to carry a lifeboat. (Courtesy of the Brown-Gabriel Collection.)

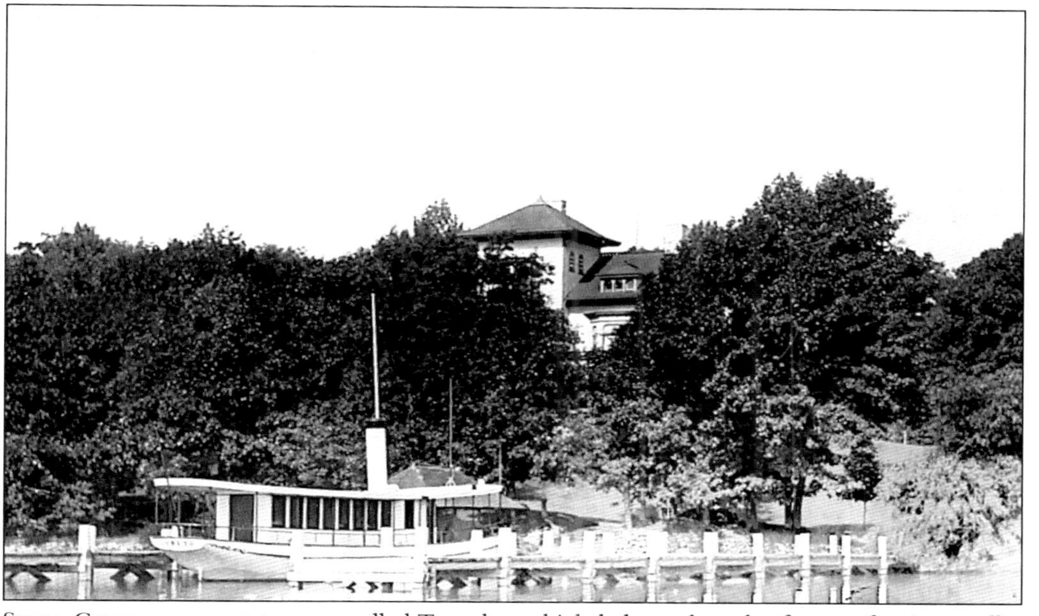

Stone Gates was an estate once called Tyrawley, which belonged to the famous furniture seller John M. Smyth. The *Loreto*, pictured here in front of the Smyth home, was one of the first private steamers on Geneva Lake. The boat was quite heavy and drew a considerable swell. Mr. Smyth had to remind his family not to run the vessel at full throttle, and at one time reportedly changed the propeller to a smaller size when he learned that his sons were having friendly races with other steamers! (Courtesy of the Brown-Gabriel Collection.)

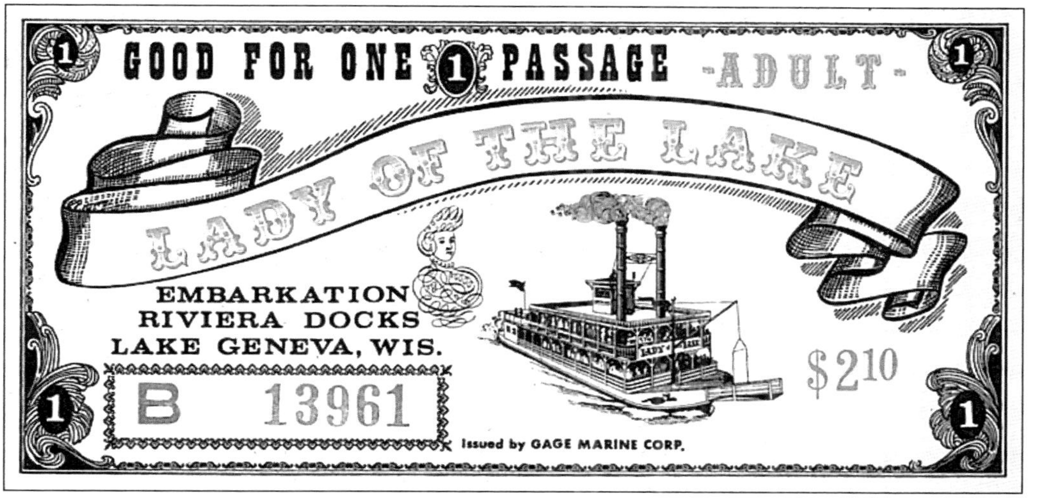

The first *Lady of the Lake* was launched in 1873. This majestic side-wheeler steamboat was 82 feet long. She carried passengers for several different excursion companies for the next 20 years until she just wore out. Almost 60 years later, Russell and William Gage, owners of the Gage Marine Corporation and operators of the Lake Geneva Cruise Line, wanted to create a nostalgic link to the lake's elegant past. They commissioned a new *Lady of the Lake*, and their dream came true when this replica of a Mississippi paddle-wheeled river boat was built in 1963.

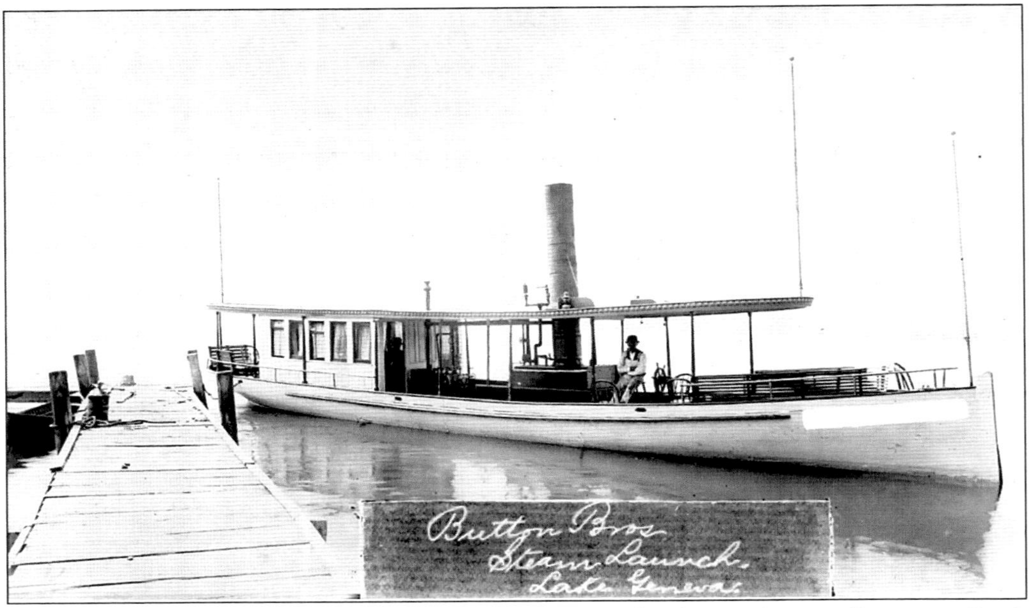

Built in 1880 for Judge T. F. Withrow, the Shadyside was 62 feet long and unusually narrow. Frank and Silas Button, local boatmen soon to become florists, purchased it in 1885. (Courtesy of the Brown-Gabriel Collection.)

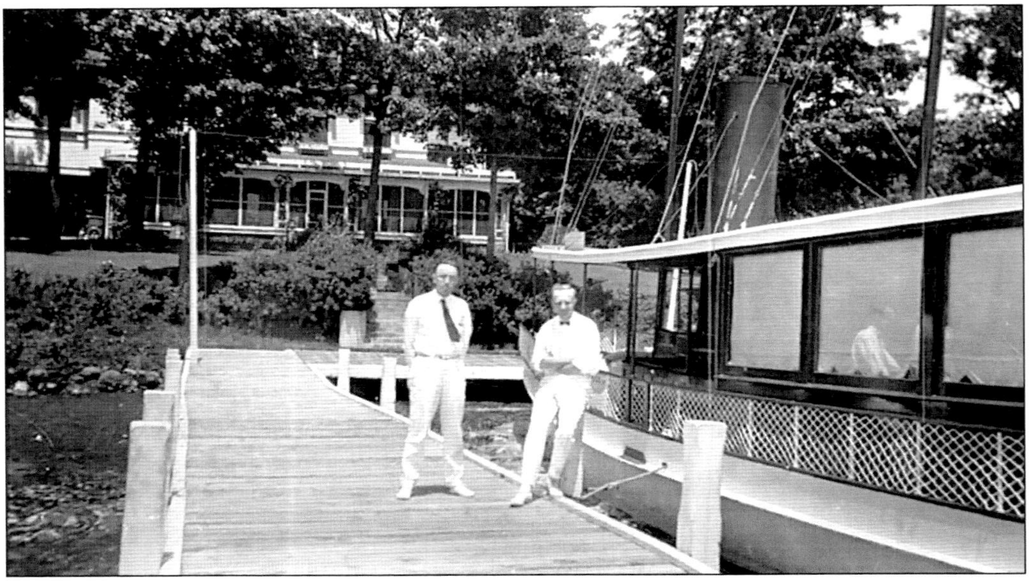

This steam vessel was built at the turn of the century and was christened the *Gertrude*. Long considered the prettiest yacht on Geneva Lake, she was purchased in 1910 by Henry C. Lytton, founder of Lytton's Department Store, and is shown here in front of his home. In 1912, the estate was sold to P.K. Wrigley, and the boat was sold to Sidney Smith and renamed the *Minerva*. Her name and owner changed again 25 years later, and the *Doreen* could be seen on Geneva Lake until 1954. (Courtesy of the John P. Urlakis Collection.)

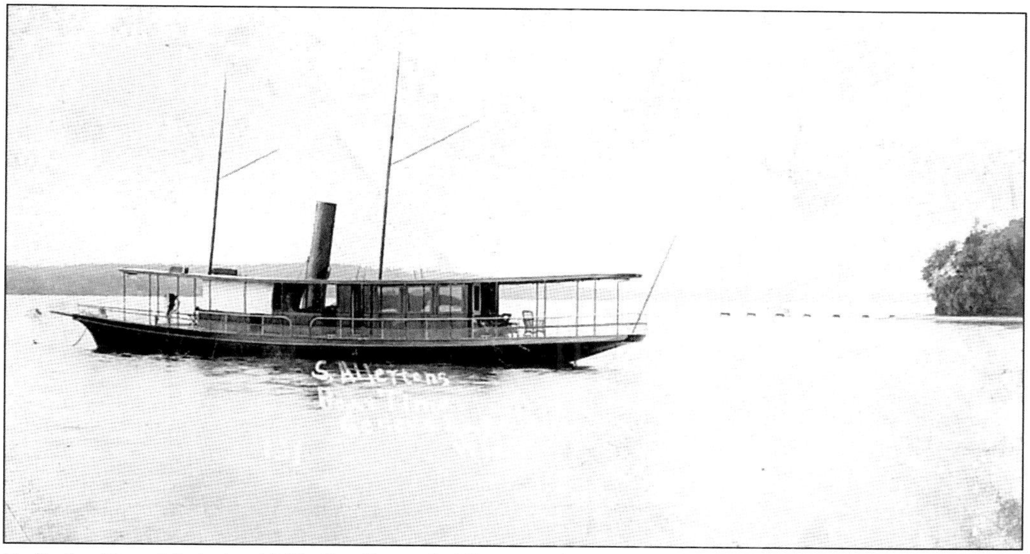

Built in New York in 1883 for Samuel Allerton, the *Time* had a sleek, glistening black hull trimmed with red and gold. Near the bow was an ornately carved scroll of Father Time, which was covered in gold leaf. S.B. Chapin renamed her the *Marietta* after his daughter when he purchased the boat in 1897. She was a popular boat enjoyed by the Chapin family until 1917, when she lost several hull planks, was deemed unsafe, and cut up and sold for parts. (Courtesy of the Brown-Gabriel Collection.)

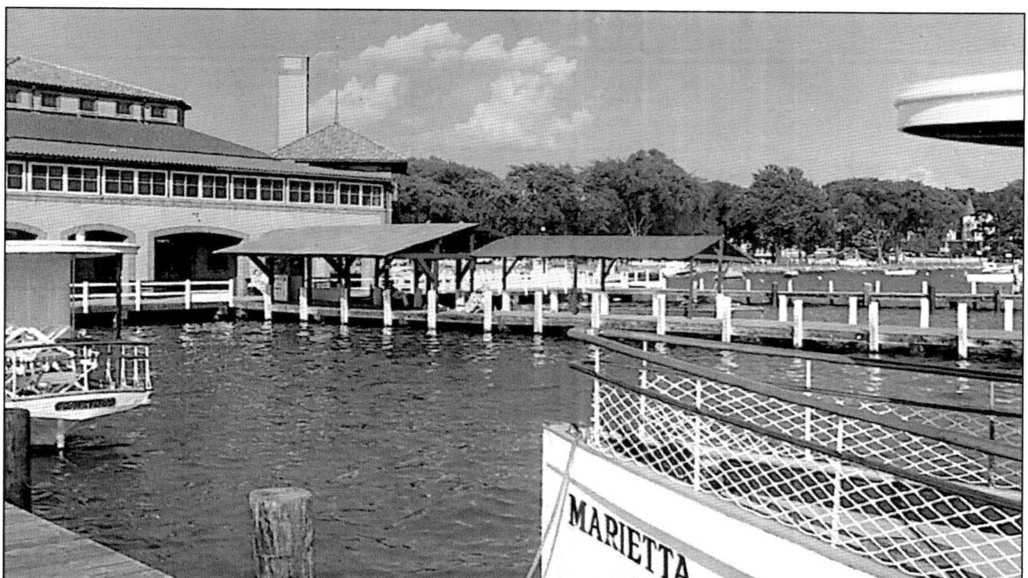

Originally built for James H. Moore and called *Loramoor,* this steamer was purchased in 1916 by S.B. Chapin and rechristened the *Marietta* (this was the second vessel of that name owned by the Chapin family). The boat was used extensively by the Chapin family until 1938, when she was sold to a boat excursion company, and her steam engine converted to gas. (Courtesy of the Joy Peterkin Rasin Collection.)

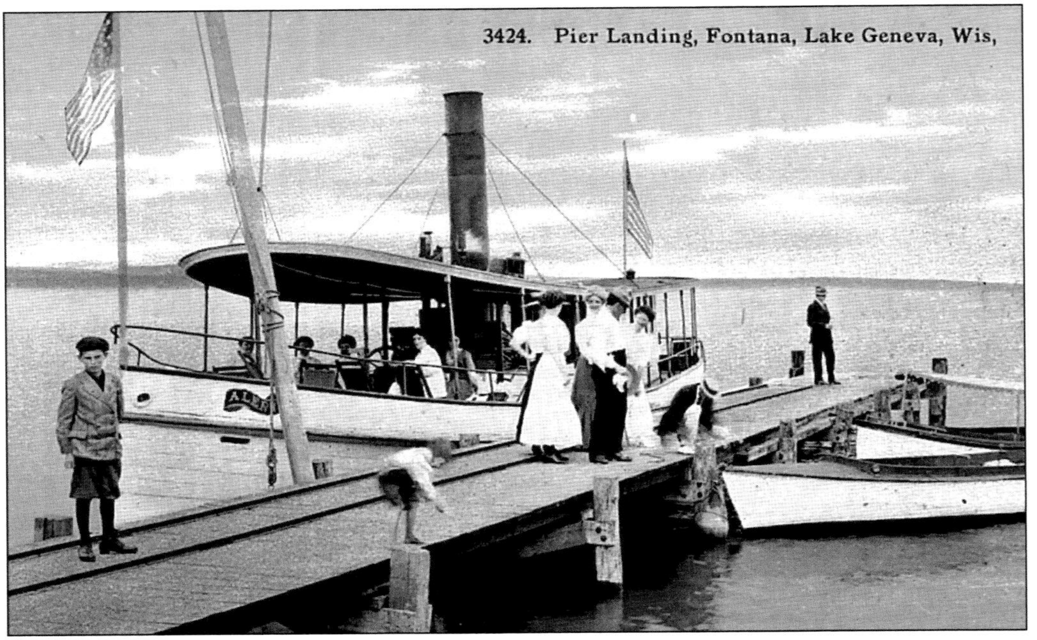

This steam vessel, the *Alert*, was in excursion service from the 1890s until 1922. The rails on the dock are for a coal car to provide fuel to power the steam engines.

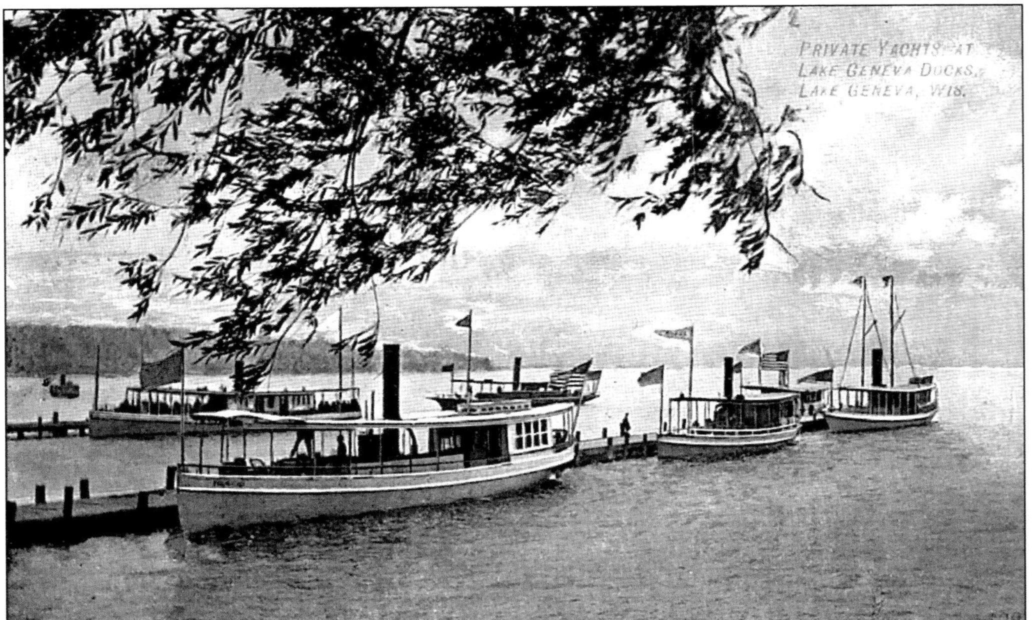

We hope you have enjoyed this journey around Geneva Lake and that you were able to catch a glimpse into the area's history. Glad you were here!

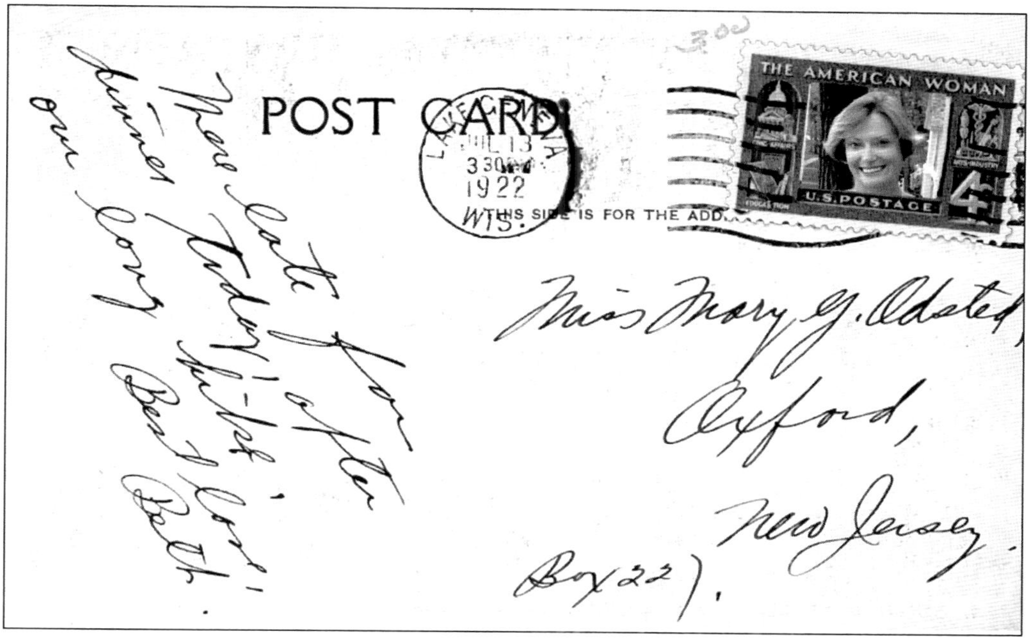
POST CARD
LAKE GENEVA JUL 13 3 30 1922 WIS.
THIS SIDE IS FOR THE ADD...
THE AMERICAN WOMAN
U.S. POSTAGE
Miss Mary G. Odsted,
Oxford,
New Jersey.
Box 227.

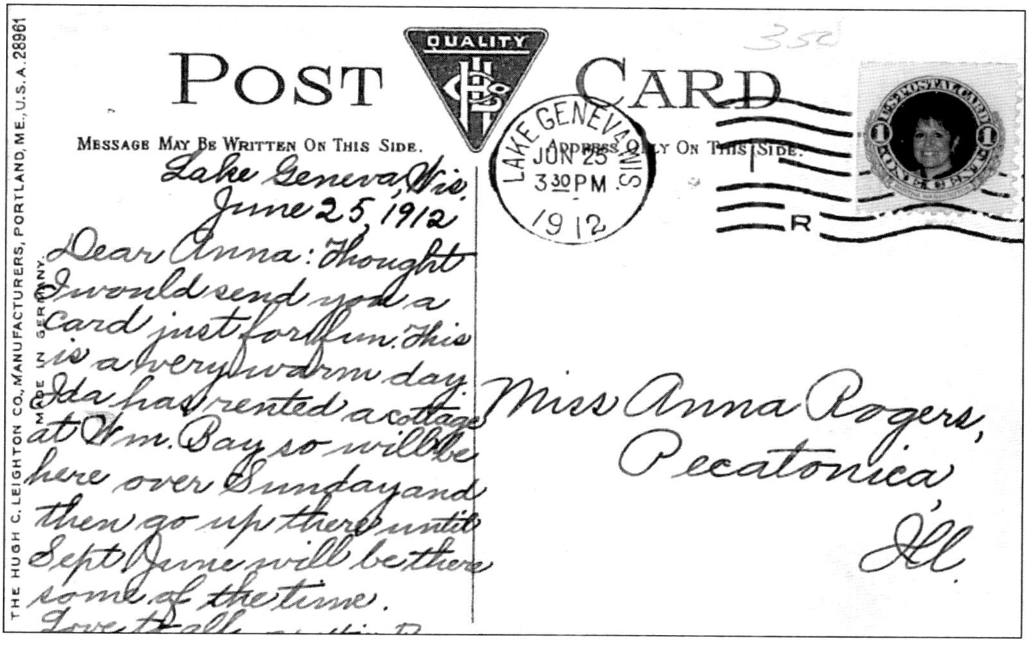
THE HUGH C. LEIGHTON CO., MANUFACTURERS, PORTLAND, ME., U.S.A. 28961
MADE IN GERMANY
POST
QUALITY
CARD
MESSAGE MAY BE WRITTEN ON THIS SIDE.
ADDRESS ONLY ON THIS SIDE.
LAKE GENEVA, WIS. JUN 25 3 30 PM 1912
Lake Geneva, Wis.
June 25, 1912
Dear Anna: Thought I would send you a card just for fun. This is a very warm day. Ida has rented a cottage at Wm. Bay so will be here over Sunday and then go up there until Sept. June will be there some of the time.
Miss Anna Rogers,
Pecatonica
Ill.

References

Discover Lake Geneva: A Historic Guide of Lake Front Homes, Lake Geneva Cruise Line. Gage Marine, 2003.
Dunn Jr., Walter S. *Images of America: Walworth County*. Chicago: Arcadia Publishing, 1998.
Fogle, Phil. *Grassroots—Lake Geneva.* Williams Bay, Wis.: Big Foot Publishing Company, 1986.
Gage, Maggie, "Winds of Change are Kind to the Lake Geneva Yacht Club." *Lake Geneva Magazine*, May/June 1988.
Geneva Lake Area Intensive Survey: An Architectural /Historical Report. August 1985.
Gray-Fow, Dr. Michael. *Boys and Men: A Hundred Year History of Northwestern Military and Naval Academy*, 1888-1988.
Larkin, Larry. *Full Speed Ahead*. Sealark, 1972.
Larkin, Larry. *Grand & Glorious: Classic Boats of Lake Geneva*. Boston Mills Press, 2002.
Pufahl-Firestone, Margaret. *Nostalgic Lake Geneva.*
Seymour Lundahl, Eva. *Main Street Lake Geneva.*
Seymour Lundahl, Eva. *Lovely Lake Geneva*. Los Angeles: New Age Publishing Co, 1950.
Shofner-Russell. Betsy, *Wish You Were Here*, unpublished.
Shoberg, Thel. *Fontana Sesquicentennial Historical Handbook*. 1986.
Vandemark Vollbracht, Pamela. *Yesterday, Today and Forever*. Curtis Media, Inc., 1994.
Wolfmeyer, Ann and Mary Burns Gage. *Lake Geneva, Newport of the West, 1870-1920*. Lake Geneva Historical Society, 1976.

Additional Sources

Eleanor Foundation Web Site. 2005. www.eleanorfoundation.org
Geneva Lake Area Chamber of Commerce Staff. *Lake Geneva, It's Always Been the Place.* 1999–2002. www.lakegenevawi.com
Holiday Home Employee Orientation Manual. 2004. www.holidaycamp.org
Lake Geneva Country Club
Lake Geneva Regional News
The Geneva Lake Conservancy